CONTROLLING
the use of
THERAPEUTIC
DRUGS

CONTROLLING
the use of
THERAPEUTIC
DRUGS
An International
Comparison

Edited by William M. Wardell

American Enterprise Institute for Public Policy Research
Washington, D.C.

Library of Congress Cataloging in Publication Data
Main entry under title:

Controlling the use of therapeutic drugs.

(AEI studies ; 178)
Includes bibliographical references.
1. Pharmaceutical policy.   2. Drugs—Laws and
legislation.   3. Drug utilization.   I. Wardell, William M.
II. Series: American Enterprise Institute for
Public Policy Research.   AEI studies ; 178.
[DNLM: 1. Drug evaluation.   2. Quality control.
3. Legislation, Drug.   QV771 C764]
RA401.A1C66   614.3'5   77-16802
ISBN 0-8447-3278-8

AEI studies 178

Printed in the United States of America

CONTRIBUTORS

WILLIAM M. WARDELL, M.D., Ph.D., is associate professor of pharmacology and toxicology, assistant professor of medicine, and director of the Center for the Study of Drug Development at the University of Rochester Medical Center in Rochester, New York. He is a former chairman of the Clinical Trials Methodology Section and currently chairman of the Drug Regulatory Committee of the American Society for Clinical Pharmacology and Therapeutics, and is an adjunct scholar of the American Enterprise Institute.

STEEN ANTONSEN, Dr. Pharm., is director of the Danish National Health Service's Pharmaceutical Laboratories.

LARS ERIK BÖTTIGER, M.D., is professor and chairman of the Department of Medicine at the Karolinska Institute and Hospital in Stockholm, Sweden. He is also editor for, and a member of the board of, the Swedish Association for Medical Sciences and coeditor of the Acta Medica Scandinavica.

MAURICE FREDERICK CUTHBERT, M.B., B.S., Ph.D., is a principal medical officer at the Medicines Division of the United Kingdom's Department of Health and Social Security and medical assessor to the Committee on the Review of Medicines.

J. P. GRIFFIN, B.Sc., M.B., B.S., Ph.D., is senior principal medical officer in the United Kingdom's Department of Health and Social Security and is currently medical assessor to the Committee on the Safety of Medicines and to the Medicines Commission.

MAGNE HALSE, Cand. Pharm., is director of the National Centre for Medicinal Products Control in Oslo, Norway, and a member of several governmental committees on the reorganization of pharmaceutical services and on drug control.

EIGILL F. HVIDBERG, M.D., D.M., is professor of clinical pharmacology at the University Hospital in Copenhagen, Denmark. He is also a member of the Registration Board, the Medicines Committee, and the Drug Information Board of the Danish National Health Services, president of the Danish Clinical Pharmacology Society, and chief editor of the Danish Medical Association's *Register of Medicines.*

WILLIAM H. W. INMAN, M.A., M.R.C.P., M.F.C.M., is a principal medical officer at the Medicines Division of the United Kingdom's Department of Health and Social Security and medical assessor to the Adverse Reactions Subcommittee of the Committee on Safety of Medicines.

HERMANN KAMPFFMEYER, M.D., is *Privatdozent* and lecturer in clinical pharmacology in the Institute of Pharmacology at Munich University in Germany.

PER KNUT M. LUNDE, M.D., is associate professor of clinical pharmacology at the University of Oslo and head of the Division of Clinical Pharmacology and Toxicology in the Central Laboratory at Ulleval Hospital in Norway.

ZDENĚK MODR, M.D., CSc., is head of the Third Research Unit of Internal Medicine at the Institute for Clinical and Experimental Medicine in Prague, Czechoslovakia. He is also chairman of the Central Committee for Rational Pharmacotherapy.

JOHN P. MORGAN, M.D., is associate professor in charge of pharmacology at the Center for Biomedical Education of the City College of New York.

RUDOLF PREISIG, M.D., is chairman of the Department of Clinical Pharmacology at the University of Berne, Switzerland, and a member of the Committee on Drugs of the Swiss Drug Administration.

EDWARD M. SELLERS, M.D., Ph.D., F.R.C.P.(C), is head of the Division of Clinical Pharmacology at the Clinical Institute, Addiction Research Foundation and Toronto Western Hospital, in Toronto, Canada. He is also head of the Clinical Research Unit of the Addiction Research Foundation and an associate professor of pharmacology and of medicine at the University of Toronto.

SIRJE SELLERS, B.Sc.(Med.), Ll.B., is associated with the law firm of Melnik and Saunders, in Toronto, Canada.

LUDVÍK ŠTIKA, M.D., is a neurologist at the Policlinic of the District Institute of National Health in Prague, Czechoslovakia. He is also a member of the Central Committee for Rational Drug Therapy and chairman of its working group on computerized drug consumption studies.

A.W. S. THOMPSON, M.D., D.P.H., F.R.C.P., was director of clinical services in the New Zealand Department of Health from 1955 until his retirement in 1975.

MICHAEL WEINTRAUB, M.D., is associate professor of pharmacology and toxicology and of medicine at the University of Rochester Medical Center and chairman of the Pharmacy and Therapeutics Committee at Strong Memorial Hospital, in Rochester, New York.

CONTENTS

FOREWORD

The quality of utilization of therapeutic drugs is an issue of great importance, and the costs of drugs—particularly as they are increasingly borne by third parties such as insurance companies and governments under national health systems—have begun to attract increasing attention in recent years. As a result of these concerns, the United States is beginning to move toward control of drug utilization on a large scale, with two distinct aims: constraining costs and improving the quality of utilization. The extent of the controls on drug use being implemented or planned in the United States, together with their rapid increase in number, has important public policy implications that are not widely recognized. This book explores those implications.

An important aid to understanding the options and implications for the United States is to examine both the experience of other countries and the systems that already exist here. Since elaborate systems for controlling drug utilization have been in place for decades in several other countries, we sought descriptions of them, so that they could be analyzed and compared. This volume explores the reasons for the trend toward control of drug utilization and the characteristics of the existing systems: their objectives; their performance measured against their goals; and their impact on the development of new therapies, as well as on the costs and quality of utilization of existing ones.

Countries with different systems of utilization control were selected for examination on the basis of their importance for drug development or their utilization control systems. Experts in these countries were asked to describe the systems from their own perspective.

Each author was asked to cover certain points: the history of the system for regulating drugs; postgraduate education in clinical pharmacology and therapeutics; controls over access of drugs to the market (for both new and existing drugs); controls over drug utilization after the point of marketing; bases for controls (voluntary, legal, third-party payment regulations, and others); specific avenues of control (promotion, prescribing, surveillance, and others); performance of the system (including mechanisms for evaluation); contributions to the improvement of drug utilization; and features peculiar to the particular country or health service. Because of the wide variety among national systems, the authors were not expected to keep rigidly to the format, but rather to address the issues in general terms.

It should be clearly understood that each author speaks as an individual and not as an official representative of his country's system. The authors were selected for their knowledge of their own systems, rather than for their particular point of view. Similarly, in the introductory chapter, the editor speaks only for himself and not for any of the other contributors.

Some papers are written from the point of view of an administrator of the control system (for example, the papers on the U.S. hospital formulary systems and on the Czechoslovakian system); some see the system as it affects the practicing or academic physician (the papers describing the German and the U.S. third-party payment systems); and some combine both viewpoints (those on New Zealand, Norway, Switzerland, Sweden, and Denmark). This variety in viewpoints—which is believed to be a healthy feature of this volume—should be kept in mind by the reader in interpreting the results. Thus, a person who administers and operates a system of drug utilization control will have a perspective that differs entirely from that of someone in practice under that system. We believe that the descriptions presented here are valuable resource materials and that they raise fundamental public policy questions not generally appreciated about drug utilization control systems.

In addition to summarizing these key public policy issues and the essential features of other systems described in this volume, the editor's introductory chapter describes in some detail the background, mechanisms, and reasons for the systems currently in place or being proposed in the United States. Since that chapter was written, the final version of the Carter administration's proposed Drug Regulation Reform Act of 1978 (S. 2755 and H.R. 11611) has been introduced into Congress. The provisions of the bill dealing with drug utilization incorporate virtually all the features of the draft version discussed in the Introduction. The final version of the bill would also authorize the secretary of HEW to conduct drug education programs for the public and for health professionals and, after consulting with the Federal Trade Commission, to require sellers of drugs to post prices of prescription drugs.

WILLIAM M. WARDELL
University of Rochester
March 25, 1978

INTRODUCTION

William M. Wardell

The main focus of this book is on controls over drug use *after* the point of marketing. It deals with systems for distributing and paying for drugs, therapeutic practices, physician prescribing, and patient compliance. The systems that regulate research on drugs prior to their approval for the market are also important, however, because to a regulatory agency, the way a drug is likely to be used once marketed may determine whether it will be allowed on the market at all. [1]

Over the past decade a trend toward instituting control over the use of therapeutic drugs by physicians and patients has been gaining momentum in the United States. There are two general aims: improvement of the quality of drug prescribing and reduction of drug costs. The impetus for control comes from four sources: the Congress; the Department of Health, Education, and Welfare (HEW); nongovernmental third-party payers for drugs; and some (but not all) consumer representatives. The Congress and consumer groups have been interested in both aims; nongovernmental third-party payers have mainly addressed the control of costs. Within HEW the Food and Drug Administration (FDA) has addressed itself primarily to improving the benefit-to-risk aspects of prescribing, whereas other divisions of HEW are concerned largely with controlling costs.

Background to Control of Drug Use

Quality of Use. The recent increase in attention to the quality of drug use has two distinct aspects. The first is a desire to improve the stan-

---

[1] For this reason, in the chapters that follow the authors were asked to describe the relevant portions of the premarketing drug regulatory system in their countries, together with other pertinent factors such as educational practices in clinical pharmacology and therapeutics, and any relevant characteristics of the system by which health care is organized.

dards of drug prescribing and use. Although—apart from anecdotal "horror stories"—there are relatively few hard data on the quality of prescribing, it is often said that there is considerable room for improvement. Examples exist of drugs having been prescribed in an inappropriate—or allegedly inappropriate—fashion. One such example is the prescribing of chloramphenicol for conditions other than those for which it is definitely indicated.[2] Other examples are the inappropriate use of tetracyclines in young children,[3] the excessive use of major tranquillizers in some mental hospitals, and the use of vitamin B_{12} for conditions other than pernicious anemia.

Data are needed to give a comprehensive picture of the quality of drug prescribing. More factual studies should include wider considerations, such as the standards of all therapeutic and diagnostic modalities. With the limited evidence available, it would seem that the quality of medical care could be improved if standards of drug utilization were improved, but the extent of this potential improvement in relation to other remediable deficiencies in health care is not known.

The second aspect of the quality of drug use focuses on the regulatory agency's approval of a drug for the market. In the present scheme, a regulatory agency must address the problem of having to grant approval despite uncertainty about how the drug will actually be used in medical practice and what the total impact of such use, for good or ill, will be. The marketing of a newly approved drug occurs with great intensity: the drug moves almost overnight from scientifically controlled study in a few hundred or thousand patients with no commercial promotion, to maximal promotion and relatively uncontrolled treatment situations that may involve several million patients in the first year of marketing alone. Faced with such uncertainties, there is a natural tendency for a regulatory agency to err on the side of conservatism. Former FDA Commissioner Dr. Alexander Schmidt described some drugs as being held to ransom in the regulatory process because of doubts about how they would be used if approved for release.[4]

---

[2] Even this case is not entirely clear-cut since appropriateness depends on location and other factors. For example, chloramphenicol is believed to be the most widely prescribed antibacterial drug in mainland China, presumably because of its low cost and broad antibacterial spectrum; it is occasionally severely toxic, however, which makes it unacceptable for widespread use in industrialized Western nations.

[3] Wayne A. Ray, Charles F. Federspiel, and William Schaffner, "The Mal-Prescribing of Liquid Tetracycline Preparations," *American Journal of Public Health*, vol. 67 (August 1977), pp. 762-63.

[4] Alexander M. Schmidt, "The Congress, FDA, and Medical Practice" (presidential guest lecture, presented before the Chicago Gynecological Society, Chicago, Illinois, October 15, 1976); also "Informal Remarks" (presented at the E. F. Hutton &

If drugs were used perfectly, few regulatory constraints on their development, introduction, or use would be necessary. Improvement of the manner in which drugs are used and better feedback of information about the use and impact of new drugs—both before and after the point of marketing—are of special importance in devising more effective systems of drug development and regulation that will facilitate the development of new therapies and make them rapidly available to patients who need them, while minimizing hazards to the public.

One improvement would be to use postmarketing surveillance (PMS) to avoid prolonged premarketing barriers. Virtually all parties to the process of drug development have agreed in recent years that improved PMS is desirable, but there is some uncertainty whether the benefits of PMS will exceed its costs. In mid-1975 research guidelines proposed by the Pharmaceutical Manufacturers Association (PMA) endorsed the need for better postmarketing surveillance.[5] In 1975 Senator Edward Kennedy proposed the addition of a formal postmarketing requirement to the drug regulatory process, with enough flexibility for this to be used instead of or in addition to the present Phase III (late premarketing) clinical studies, or not at all.[6] His bill also proposed extensive utilization controls for implementing PMS.[7] In response to that bill, Alexander M. Schmidt, then commissioner of the FDA, acknowledged the increasing expense and delays inherent in the present U.S. regulatory approach and proposed similar but more extensive changes, involving a more flexible approval and withdrawal process coupled with more control over the postmarketing phase of a drug's history. Schmidt believed that these changes "might permit earlier appearance in the United States of many drugs, in return for a

---

Co. luncheon, Chicago, Illinois, February 1977). Similar ideas have been expressed by the current commissioner, Dr. Donald Kennedy. See, for example, his address in *The Industry and Government: Emerging Health Policy*, Proceedings of the Second Fall Meeting of the Health Industry Manufacturers Association, October 22, 1977, p. 3.

[5] Pharmaceutical Manufacturers Association, *Postmarketing Surveillance Guidelines*, 1975.

[6] U.S. Congress, Senate, Subcommittee on Health of the Committee on Labor and Public Welfare, *S.2697: Federal Drug and Devices Act*, 94th Congress, 1st session, November 1975. See also, U.S. Congress, Senate, Subcommittee on Health and Scientific Research of the Committee on Human Resources, *S.1831: 1977 Amendments to the Food, Drug and Cosmetic Act*, 95th Congress, 1st session, July 1977.

[7] William M. Wardell, "Monitored Release and Postmarketing Surveillance: Foreign and Proposed U.S. Systems," in Samuel A. Mitchell and Emory A. Link, eds., *Impact of Public Policy on Drug Innovation and Pricing* (Washington, D.C.: The American University, 1976), pp. 289-330.

longer investigational phase controlled by FDA. This seems to me to be a reasonable trade-off." He then went on to say:

> I would not lightly venture into this area. It does, indeed, approach on the outer limits of where I think FDA ought to be. This matter requires national debate, and perhaps specific legislative direction. In any case, we would need to have the support and the assistance of the medical profession in any such venture.[8]

Similar postmarketing features appear in the subsequent Senate Health Subcommittee bill and in three other bills introduced in 1977. Furthermore, in response to a challenge from Senator Kennedy, an independent Joint Commission on Prescription Drug Use has been set up with industrial and other funding to consider all aspects of drug utilization. This commission may recommend utilization controls if the quality of drug use is deemed to be significantly deficient.

Drug Costs. The other reason for controls is to constrain the cost of prescription drugs. The cost of health care in general has caused increasing concern, particularly as the United States considers some sort of national health insurance scheme. In this context, prescription drugs have received more and earlier attention than have other components of health care, even though they account for somewhat less than 10 percent of the total cost of health care.[9] In countries with a national health service where the government pays for all or most prescription drugs, cost-constraint programs have been in operation for many years. Longstanding examples exist in the United States also. Several examples of both U.S. and foreign systems are described in this book.[10]

---

8 Alexander M. Schmidt, "The FDA in 1985" (presented at the Tulane Medical Symposium, New Orleans, Louisiana, November 5, 1975), p. 14.

9 The exact amount and the percentage of total health care costs that are spent on prescription drugs are difficult to calculate and are the subject of debate. Much depends among other things on definitions of "drug," "prescription drug," and "health care costs," and on the availability of data under the various definitions of each. It is not my intention to enter this debate. If the estimates of both government and industry are taken together, the range in the United States is approximately 7 to 11 percent for 1975, a decline from the preceding decade. This is the basis for my use of the term "somewhat less than 10 percent."

10 An extensive review of the comparative aspects from the pharmaceutical industry's viewpoint is given in Armistead M. Lee, "Comparative Approaches to Cost Constraints in Pharmaceutical Benefits Programs," in Mitchell and Link, *Impact of Public Policy on Drug Innovation and Pricing*, pp. 115-70.

Recent Controls Aimed at Improving Quality of Use

Among the controls recently introduced or proposed in the United States, the initiatives have primarily come from the Congress and the Food and Drug Administration, with additional input from other parties as will be described.

Congressional Initiatives. One act and three bills particularly deserve consideration.

A provision of the Medical Device Amendments (1976) to the 1938 Food, Drug and Cosmetic Act states that because of the potentially hazardous nature of some medical devices, certain types may be sold or distributed for use only by prescription, by certain categories of health professionals, or in certain settings, such as hospitals or clinics. Comparable provisions for restricting distribution and use of drugs do not yet exist (as demonstrated by FDA's loss of the methadone case [11]), but the preface to FDA regulations implementing the device law anticipates similar approaches to drugs in the future.[12] Such restrictions are contained in some drug bills now pending, including the FDA's own draft bill.

Among the drug bills that have been introduced are the Drug Safety Amendments of 1977 (H.R.8891, introduced by Representative Paul Rogers), the Comprehensive Drug Amendments of 1977 (S.2040, Senators Jacob Javits and Harrison Williams), and the 1977 Amendments to the Federal Food, Drug and Cosmetic Act (S.1831, Senators Edward Kennedy, William Hathaway, and Claiborne Pell).

In broad terms, the combined effects of the first three bills as they relate to controls over drug utilization are:

- They provide for patient package inserts (PPIs), that is, brochures that contain information about the drug for the patient.
- The FDA commissioner could issue limited or conditional approval of new drugs before marketing or before final approval of a new drug application (NDA) and set conditions for the use and distribution of a drug. One bill combines this feature with the

---

[11] In 1974 FDA attempted to prevent the distribution of methadone through retail pharmacies, in order to restrict its use to methadone maintenance programs. This was challenged in a suit by the American Pharmaceutical Association, which prevailed. FDA was told that it had no authority to restrict the distribution of a drug. American Pharmaceutical Association v. Mathews (D.C. Cir. 1976).

[12] "Medical Devices—Proposed Investigational Device Exemptions," *Federal Register,* vol. 41 (August 20, 1976), pp. 35282-313; "Device Legislation Could Have Major Implications for Pharmaceuticals," *Research from Washington,* May 3, 1976, p. 27.

formal addition of a postmarketing phase (Phase IV) to the three existing premarketing phases of regulated clinical drug investigation. One bill seeks to change the standards for removal of a drug from the market from the present "imminent hazard" to "serious and substantial risk of harm to any segment of the public or material deception of the consumer."

- A drug hearing board would be set up to review the scientific evidence about a drug's properties. Among the criteria for regulatory approval, this board would introduce judgments on the relative benefits and risks of a drug and the importance of the conditions for which it is prescribed.
- Labels would warn physicians and patients that a drug or device is approved only for the listed indications.

Food and Drug Administration Initiatives. Controls of drug utilization have been a particular concern of FDA for several years, and various modes of utilization control are contained in a bill from FDA and HEW entitled the Drug Regulation Reform Act of 1978, the first public draft of which appeared in December 1977.[13] Because of the importance of this draft bill, the development of the concepts it contains insofar as they refer to drug utilization controls will be briefly summarized.

In submissions to the Department of Health, Education, and Welfare's Review Panel on New Drug Regulation in 1976, FDA Commissioner Schmidt listed four new or increased powers he desired for FDA, including "the ability to assure that a drug will be used only in accordance with the approved labeling."[14] Schmidt's four points were subsequently amplified by FDA's associate chief counsel for drugs, William Vodra, in testimony before the same panel in February 1977. Among seven new or stronger powers which Vodra deemed desirable were the following:

> FDA should have broad authority to regulate the conditions of manufacture, *distribution and use* of a product. . . . Conditions of distribution would provide for a new level of restriction beyond the prescription level [which would] be established if the Commissioner found it is necessary to assure that the benefit-to-risk ratio of the drug was acceptable. [Emphasis added.][15]

---

[13] *Food, Drug and Cosmetic Reports* (hereafter cited as *FDC Reports*), vol. 39 (December 12, 1977), pp. B1-B44.

[14] Alexander M. Schmidt, statement submitted to the HEW Review Panel on New Drug Regulation, 1976.

[15] *FDC Reports*, vol. 39 (February 28, 1977), pp. 15-28.

Vodra discussed several types of utilization control, including restriction of the drug to certain settings (for example, to hospitals, to certain types of practitioners, or to both). He advocated the regulation or control of practitioners' access to drugs by local drug utilization review committees, which he felt could be part of the Professional Standards Review Organization (PSRO).

It is my belief that, if FDA has the seven powers enumerated above, and [if] these powers were not limited simply to the immediate period after marketing approval, but would [extend] throughout the life of a marketed drug, we could face the issue of whether FDA should vary the quantity of data necessary to approve an NDA without regard to whether the *premature approval* was conditioned upon a particular *Phase IV* design or not.

Thus, the public policymakers of our society should express their willingness to exchange (a) some delay in general availability of a product to permit additional testing, or (b) *earlier release of a drug accompanied by extensive federal control*, except in those cases where the benefits from the earlier release clearly exceed any anticipated social costs in terms of unanticipated risks and intensive federal enforcement activity. [Emphasis added.] [16]

The FDA's authority with respect to risk-benefit considerations is addressed in one congressional bill (S.2040), which would give the commissioner authority to:

attempt to eliminate any product presenting an unreasonable risk of disease, injury, or death when compared to its benefit; [and] establish a capability within the Administration to engage in product evaluation and benefit-risk analysis.[17]

With the advent of a new commissioner, FDA has continued to develop plans to increase control over drug utilization and to integrate this with existing controls over the later stages of drug development. In testimony on the revised Senate Health Subcommittee's bill (S.1831), FDA Commissioner Donald Kennedy stated that the FDA was in the midst of a "fundamental and comprehensive revision" of the drug law and that the Carter administration planned to submit its own version of the drug law overhaul to Congress in early 1978. Commissioner

---

[16] Ibid., pp. 16-20.

[17] U.S. Congress, Senate, Subcommittee on Health and Scientific Research of the Committee on Human Resources, *S.2040: Comprehensive Drug Amendments of 1977*, 95th Congress, 1st session, August 1977.

Kennedy indicated that Senator Kennedy's bill did not go far enough to satisfy him:

> Nothing less than a comprehensive rewrite will suffice; more patchwork efforts to make 1938 concepts fit contemporary science and a modern health-care system will only further amplify the inconsistencies and contradictions that now encumber our work.

Among FDA's recommendations were three guiding principles:

- All drugs for human use should be regulated according to the same standards and rules;
- Particular requirements imposed upon one group of drugs but not another should derive from differences between the groups that logically and directly relate to consumer and patient protection; and
- Because science is dynamic, the regulatory system and individual regulatory decisions must be capable of prompt and orderly internal change.[18]

Commissioner Kennedy went on to ask:

> What are our most pressing needs? At the beginning of the drug development process, we require greater flexibility in the clinical testing and marketing of drug products, particularly those entities which may represent significant or urgently sought therapeutic breakthroughs. At the other end of the process, we must have the ability to keep the use of particular marketed drugs in our society under strict controls, and to halt their use summarily where necessary if toxicity or adverse reactions appear. In the middle, drug testing and marketing should be a more integrated and gradual process than it is today. An ideal regulatory system, in our view, must permit a new drug to be used in an increasingly large number of individuals who can benefit from its effect in decreasingly sophisticated medical settings—beginning with the research scientist in the laboratory and going towards the family physician in the community.

> I believe it is also essential that the law articulate clearly the two key standards for decision making on drugs—those related to safety and efficacy—in a way that is clearly understood by our whole society. No drug is safe in the absolute sense; not every drug is efficacious in all applications. Some

---

18 Donald Kennedy, statement before the Subcommittee on Health and Scientific Research, Committee on Human Resources, U.S. Senate, July 26, 1977, p. 7.

drugs, like amphetamines, are useful in very limited clinical indications but for certain individuals are outrageously dangerous and damaging in actual use and thus to society. No drug should be permitted on the market unless it can be established by rigorous experiment to alter the course of some ailment or disease—that is, it must be effective. Once we answer that threshold question in the affirmative, we then must judge its risks and benefits and ask whether the benefits justify the risks to the individual and to society. This benefit/risk determination should be an explicit feature of any statutory revision. Thereafter, we must have the flexibility to guarantee distribution and use, in accordance with sound medical and scientific judgment, for the indicated conditions—without stationing ourselves as the policemen in every prescriber's office or community pharmacy.[19]

Commissioner Kennedy's testimony identified key points in his own policies that paralleled or differed from those in Senator Kennedy's bill:

Distribution controls: "Should apply to all drugs for which such controls are indicated, not only for Phase IV drugs" (that is, FDA's perceived need for distribution controls is independent of whether the drug needs further study after marketing approval).

Faster approval: "We want to be able to expedite the approval of important therapeutic advances, perhaps using such postmarketing authorities as are found in [Senator Kennedy's] Phase IV."

NDA suspension: "We also favor expedited procedures for removing already-approved drugs from the market when subsequent knowledge or experience so requires."

Patient package inserts (PPIs): "FDA's authority to require patient package inserts . . . should not be limited to drugs that have not completed the drug approval process," that is, FDA should be able to determine which drugs require PPIs.

Warning against nonlabeled uses: Instead of the general warning in the Kennedy bill, FDA favors specific warnings for uses known to be harmful or ineffective.

Safety and efficacy: FDA regards it as essential that the law clearly articulate these two standards for decision making so that they are understood by the whole U.S. society.[20]

---

[19] Ibid.
[20] Ibid., pp. 1-18.

At the hearing, former Commissioners Alexander Schmidt and Charles Edwards endorsed Phase IV monitoring for both new and old drugs. Edwards cautioned, "The one thing we have to be careful of is that we don't build Phase IV in and add even more delay to the procedure of processing new drug applications." Senator Kennedy responded, "Of course, the purpose is to expedite it." [21]

Long before the current bills had been proposed, FDA was using powers it already possessed in fact—if not in law—to require Phase IV studies. Although this authority is not specifically provided in the law or in regulations,[22] in practice it is virtually impossible for a company to resist a "suggestion" by FDA that it could approve a drug's NDA earlier if Phase IV surveillance were carried out. In fact several NDA approvals have been contingent on a PMS program in the United States, the first being L-Dopa in 1970.[23]

In addition, FDA has recently begun to use its existing powers of utilization control more aggressively. In June 1977 for the first time FDA invoked power given to it under the 1962 amendments to withdraw a drug (phenformin) from the market, before holding a hearing, because of a perceived "imminent hazard" to health. This action was taken by the secretary of HEW in response to a petition from Ralph Nader's Health Research Group.[24]

---

[21] *FDC Reports*, vol. 39 (August 1, 1977), p. 12.

[22] See note 11 above, on FDA's loss of the methadone case.

[23] William M. Wardell, Michael C. Tsianco, Sadanand N. Anavekar, and Henry T. Davis, "Postmarketing Surveillance of New Drugs," Experimental Technology Incentives Program, National Bureau of Standards, NBS-GCR-ETIP-76-35 (Washington, D.C., December 27, 1976).

[24] *FDC Reports*, vol. 39 (August 1, 1977), p. A-2, and *FDA Drug Bulletin*, vol. 7 (August 1977). It is not clear why the particular hazard associated with phenformin—lactic acidosis—should suddenly in 1977 be considered an "imminent hazard." This effect has been widely known since the early 1960s (phenformin was approved for market in 1959 in the United States), and warnings about lactic acidosis have been included in the labeling of phenformin since 1964. As recently as January 1977, the labeling was revised to reduce the upper limit of the recommended dosage and to restrict the use of phenformin to patients who could not be adequately treated by sulfonylureas or insulin. At the time of the ban, FDA was already negotiating with the manufacturer to keep the drug available to those patients for whom it is needed; subsequently FDA has found it necessary to send out a general warning to patients against discontinuing phenformin without consulting their physician. Phenformin was the only big uanide drug available in the United States (though other countries have drugs such as metformin as well); thus an entire drug class has been removed by administrative fiat. It is doubtful whether all the implications of this ban have been fully considered, especially the hazards for elderly diabetics who will need to learn to use insulin for the first time. It would be very instructive if the full effects of this rather blunt instrument of utilization control could be determined.

The draft of FDA's drug regulation reform bill of December 1977 contains a number of provisions that give FDA more power to control drug utilization, including:

- easier withdrawal of a drug on the grounds of toxicity or lack of efficacy of the drug as used (Section 101)
- requirement that the manufacturer conduct postmarketing surveillance and investigation, restrictions on availability, and reporting requirements for practitioners (Section 106)
- limitation on the quantity and number of prescriptions to assure safe and effective use of any drug (Section 107)
- restriction of drug use to specific types of patients or health care facilities, and monitoring of prescriptions (Section 108), and
- requirement for patient information labeling (Section 305).

Other Initiatives. Drug abuse controls are another means by which federal control is exerted over drugs. Both the Drug Enforcement Administration and the Department of HEW have been directed, by the President's message to Congress on drug abuse, to examine the production and prescribing of these drugs, especially barbiturates.[25]

The HEW Review Panel on New Drug Regulation, in a report of April 25, 1977, recommended giving FDA power to limit the distribution of drugs possessing "unusual benefit and high toxicity" in "highly limited circumstances."[26] Noting that "there are serious problems associated with distribution controls," the panel urged strict procedures for and limits on the FDA process of imposing restrictions— including the requirement that FDA give an annual explanation to the drug's sponsor of the grounds for continued limitation. The restricted distribution concept is similar to that in Senator Kennedy's currently pending bill S.1831 and in its 1975 predecessor, and has been adopted in part in the FDA's drug regulation reform bill.

To date, the Joint Commission on Prescription Drug Use has discussed various topics. These include: effects of formularies on patterns of drug use; an ad valorem tax on drugs to finance studies or compensate victims of adverse drug reactions; the means of determining the costs and the benefits to society of proposed systems; the impact of Phase IV surveillance on the processes of drug approval and

---

[25] Peter G. Bourne, M.D., address to the medical section of the Pharmaceutical Manufacturers' Association by the special assistant to the President of the United States, Arlington, Virginia, November 21, 1977.

[26] HEW Review Panel on New Drug Regulation, "Prescribing Drugs for Unapproved Uses" (Washington, D.C.: Department of Health, Education, and Welfare, February 28, 1977).

removal; methods of surveillance; and restricted as opposed to general release with postmarket monitoring.[27]

Cost Controls

The maximum allowable cost (MAC) program of the Department of Health, Education, and Welfare uses fiscal controls to encourage the use of lower-cost sources for drugs used primarily in government Medicaid programs, when such drugs are available from more than one supplier.

Recent events have set the stage for considerably more generic substitution (that is, the use of the same substance from a different manufacturer) in dispensing. Several states' antisubstitution laws have been repealed, and for some purposes restricted formularies have been created at both the state and federal levels. In at least one state (New York), the FDA has become directly involved in promoting substitution by endorsing (and in effect guaranteeing) the pharmaceutical equivalence and bioequivalence, and hence the claimed therapeutic equivalence, of substitutable drugs on the state's list. After April 1, 1978, all prescriptions in New York State must be written on newly printed forms that facilitate substitution.

Hospital formularies carry the principle of substitution a step farther by restricting physicians' choices among similar but not identical drugs in a given pharmacological class (as distinct from a choice between different brands of the same substance).

The HEW Review Panel described the influence of government reimbursement policies as follows:

> A potentially significant means of indirect regulation of unlabeled uses of prescription drugs is the third party payer. The Social Security Administration, on the authority of Section 1862(a) (1) of the Social Security Act, which excludes from payment items or services not "reasonable and necessary for diagnosis or treatment," has adopted a policy of denying payment in cases of drugs used for reasons not authorized by the approved label. The policy is based on an interpretation of "reasonable and necessary" as "medically effective, safe, nonexperimental and accepted to some degree." Although Section 1802 of the Act explicitly prohibits interference with the medical care provided beneficiaries, the position of the Social Security Administration has not been challenged in court.

---

[27] *FDC Reports*, vol. 39 (August 1, 1977), p. 18.

While this policy is presently limited to Medicare coverage, other third party payers may be piggy-backing on the Medicare mechanism to narrow their own tort liability. Third party payer costs will be limited to the small percentage of all medications prescribed because such payment does not include the extensive outpatient market. Nevertheless, denial of payment for drugs being given for unapproved uses in the hospital may call the attention of patients to the issue, and it is likely that the physician may be encouraged to be generally more cautious about the prescription of drugs for such unapproved uses.[28]

In general, consumer groups are solidly behind the movement toward generic substitution because of their belief in its potential for lowering the purchase price of prescription drugs. The American Association of Retired Persons, for example, strongly supports generic prescribing. Groups representing patients with high-disability diseases, however, have not in general developed policies toward these fiscally oriented controls over prescriptions, possibly because they are aware of the personal medical impact of the diseases themselves and the need for improved therapies. It is unlikely that either consumer or patient groups fully understand the complex relationship (to be explored later in this chapter) between current drug prices, profits, and utilization controls on the one hand, and research into improved therapies on the other.

Measuring the Impact of Utilization Controls

As shown in the previous sections, the amount of control over drug use in the United States is already considerable and is expected to increase greatly. Controls over drug use will have wide-ranging effects on costs, on the quality of prescribing, and on research and development of new drugs.

Control of Drug Costs. One of the main reasons for instituting controls on utilization is to contain costs, particularly under a national health service where the drug bill is a clearly distinguishable portion of a nation's health expenditure. Although the outlay on drugs can be readily constrained by a control system, two questions have not been satisfactorily answered. The first is whether the total cost of administering a control scheme can be offset by the actual saving in

---

[28] HEW Review Panel on New Drug Regulation, "Prescribing Drugs for Unapproved Uses," p. 11. It is my understanding that the particular policy outlined here, although unchallenged in court, is neither observed nor at present enforced.

drug costs. There is evidence that at least in some cases, such as the Manitoba system, the saving may be less than the cost of administering the system.[29] It remains to be seen whether the U.S. MAC system will save as much as predicted, in view of the high cost of administration; alternative approaches may be more cost-effective.[30]

The second question relates to the overall effect of savings in drug costs on the total cost of health care. Since the drug component is a relatively small percentage of the total, even a relatively large reduction in drug expenditures could not reduce total health care costs significantly. It is at least possible that cost constraints on drugs could change health care delivery patterns into more expensive modes (for example, by lengthening the time of hospitalization), or could prolong a patient's loss of earnings. (It is also possible that the opposite would happen.) The point is that the actual effects of drug cost-constraint systems are unknown. Until hard data are obtained to answer these questions, it is not valid to assume that cost constraints on drugs will actually constrain the total cost of health care.

Control of the Quality of Prescribing. Advocates of the use of utilization controls to improve the quality of prescribing believe that it opens the way to optimizing benefit-to-risk ratios in the use of drugs. Such controls have important implications for both the quality of therapeutics and the regulation of new-drug development.

Utilization controls would deserve serious consideration if it could be shown that they improve the quality of therapeutics both for individual patients and for society as a whole (for example, if they generally structure drug use to "beneficial" indications without denying care to those patients who would benefit from an unapproved use).

It is true that control of utilization has reduced the inappropriate use of toxic drugs in the case of chloramphenicol restrictions in New Zealand and Sweden,[31] for example, but in most situations the outcome, in terms of the risks and benefits, has not been fully examined. Indeed, there is usually no procedure for examining the outcome in those situations where most controls are exerted, such as admission of drugs to formularies.[32] Most schemes that are intended to alter benefit-risk ratios are implemented through the special use of existing cost-control

---

[29] Rene Chartier, address delivered at the Horner International Seminar, The Algarve, Portugal (April 23, 1977).

[30] Roy Wiese, Jr., "Utilization Management Techniques: Texas Medicaid Drug Program" (presented at the National Medicaid Meeting, Health Care Financing Administration, Albuquerque, New Mexico, October 17-19, 1977).

[31] See chapters 7 and 10.

[32] This is explored further by Dr. Michael Weintraub in chapter 1.

systems. In the systems described in this book, however, usually neither the net cost savings nor the full medical benefits have been assessed in relation to the disadvantages.

In the case of the regulation of drugs, both past and present FDA commissioners have stated that if the agency knew drug use would be confined to specific and restricted indications, it would be more ready to approve new drugs. There is, however, a risk that these restrictions would simply add new postmarketing hurdles to the existing premarketing ones, thus defeating the aims of the exercise. That this is not the intent of the proponents of a regulated Phase IV is expressed by Senator Kennedy himself as already quoted.[33]

Impact on Research. Another very important influence of drug utilization controls is on research. Tight controls on drug utilization would, if they have the same substantial impacts on the world's main drug markets as they have been shown in this book to have in other countries, raise the prospect of a radical, and so far generally unanticipated, change in the structure of drug research.

The prospective returns on investment in research by profit-making companies are very likely to be reduced by utilization controls, both those aimed directly at drug costs as well as those intended to improve prescribing. If this occurs in the main world markets (themselves the main drug-developing countries), the level of industrial investment in research and development will necessarily decline and research investment will be reduced or redirected into products with less likelihood of being controlled. The implementation of both types of controls in the United States would be the first serious attempt in history to control utilization in the world's largest single market. (At present the U.S. government pays for approximately 22 percent of prescription drug sales in the country.[34]) If, as a result, the private sector's investment in research and development (R&D) should fall, there would be a delay before the impact of this decline would be recognized. This delay in recognition would be due to the rudimentary state of our ability to measure the level of research and to quantify the therapeutic innovations that result, and to the length of time that must elapse between research investment and any measurable outcome from it.[35] There could be a significant shortfall in R&D investment

---

[33] *FDC Reports*, vol. 39 (August 1, 1977), p. 12.

[34] Irwin Lerner, "Issues and Prerogatives" (presented before the Pharmaceutical Advertising Club, Hotel Biltmore, New York, March 17, 1977), p. 10.

[35] Ronald W. Hansen, "The Pharmaceutical Development Process: Estimates of Current Development Costs and Times and the Effects of Regulatory Changes" (report submitted to the National Science Foundation, Grant no. 75-19066, Washington, D.C., August 1977, forthcoming).

and a very large decrease in research output before society became aware of the difference. The ultimate result might be government intervention to make up the shortfall in research, although recent federal expenditures on research hardly encourage optimism about such action. In the interim, the years of delay in therapeutic progress could be very costly to patients. It is this cost that has to be weighed against any short-term saving on drug costs (if saving does in fact outweigh the cost of controls) and the putative improvement in the quality of prescribing that are the aims of existing and planned utilization control systems.

One of the outcomes of the above scenario could be a major restructuring of the present relation between the public and private sectors in the management of research into new therapies. At present government sponsorship is primarily of basic biomedical R&D. If government were to become the main sponsor of applied therapeutic R&D, a new set of problems could emerge. It is conceivable that the research-based pharmaceutical industry would eventually become a contract research organization, resembling in many ways the present defense and aerospace industries. The implications for drug research and procurement and for therapeutic progress are hard to predict, but some obvious dissimilarities between research in therapeutics and in the defense industry suggest that the patient would not necessarily benefit from this change. The procurement techniques that led to successful solutions of the engineering problems of space exploration are not ideally suited to therapeutic research; even as large a biomedical program as the war on cancer has not had as spectacular a payoff as its aerospace counterparts.[36] Much thought and debate needs to be devoted to any policy that would radically change—even if unintentionally—the present structure of both basic and applied biomedical R&D.

The funding of research directed toward new therapies is complex, and little is known about how to optimize the overall process.[37] In broad terms, it is generally thought that the federal government supports research of a fundamental nature aimed at understanding biological processes and diseases, while the pharmaceutical and medical device industries underwrite applied research into practical applications and development. In fact, however, the demarcation lines are

---

[36] G. B. Kistiakowsky, "The Arms Race: Is Paranoia Necessary for Security?" *New York Times Sunday Magazine*, November 27, 1977.

[37] Edward J. Burger, Jr., "The Current Role of the Federal Government in Drug-Related R&D: What Is It and What Should It Be?" in Mitchell and Link, *Impact of Public Policy on Drug Innovation and Pricing*.

increasingly blurred as the private sector addresses more fundamental problems while government institutes conduct applied work. In 1974 the total expenditure on biomedical R&D in the United States was $4.3 billion, of which $2.8 billion (65 percent) came from the federal government and $1.2 billion (28 percent) came from industry—the majority of it from the pharmaceutical industry. The budget of the National Institutes of Health (NIH) in 1974 was $1.99 billion, of which $168 million (8.4 percent) was on clinical trials alone. Over the several years that are required to complete each trial, the total cost of clinical trials was estimated to be $848 million.[38] As an example of the growing governmental support for applied R&D, the National Heart and Lung Institute increased its support of clinical trials nearly fifteenfold from 1962 to 1974.

Although government expenditure specifically on drug research is growing, that of the private sector is still many times greater. In 1975, a year in which the U.S. pharmaceutical industry reported spending nearly $1 billion on R&D for pharmaceuticals for human use,[39] it was reported that NIH had dedicated a total of $657 million to drug R&D over the previous *fifteen* years.[40]

Research in vaccines and antisera has special relevance to the future structure of the drug R&D effort. For a number of reasons government participation in this type of research has been increasing and that of commercial producers declining. The *Reports and Recommendations* of the National Immunization Work Groups in March 1977 describes the problem as a threat to maintaining the production and supply of vaccines:

> Demand for vaccines [including antisera] is of two general sorts: some are required for a substantial segment of the population (general use vaccines) while others are needed only for limited populations (special use vaccines). Private production of general use vaccines has been traditionally accomplished by industry in response to a significant demand which makes investment reasonable on a free market basis. Government support is needed, however, for development and production of limited use vaccines which are inherently unprofitable and cannot be expected to be undertaken spontaneously by private industry.

---

[38] Ibid., pp. 383-84.
[39] Pharmaceutical Manufacturers Association, Annual Survey Report of the Ethical Pharmaceutical Industry Operations 1975-76, November 1976, p. 18.
[40] "The Current Role of Federal Government in Drug-Related R&D," p. 395.

The availability of adequate supplies of general use vaccines and special use vaccines for both public and military use, while not yet an acute problem, is certainly a potential problem for several reasons:

- While the potential capability of American industry to supply vaccine requirements is unarguable, *there has been a steady attrition of specific pharmaceutical manufacturers from the entire field of biologics.* A relatively low profit margin, high production risks, increasing costs of research and development, difficulties in clinical testing, and increasingly stringent governmental standards of safety and efficacy are all formidable constraints to private investment. [Emphasis added.]
- Failure to solve the liability and informed consent problems and any marked change in the already delicate balance between the industry and the highly structured regulatory process in the direction of a more adversary position could drive the remaining few firms from a commitment to vaccine production under the present system.
- A firm's desertion of the field of biologics manufacture means dissolution of an expert staff and removal of commitment to further activity in the biologics field. For example, whereas numerous firms of diverse size were recently committed to manufacturing viral vaccines and serums, there has been a notable attrition of pharmaceutical houses from the manufacture of viral vaccines.

Thus, unless the above problems are dealt with effectively, production and supply as well as research and development of present and potential vaccines and serums could be threatened, despite the absence of a current crisis. [Emphasis added.] [41]

The report goes on to propose solutions, emphasizing in particular the preservation of effective components of the present system:

---

[41] National Immunization Work Groups, *Reports and Recommendations* (submitted to the Office of the Assistant Secretary for Health, McLean, Virginia, March 15, 1977), pp. 1-2. Since the report was published, one of the major remaining vaccine producers (Merrell-National) has decided to cease production of vaccines. Subsequently it has been noted that "only one firm, Merck, is currently producing live measles, rubella, and mumps virus vaccines, compared with seven producers within the past 15 years." *FDC Reports*, vol. 39 (April 11, 1977), p. T&G-6; Ivan Husovsky, memo to employees, Merrell-National Laboratories, Cincinnati, Ohio, September 23, 1977.

It is essential to preserve the effective components of the present system, particularly the excellent function of its governmental, advisory, and industrial components. Their current effectiveness stems mostly from the high concentration of expertise represented within each of these components. Any proposed solution to the broad newly perceived social and economic policies should not dilute or distort this expertise. However, the areas needing new approaches include liability, informed consent, public and professional acceptance, and clinical research.[42]

The report then goes on to discuss functions and operations of the proposed National Immunization Commission:

The Commission should consider that present sentiment is strongly in favor of preserving the efficiency, expertise, and cost control advantages of private industry. To accomplish this objective, the Commission should be thoroughly familiar with the problems and exigencies of commercial vaccine research, development, production, marketing, and distribution. It should engage in long-term planning to assure the continued viability of these functions within private industry with special emphasis on new, rare, and improved vaccines. Such planning should specifically include contract support for research, development, and production of important vaccines. In any case, the Commission must be responsible for ensuring the production and supply of the nation's needed vaccines, including the obligation to consider in depth the pros and cons of a national production facility should it appear that private production sources may disappear.[43]

The area of vaccines is one in which the government has already been involved and in which the discovery procedures and likelihood of results are far more predictable than is the case with drugs. The special problems of R&D and production that are now seen with vaccines may thus be the first indication of what may occur for other pharmaceuticals as the decline in return on R&D is accentuated by utilization controls.

Controls in Other Areas of Medicine. Control of drug use is in a sense a model of, and a method for anticipating, other control systems that may develop in the United States. Historically, controls on drugs have preceded controls over other aspects of medicine because drug use is

---

[42] National Immunization Work Groups, *Reports and Recommendations*, p. 7.
[43] Ibid, p. 9.

easier to administer than are other aspects of medical practice such as surgery or diagnosis. Overutilization and adverse reactions in the drug sector are better publicized; the pharmaceutical component is easy to distinguish from other medical inputs; pharmaceuticals are a separate budget item; and there is a readily identifiable agent—the manufacturer—for whom mechanisms of controlling research and distribution are already in existence. Thus, when there is a perceived political gain to be made from regulation in medicine, pharmaceuticals offer a natural first target.

With the advent of third-party payment schemes for other areas of medical care, the techniques learned for drugs are being applied to these other areas. For example, a second opinion is now required before surgery, under some systems,[44] and controls are being developed for other therapeutic and diagnostic procedures.[45]

In the case of medical devices, the trend is to bring more high-cost items and procedures under cost constraints, a noteworthy example being that of the computed tomography X-ray scanner. Third-party payer's policies on the purchase of these machines and reimbursement for their clinical use are in some ways analogous to controls on drugs and are setting precedents for utilization controls on other devices and procedures.[46] Large medical devices present some new problems, however, that do not arise with drugs; one is the distinction between the cost of acquisition (a capital investment) and the cost of use. Containment of such capital costs is analogous to regulating new hospital construction and differs from constraints on utilization.

The Professional Standards Review Organization (PSRO) program and constraints on Medicare and Medicaid reimbursement were designed as brakes on utilization expenditures and as ways of controlling the dollar costs of products and services.[47] It is not clear,

---

[44] B. Z. Paulshook, " 'Unnecessary' Surgery: Who'll Have the Final Say?" *Medical Economics* (March 7, 1977), pp. 75-80.

[45] Council on Wage and Price Stability, "The Complex Puzzle of Rising Health Care Costs: Can the Private Sector Fit It Together?" (Washington, D.C.: Executive Office of the President, December 1976).

[46] See, for example, Institute of Medicine, "A Policy Statement: Computed Tomographic Scanning" (Washington, D.C.: National Academy of Sciences, April 1977); and also Walter J. McNerney, president, Blue Cross, as quoted in *PMA* [Pharmaceutical Manufacturers' Association] *Newsletter*, vol. 19 (May 9, 1977), p. 2.

[47] For an example of specific third-party constraints, see Genesee Valley Medical Care, Inc., "Medical Waiver of Liability and Regulation under Public Law 92-603," *Medicare Bulletin* (September 1977). For a description of the legislative history of the PSRO law, see Clark Havighurst and James Blumstein, "Coping with Quality/Cost Trade-Offs in Medical Care: The Role of PSROs," *Northwestern University Law Review*, vol. 70, no. 1 (March-April 1975), pp. 38-41.

however, whether policies that reduce the immediate financial outlay of third-party payers actually reduce the total cost of medical treatment or the total cost of the disease, or whether these policies may have wider impacts by retarding medical progress. With the exception of a few case studies of drugs, these questions have received little systematic research.[48]

Foreign and U.S. Utilization Control Systems

Details of various national systems are given in the chapters that follow. The main features, comparisons, and contrasts are summarized here.

Controls from Third-Party Payers. By far the most widespread mechanism of utilization control is that of third-party payers. In nearly every country described here in which payment for drugs is financed in some degree by a third party, drugs must pass through a two-stage process in order to be prescribed. In the first stage the drug is screened for safety and efficacy to determine whether it should be permitted onto the market; in the second stage the drug is screened for admission to a formulary, thus qualifying it for third-party reimbursement. Most of the controls over utilization occur at the point of admission to the formulary, and at this stage questions of cost and of quality of prescribing arise. In many of the examples, the state is the third-party payer, but a similar two-stage approach is used by many private third-party payers as well. The United States has examples of both state and private third-party payer control of utilization.

An exception to this general two-stage procedure exists in the case of the United Kingdom where the formulary step is essentially lacking. Instead there is a price-negotiation program in which government and industry set the prices of drugs once they are approved for the market. In addition, every practitioner's prescriptions are subjected annually to a randomly chosen audit of one month's duration to detect high and costly prescribers.

---

[48] For studies that consider the costs and benefits of drug therapy see Bengt Jönsson, *Cost-Benefit Analysis in Public Health and Medical Care* (Lund, Sweden: Institute for the Study of Health Economics, 1976); Sam Peltzman, *Regulation of Pharmaceutical Innovation: The 1962 Amendments* (Washington, D.C.: American Enterprise Institute, 1974); William Wardell and Louis Lasagna, *Regulation and Drug Development* (Washington, D.C.: American Enterprise Institute, 1975); and Burton Weisbrod, "Costs and Benefits of Medical Research: A Case Study of Poliomyelitis," *Journal of Political Economy*, vol. 79, no. 3 (May–June 1971), pp. 527-44. For a recent assessment of the political reaction to some of these studies, see David Seidman, "The Politics of Policy Analysis: Protection and Overprotection in Drug Regulation," *Regulation*, vol. 1, no. 1 (July-August 1977), pp. 22-37.

In the special case of Norway, criteria such as "medical need" and "relative efficacy" have been applied for forty-five years at the first stage rather than the second. As a result, Norway has probably the smallest number of drugs actually available on the market, although other countries, by formulary controls, may have equally few drugs that are widely used. Czechoslovakia is another special case in which additional controls are exerted at the first stage. Approximately half the 2,000 registered drugs are not regularly imported and have to be obtained by an "extraordinary import procedure."

The majority of third-party controls are primarily to constrain costs. The simplest and most direct mechanism exists in West Germany, where insurance companies can claim restitution from a physician for the value of that portion of his prescribing costs that exceeds 40 percent above "average."

The extent to which formulary controls are used to attempt to improve the quality of prescribing varies widely among countries. The most detailed formulary-control systems described in this volume are in New Zealand and Czechoslovakia. Australia, another country with strict utilization controls (not described here), is distinguished by the fact that its entire program for federal reimbursement of pharmaceuticals is managed from a single computer installation in Canberra, which records every such prescription.[49]

Controls Inherent in the Structure of Medical Practice. In some countries (the United Kingdom, New Zealand, Czechoslovakia, and several others to varying extents), the practice of medicine is concentrated into either hospital practice involving specialist physicians or outside practice involving general practioners. In such countries, some control over the quality of prescribing can be exerted by restricting drug use, either initially or permanently, to hospitals or hospital-based practice. These controls may be through regulation of either access to the market or reimbursement. The advantage of this approach is that it places drugs at least initially (and in some cases permanently) in the hands of specialists who presumably know how to use them best, and who in the course of ordinary medical practice—which involves easy referral —educate their general practitioner colleagues by example. The disadvantage is that it depends on, and may accentuate, a two-tier structure of medical practice, and could lead to substantial inefficiencies and inconvenience for the patient. The actual effect on the quality of medical care is, again, unknown.

---

[49] A. E. Shields, "Drug Distribution and Payment System in Australia—Pharmaceutical Benefit Schemes," Pharmaceutical Benefits Branch, Australian Department of Health, Canberra A.C.T., November 1976.

General Differences. A wide variety of countries are represented in this volume, from small, homogeneous countries with a long tradition of national health care, to large, heterogeneous countries, some of which have national health care systems that include comprehensive payment for drugs and some of which do not. Although some countries automatically assume that the way to better prescribing is through regulation, others, particularly the Scandinavian countries, feel that postgraduate education of physicians is a more desirable approach. In addition certain differences in governmental philosophies toward drug pricing derive from whether pharmaceuticals are a line item in an import budget (as in Norway, Czechoslovakia, and New Zealand) or an integral part of an industrial economy with a strong impact on export trade (as in Switzerland, Germany, and the United Kingdom).

The systems described in this book reveal an obvious similarity of goals combined with very diverse approaches toward attaining them. But there is a general lack of systematic evaluation of whether these goals—either the apparently straightforward ones of cost containment or the more complex ones of improving the medical quality of drug use—are actually achieved. It is surprising to find no widespread procedure for setting up precise goals for any utilization control system, nor for fully evaluating the results to determine whether the goals have in fact been met. This is one of the main unexpected points that emerged from this international comparison, and it has obvious implications for the design of the systems that are currently being implemented or planned for the United States.

Conclusions

From the description in this book of the situation in the United States and elsewhere, it appears that most utilization-control systems have originated for the purpose of constraining drug costs under third-party payment schemes.[50] In some countries these control systems have easy access to large computerized data bases that already exist for purposes of reimbursement and accounting and that typically have information for each prescription identifying the kind and amount of drugs used, the prescribing physician, and the dispensing pharmacist. Some systems have, in addition, information on the patient's identity and the medical indication for which the drug was prescribed. These

---

[50] See also Albert I. Wertheimer, ed., "Proceedings of the International Conference on Drug and Pharmaceutical Services Reimbursement," sponsored by the National Center for Health Services Research, Department of Health, Education, and Welfare Publication No. (HRA) 77-3186 (Washington, D.C., 1977).

systems are readily adaptable to setting up and enforcing elaborate utilization controls. Criteria can be set for the identity and quantity of drug, the condition for which it is prescribed, the type of physician or pharmacist, and the patient, or any combination of these. Failure to meet all the criteria can be made grounds for rejecting reimbursement of the prescription's cost by the third-party payer. These systems thus have the potential for complete control over the way in which reimbursable drugs are used. In some countries, the systems have been adapted to varying extents to improve the quality of utilization of therapeutic drugs. More recently, it has been proposed to use utilization control schemes to control at least the early stages of drug use after marketing. For this purpose, the premarketing investigation of a drug's development is integrated with its early postmarketing experience.

In some countries both main objectives of utilization control are merged within one system. For example, a country with a structured health service and a national formulary may implement constraints on utilization, under the rules of third-party reimbursement, in order to monitor the early progress of a drug after it has been approved for marketing.

In the United States the two functions of cost constraint and improving the quality of prescribing are at present separate. Certain parts of currently proposed bills, however, would involve the FDA in cost-containment activities. For example, its rulings on the therapeutic equivalence of different products would imply a guarante of bioequivalence that is needed and used in the MAC program. Cost containment would be a new role for FDA, and one not envisioned among its original functions.

There are large differences between the systems in countries that are drug consumers and those that are drug developers. The former perceive utilization controls largely as cost-control weapons that enable the consumer David to fight the Goliath of the multinational pharmaceutical industry. In contrast, the drug-developing countries are less likely to control domestic drug costs, probably because to do so might damage the export prices obtainable for the same drugs.

Although the objective of most utilization-control systems is to save money, there has not yet been a good demonstration of the saving related to even this narrow objective (taking into account the cost of administering the system).[51] Nor has there been a cost-benefit

---

[51] See also IMS [International Marketing Systems] America Ltd., *Description and Evaluation of Four Institutional Drug Utilization Review Programs* (Ambler, Pennsylvania, February 1977).

study in a wider sense that weighs the cost of illness against the cost of drug therapy and the saving achieved by utilization constraints. The cost of illness and the cost-savings achieved by effective therapy have seldom been measured by anyone and obviously need research.

In improving drug utilization, the main alternatives to compulsory forms of control are voluntary processes such as peer review and education. Peer review, as practiced by a hospital formulary committee and by the drug utilization panels of a hospital's pharmacy and therapeutics committee is described in chapter 1.[52]

Other alternatives include better information for the patient. One channel for this is the patient package insert (PPI), two of which already exist (for oral contraceptives and for estrogens used postmenopausally), and two others (for progestogens and for intrauterine devices) have been ordered by FDA. This is in general a desirable trend, but the issues are not as clear-cut as they seem at first sight, and more research is needed to determine the most effective type of PPI. There has been little objective study of what information, and how much, should be included—and what should not—to benefit the patient most; nor is there any information about how much improvement in the quality of drug use will result from different levels of information.

Another alternative to stricter regulation is stricter legal liability of a manufacturer for his products.[53] The consequences and public policy implications are far-reaching but have not been fully explored. The liability issues that have arisen as a result of the 1976 swine flu program in the United States are believed by some to imperil all future national immunization programs in this country. Claims against the U.S. government for alleged injuries from swine flu immunization now exceed $3 billion, compared with the actual cost of the program itself, which was a little over $100 million.

Utilization-control systems, in addition to any direct effect on drug prescribing, provide a means of enforcing other influences on the drug market, including generic substitution and price controls. Along with other regulations, such as the compulsory licensing of patents in

---

[52] See also, Douglas E. Miller and William N. Kelly, "A Drug Utilization Review Program with Teeth in It," *Hospital Formulary*, vol. 12 (March 1977), pp. 194-95.
[53] Richard A. Epstein, "Medical Malpractice: Its Cause and Cure," in *The Economics of Medical Malpractice*, Simon Rottenberg, ed. (Washington, D.C.: American Enterprise Institute, 1978), pp. 245-67; Clark C. Havighurst, "Legal Responses to the Problem of Poor-Quality Blood," in David B. Johnson, ed., *Blood Policy: Issues and Alternatives* (Washington, D.C.: American Enterprise Institute, 1977), pp. 21-38.

some countries (for example, Canada), these mechanisms will make it possible for third-party payers to control the pharmaceutical companies' returns on investment in drug research. Such controls already exist in some of the drug-consumer countries, but since these are small individual markets the full impact on expected return on investment has not been felt. The real impact will occur as the drug-developing countries impose utilization controls. When this happens, it will signal the beginning of a major change in the entire structure of therapeutic R&D, including a fundamental rearrangement of the relations between the functions of the public and private sectors in this endeavor.

The magnitude—even the existence—of this potential problem is not generally appreciated. The full public policy implications of the impact on therapeutic progress have scarcely begun to receive attention. One indication of the scope of the problem is the extremely small number of countries that are now responsible for originating nearly all new therapeutic drugs.[54]

At present, with applied drug development largely in the hands of the private sector, decisions to fund projects that could yield better drugs depend in large part on the anticipated returns from sales to tomorrow's patients, while the funds for implementing these decisions come from profits on sales of existing drugs to today's patients. Controls on the profits from today's new drugs and hence on the return on investment in therapeutic drug R&D inevitably raise the important public policy question of who will fund drug research and development in the future. The answers will determine the structure and future of drug (and device) research. The serious problems with vaccine R&D in the United States illustrate what could happen to such research in the future.

In view of existing U.S. and foreign experience, I would suggest the following objectives for sound public policy decisions as this nation moves toward utilization controls.

(1) The goals of any proposed utilization-control system, or of any particular aspect of such a system, should be clearly defined. If the aim is to control costs, to improve drug utilization, or both, this should be stated. Formal evaluation should be part of the design and implementation of the system in order to determine whether the stated

---

[54] William M. Wardell, Mohammed Hassar, and Jean DiRaddo, "National Origin as a Measure of Innovative Output: The National Origin of New Chemical Entities Marketed in the U.S." (manuscript prepared for the National Science Foundation, Grant no. 75-19066, Washington, D.C., August 1977).

goals are actually being achieved. In particular, evaluation should also seek to detect and measure any undesired effects, especially on R&D.[55]

(2) For any system that is designed to constrain drug costs, the evaluation should, at a minimum, measure the total amount actually saved on drugs and compare it with the total cost of setting up, implementing, and administering the cost-constraint system.

(3) In addition to these elementary cost-accounting procedures, formal and more extensive cost-benefit analyses should be undertaken to assess the total medical impact of utilization-control systems as measured by rates of mortality and morbidity, gain or loss of earnings, and comparative total cost of all forms of treatment for each disease in question.

(4) Detailed attention should be given to the effects of utilization controls (particularly cost constraints) on the expected rate of return from research and on the discovery and development of drugs and medical devices in the future. The advantages and disadvantages of the present balance between the functions of the public and private sectors should be fully described, and data should be obtained on the current levels of research activity and output in the United States to provide a baseline against which future changes can be assessed. The implications and outcomes for R&D of the range of changes likely to flow from utilization controls should be carefully defined. Special cases where detailed study would illuminate the general problems should be identified and examined in depth. Some examples that have already been given in this chapter are vaccine R&D in the United States; governmental participation in research, as exemplified by the drug development programs of the National Cancer Institute; and the effects of U.S. and foreign drug utilization-control systems.

(5) In the overall task of improving utilization, alternatives to regulation need careful consideration. In several countries, particularly Scandinavia, physicians and patients are instructed in pharmacology and therapeutics as part of overall continuing education. This is one realistic alternative approach to improving utilization, although a clear distinction needs to be made between education aimed at cost con-

---

[55] The scientific standards for efficacy set up by the 1962 Drug Amendments in the United States, although medically and scientifically desirable, have been powerful influences toward monopoly and increased prices in pharmaceuticals and the elimination of small companies from pharmaceutical research. Ironically, the 1962 law arose principally out of hearings of the Senate Subcommittee on Small Business and Monopoly, hearings whose original purposes included investigation of high prices and alleged monopolistic practices of the pharmaceutical industry. This irony points to the need for evaluation of the real impact of controls.

straint and education aimed at improving the quality of prescribing. Often these two educational aims are implicitly assumed—erroneously in my opinion—to be synonymous. Educational approaches for physicians and patients have been endorsed by FDA [56] and should be expanded.

Approaches involving regulation or other forms of control are premature if their effectiveness is unknown and if the relative effectiveness of alternative and less restrictive measures such as education have not been thoroughly explored.

The implications of utilization controls and their potential for fundamental change in the present system are formidable. Utilization controls are already being planned and even implemented in the United States without much evaluation or even the intent to evaluate their effects. Evaluation of the fundamental public policy issues is therefore all the more necessary before the chance to measure the effects of such controls is lost forever, together with the opportunity to maximize their total benefits and to minimize their harm.

---

[56] Sherwin Gardner, "FDA Trends Affecting Medical Practice" (presented at the General Membership Meeting of the Montgomery County Medical Society, Indian Spring Country Club, Silver Spring, Maryland, November 1976).

PART ONE

EXISTING SYSTEMS IN NORTH AMERICA

1

THE UNITED STATES: HOSPITAL FORMULARIES

Michael Weintraub

Introduction and Definition

Early formularies contained lists of remedies and their formulas. They instructed pharmacists how to compound the standardized recipes believed to be most efficacious. These formularies also served to inform physicians of the ingredients and the strength of what they were prescribing. In the United States, various jurisdictions, such as the Continental army during the War of the American Revolution and (just a few years later) the New York Hospital, developed formularies specific to their patient populations and therapeutic goals.

Paton has studied the development of modern pharmacology and therapeutics through an analysis of pharmacopeias (which until the 1930s were simple formularies, as defined above).[1] Between the seventeenth and early nineteenth centuries the drug list, which had been stable perhaps since before recorded history, was reduced in length, primarily by removing "galenicals" (crude preparations of natural drugs, such as decoctions, infusions, extracts, fluid extracts, and tinctures). During the nineteenth century the list was further shortened as a result of attempts to purify and standardize the potency of the active ingredients in the drugs. However, progress in understanding therapeutic intervention, achieved through research in medicine, physiology, and pharmacology, was not matched by commensurate advancement in chemical knowledge, with the result that new medications were not developed to treat the now better understood disease processes.

---

[1] W. D. M. Paton, "The Early Days of Pharmacology with Special Reference to the 19th Century," in *Chemistry in the Service of Medicine,* ed. F. N. C. Poynter (London: Pitman Medical Publishing Co., Ltd., 1963), pp. 73-88.

The inability to synthesize and purify medications, along with an antipharmacotherapeutic attitude on the part of both practitioners and patients, led to what Schmiedeberg called a "negative phase of pharmacology," which lasted through the first decades of the twentieth century.[2] Paton dates the beginning of modern pharmacology and therapeutics in the 1930s, when the interest of physicians shifted from the diagnostic and pathologic features of disease to treatment. At the same time, advances in medicinal chemistry permitted the development of pure efficacious agents of both known and varied chemical structure. As the art of controlled investigation was refined, it became possible to establish proof of therapeutic efficacy. Concomitantly, methods of selecting the best medications for use and of regulating their prescribing in a given environment (such as a hospital) were also developed.

The New York Hospital formularies of 1933 and 1937 illustrate the change in pharmacopeias from simple listings of recipes to documents fulfilling the new needs of selection and regulation. These newer formularies reflect the economic and therapeutic needs and the therapeutic philosophy of the institutions preparing them. Selecting the best of the available agents and describing them was in part a teaching device for improving "rational" therapeutics. However, as Hatcher and Stainsby point out in their 1933 discussion of the New York Hospital formulary, economic considerations were also important.[3] They wrote that "marked economy already had occurred," but this was not quantified. It was intended that there should be more direct regulation of drug use by limitations on the physicians' prescribing choices—this through eliminating combinations, discouraging parenteral injections when oral administration would suffice, and encouraging "blind tests" to prove the clinical impression of staff members that a favorite proprietary preparation was, in fact, superior to the official preparation included in the formulary.

A committee of department representatives reviewed the evidence for the inclusion of an "article" in the formulary. They put aside the superfluous, forbade the entry of articles of secret composition, and refused to admit brand-name products when identical generic substances could be obtained. But, at heart, their principles were fiscally based. Any proprietary product could be used if "the staff is so firmly convinced that it is willing to conduct a scientific study of its uses or

[2] Quoted in C. F. Schmidt, "Pharmacology in a Changing World," *Annual Review of Physiology* (1961), p. 2.

[3] R. A. Hatcher and W. J. Stainsby, "The Hospital Formulary," *Journal of the American Medical Association*, vol. 101 (1933), pp. 1802-7.

to *provide it at departmental expense*" [emphasis added].[4] Evidently, then, at New York Hospital (and elsewhere) the challenge of the therapeutic revolution was to be faced by selecting the most efficacious and least costly medications applicable to an institution from the myriad of old and new therapeutic agents and enshrining these drugs in a formulary. Although not specifically stated, the implication of the New York Hospital formulary was that prescribing was to be restricted to the articles included in the formulary. In this "complete formulary system," physicians practicing at an institution voluntarily limit what they can prescribe to medications that are in the formulary; not every brand of a drug included in the formulary will be immediately (or ever) available. The pharmacy at New York Hospital (and others), was to choose the particular brand or supplier of multiple-source drugs.

The Pharmacy and Therapeutics Committee

The group designated to select the agents to be included in the formulary is often called the formulary committee or the pharmacy and therapeutics (P&T) committee. It has become a formal part of the medical staff self-government system. One of the first of these was formed at Western Reserve University in the 1930s. This committee was seen as an essential liaison between the hospital's chief pharmacist and the medical staff. In their 1933 article Hatcher and Stainsby described the pharmacist's role as an investigative one, although they believed that too few pharmacists were well enough trained to fill the pharmaceutical positions in progressive hospitals and to carry out therapeutic research.[5] A few years later, Spease and Porter defined the hospital pharmacist's role in the creation and maintenance of the formulary, almost as that role now exists.[6]

During the 1940s outmoded compounds, especially the last of the ineffective inorganic chemicals, were removed from formularies. They were replaced by an array of specific pharmacologic agents such as antimicrobials, steroid hormones, and purified vitamins. However, the slow pace of introductions (slow compared with what was to come) and the outbreak of World War II delayed complete revision of many formularies until the 1950s.

---

[4] Ibid., p. 1803.

[5] Ibid., p. 1804.

[6] E. Spease and R. Porter, cited by D. E. Franke in "Guiding Principles of the Formulary System," *American Journal of Hospital Pharmacy*, October 1960, p. 3.

Pharmaceutical chemists developed many compounds through molecular modification (the "me-too" drugs, as they are called by their detractors), not only providing new chemical entities but also increasing the choices within therapeutic classes. Formulary committees now had the option of selecting from many tetracyclines, thiazide diuretics, and antihistamines, to choose just three examples. Many of these were supplied by a single manufacturer under a proprietary name. In the late 1950s and early 1960s, however, patent protection began to run out on many of the brand-name compounds, permitting the committees to select one supplier of the identical agent from among several "generic equivalents" and also one agent from many similar ones (as for example, tetracycline hydrochloride rather than chlortetracycline). Until bioavailability questions arose in the 1950s to complicate the issue, genericism and economic considerations were paramount in the decisions of many formulary committees.

Effects of Nonscientific Influences on Formulary Control

Hospital formularies (and those of other jurisdictions) intended for the control of prescribing have always responded to outside influences—economic conditions, political trends, and popular opinions of medicine and therapeutics. It is not surprising then that the "revelations" of the Kefauver hearings, the rise of consumerism, the debate over (and adoption of) Medicare, and public attitudes about physicians and the cost of medical care would be reflected in formularies. In 1965 the Joint Commission on Accreditation of Hospitals included a requirement that, for a hospital to be accredited, a formulary committee must be appointed, it must meet, and it must act on the availability of medications and how they were to be used in the institution. Later, the Medicare law gave further legal (and economic) status to pharmacy and therapeutics committees. Under Medicare, hospitals would be recompensed for medications used in treatment of Medicare patients only if the drugs were either present in various official compendia or approved by the pharmacy and therapeutics committee of the hospital.

Current Functions of the Formulary Systems

The following description is based on the workings of the Formulary Committee of Strong Memorial Hospital of the University of Rochester.[7] It is typical of a university hospital's committee.

---

[7] See M. Weintraub, "Effective Functioning of a P&T Committee: One Chairperson's View," *Hospital Formulary*, vol. 12, no. 4 (April 1977), pp. 260-63; and M. Weintraub, "What's in the Hospital Formulary?" *Drug Therapy* (February 1976), pp. 45-48.

Hospital formulary committees usually have three charges. One involves an advisory function under which the committee guides and supports the department of pharmacy. Included in this aspect of the committee's work is the selection of the drugs most appropriate for inclusion in the formulary. Secondly, most committees actively develop policies and procedures on therapeutics and pharmacy services for the institution, such as policy on controlling the activities of pharmaceutical company representatives and rules on physicians' orders (automatic stop orders for narcotics, need for special signatures for certain drugs, and the institution of unit dosing). Lastly, individual committee members and the committee as a whole have an educative role. The formulary itself, along with various newsletters, presentations, and personal contacts, is to be used to communicate hospital policy on the scientific and economic aspects of therapeutics to the staff. As will be seen, all of these committee operations affect and regulate drug utilization.

Today's pharmacy and therapeutics committee is composed of representatives from the major clinical departments (surgery, medicine, pediatrics, obstetrics, for example), nursing, and hospital administration. If the institution is closely associated with a medical school, a pharmacologist or clinical pharmacologist usually participates as well. The chief pharmacist most often acts as secretary to the committee. He and the chairman, together with a drug information pharmacist if one is available, prepare the agenda and information on the medications to be discussed. Besides deciding on whether drugs should be added to or removed from the formulary, committee members serve as a conduit for information between their departmental colleagues and the committee. At the time of a complete formulary revision, which occurs infrequently, the committee may be divided into subcommittees for decisions on individual drugs.

Any member of the hospital community can propose inclusion or removal of an agent through his department representative or by a letter to the committee chairman or secretary. The letter usually includes supporting materials, references, and (occasionally) original research data. Committee deliberations take such material into consideration, and also consider the presence of alternative agents in the formulary, comparative prices, and drug utilization data, when deciding which agents to include. During formulary revision, general announcements of proposed deletions are published, with time allotted for responses by staff members. This enables any member of the hospital staff to be involved in decisions to delete drugs from the formulary.

Hospital policy and therapeutic philosophy, at least as reflected in the formulary, naturally come from the chairman, the chief pharmacist, and the most interested and knowledgeable committee members. The published formulary may also contain additional information—beyond that already mentioned—intended to instruct prescribers: data on available dose sizes, narcotic schedule classification, specific local regulations (such as triplicate prescription blanks), "spécialités de la maison" (unusual dose sizes or hospital-compounded antacids, pediatric formulations, and so on), cost data (with expensive items specially marked), reference to pharmacologic class (with cross-indexing by the American Hospital Formulary Service code), and such specific dose-prescribing information as recommended therapeutic indication and dose modification in disease.

Inherent in the formulary system, as described here, are the control and regulation of prescribing. We will now examine the specific ways in which regulation is carried out and its rationale, its benefits and disadvantages, how successful it has been, and what the future holds.

Regulation of Drug Utilization via Formulary Sanction

The major way in which the formulary regulates prescribing is through the physician's acceptance of the formulary system and hence his agreement to prescribe only medications admitted to the formulary. Physicians relinquish their option to prescribe a particular brand of medication when multiple supply sources are available, or even particular drug members of a related series (as, for example, tetracyclines). Although most hospitals allow some latitude in ordering nonformulary items, there is often a delay because such items must be ordered from a wholesale supplier or borrowed from another institution, shipped to the pharmacy, and then sent to the floor. If the only difference between the prescribed drug and that sanctioned for use by the formulary is a different supplier, the procurement delays will probably deter a physician from ordering a particular or favored brand. But if the medication is not in the formulary because it is new or not generally used in that institution, and if it is specific for the patient's condition, then the delay will obviously be worthwhile. In some institutions other roadblocks are placed between the prescription of a nonformulary item and its administration to the patient. The first barrier between ordering and administration of a nonformulary drug is a pharmacist-physician interview in which the nonformulary status of the drug is noted and formulary-sanctioned alternatives are mentioned. If the prescriber is a house-staff physician, special signatures (from the chief resident or attending physician) may be required on nonformulary items. At some institutions, special billing procedures are used that can raise the cost of nonformulary items, the justification for this being the absence of the specific drug from the hospital pharmacy and the delays and difficulties surrounding its procurement. The need for authorized signatures acts as another brake on nonformulary prescribing, since the person approving the order is expected to discuss the prescriber's choice, challenge it, if necessary, and then attest to its validity.

The main benefits intended from limiting prescribing to medications in the formulary are economic. Once the head pharmacist knows that a medication has been approved for the formulary, he can notify the suppliers to submit bids and select the one providing the item at the lowest cost. The ability to choose one of many brands permits both inventory control and volume discounts in purchasing. Since the chosen supplier's contract will be exclusive (usually for one year), he can present a low bid price and occasionally lower the cost even more because of the large volume of sales. Single bottles of medicine from several suppliers need not sit on pharmacy shelves, passing their expiration date, gathering dust, and taking up room while awaiting the rare prescription from a particular physician. Sole suppliers of a medication still under patent protection or exclusive licensing rights are also affected by this system, even if they have no direct competition from another medication. They may lower prices both in anticipation of competition and to protect their whole product line. One company has given "credits" (supplies of a new or costly drug) based on total use of its products, some of which do not have direct competitors. Although this procedure is being challenged in the courts, it can be an incentive to an institution to keep all of a company's products in the formulary, thus building credits and lowering drug expenditures. However, the ability to use competitive bidding, discounts from high-volume business, and inventory control are the main economic goals of the formulary system.

May, Stewart, and Cluff studied the ways in which removing or adding drugs to the formulary affected prescribing.[8] They found a marked decrease in prescriptions of at least one drug when it was removed from the formulary. In other cases, surprisingly little change occurred or, after an initial decrease, nonformulary-sanctioned pre-

[8] F. E. May, R. B. Stewart, and L. E. Cluff, "Drug Use in the Hospital: Evaluation of Determinants," *Clinical Pharmacology and Therapeutics*, vol. 16 (1974), pp. 834–45.

scribing rose to nearly the same level as before the drug was removed. Conversely, simply admitting a medication to the formulary does not ensure that it will be used. In one example discussed by these authors, until a supply problem arose with a drug already enshrined in the formulary, the newer entrant was not used.

Controls on Formulary-Approved Medications

There are also prescribing controls on drugs in the formulary. While the basis of these restrictions is frequently economic, they also aim at achieving scientific, philosophic, or instructional goals.

Kunin, Tupasi, and Craig studied the impact of requiring an infectious disease consultation before a prescription for an oral cephalosporin (cephalexin) was filled by the pharmacy.[9] During the period of prescribing control (when an infectious disease consultation was required), the amount of cephalexin used dropped from 600 grams per month to 33 grams per month. Use of ampicillin and tetracycline increased but did not replace the "lost" cephalexin.

The main defect in this study, as in nearly all existing studies of its type, is that the authors did not measure the full economic cost-benefit impact, including the therapeutic outcome and the potential harm from the restrictions during the period of prescribing control. The cost of the consultations was not used to offset the savings on the drugs. Furthermore, if as few as ten additional patient-hospital days had resulted from altered antibiotic use in the three-month test period, the total apparent saving would be wiped out (assuming $100 per day hospital charge and $1 per gram cephalexin cost). Although rarely reported, data measuring the effect of formulary controls can be generated. For example, at Strong Memorial Hospital, organisms isolated from patients showed a decrease in resistance to gentamicin following control of gentamicin prescribing.[10]

Kunin and his coauthors did not discuss how much of the decreased cephalexin use resulted from physicians' self-monitoring and how much from dissuasion by the consultant.[11] Both of these represent forms of education, but the latter is the much more valuable form since the prescriber must marshal his data and organize his diagnostic and therapeutic formulation to convince the consultant.

---

[9] C. M. Kunin, T. Tupasi, and W. A. Craig, "Use of Antibiotics: A Brief Disposition of the Problem and Some Tentative Solutions," *Annals of Internal Medicine,* vol. 79 (1973), pp. 555-60.

[10] R. G. Douglas (unpublished).

[11] Kunin, Tupasi, and Craig, "Use of Antibiotics," p. 556.

In teaching hospitals, interposing consultative approval before dispensing is easiest. But if restrictions are too rigid, physicians-in-training may be denied the educational opportunity of defending their therapeutic choices. Although intended to do the opposite, restrictions on prescribing could thus limit both education and development of new knowledge—a point that will be discussed later.

Some hospitals require approval of a prescription for anticancer drugs by the cancer chemotherapy specialists before those drugs are used. Although the cost of many antitumor agents is high, they are not widely prescribed. Here the issue is related more to patient safety, proper management, and (often) research protocols than to cost or to disease resistance. Some institutions require that only physicians who are fully conversant with the unique hazards of antitumor drugs or other specialized medications should prescribe them.

In a new form of drug-use regulation being tried at some Veterans Administration hospitals (and elsewhere), the pharmacy itself monitors "dangerous" drugs and ensures that recommended laboratory tests are obtained and that action is undertaken if toxicity develops. These pharmacy watchdog functions must be sanctioned by the pharmacy and therapeutics committee and by the hospital medical staff. To some of those concerned, this intervention by pharmacists represents an abrogation of the physician's therapeutic decision making, whereas others see it as an improvement in prescribing and a safeguard against unregulated use of medications by physicians who have not kept up with new therapeutic data.

Regulation of the Activities of Pharmaceutical Manufacturers' Representatives

Another way in which the formulary system regulates prescribing is through control of the access of pharmaceutical manufacturers' representatives (PMRs) to the hospital-based staff. Pharmacy and therapeutics committees, acting as the agent of hospital staff self-government, frequently regulate the hours, the location, and even the method in which PMRs can speak to physicians. It is not unusual to declare certain meeting rooms or lounges "off limits" to PMRs. They may be required to visit the pharmacy or to register their arrival at the institution and their prospective appointments, before beginning their rounds. Some institutions require that the PMRs must have formal appointments with physicians—"dropping in" is not permitted. The studies of Coleman, Katz, and Menzels illustrate the importance of PMRs as a source of information and as a stimulus to initial and continued prescribing of a new agent.[12] By controlling the behavior of PMRs in an institution, the formulary system acts as a censoring apparatus that regulates information access and thus drug utilization. If a PMR does convince a physician that his product deserves a trial, then the committee approval system interposes data analysis and sober judgment between advertising blandishments and formulary approval.

As in any regulatory system, the effectiveness of the formulary plan depends on the quality of the people making the judgments. Pharmacy and therapeutics committees are expected to make decisions based on the evidence of a drug's intrinsic merits, its usefulness for the institution's patients, and its cost, and not on therapeutic fashion and advertising claims. What can actually occur, however, is the substitution of individual committee members' prejudices for the desires of the sponsoring physician (which are supposedly instigated by advertising). If a committee has a preponderance of members not directly involved in patient care, it may tend toward the hard line, or "Medical Letter," approach [13]—that is, "keep it out until we know more about it or until the price comes down." At the other extreme is an overpermissive, rubber-stamp attitude—such as "they'll order it anyway, so we should put it in the formulary to save trouble for the pharmacy." This response applies principally to inpatient ordering. But if the medication is predominantly an outpatient drug, not having it in the formulary raises the problem of losing hospital pharmacy income to a community pharmacy, which will probably stock a popular item or attempt to obtain it rapidly. Unless a medication is admitted to the formulary (and occasionally even if it is), an adversary confrontation between pharmacy and therapeutics committees and PMRs frequently takes place. In this sense, the committee's rules act as a negative educational force, perhaps denying the physicians working in an institution access to an important source of drug information.

Regulation through the Educational Role of the Formulary

The formulary system's educational efforts most often begin in the pharmacy and therapeutics committee. Usually the members receive pertinent references or data summaries on proposed formulary additions from the committee head and pharmacy staff. They review these

---

12 J. S. Coleman, E. Katz, and H. Menzels, *Medical Innovation: A Diffusion Study* (Indianapolis: Bobbs-Merrill, 1966), pp. 179-81.

13 *Medical Letter on Drugs and Therapeutics*, published by Medical Letter Incorporated, 56 Harrison Street, New Rochelle, N.Y. 10801.

data in the light of their own ideas and experience and the opinions of their colleagues. At the time of the committee meeting, members present their views and hear those of other members and of the pharmacy staff. Once decisions are made, the members report back to their departmental colleagues. At many institutions the chairman of the committee writes a newsletter, reporting changes in formulary content or in policies and providing descriptions of agents added, analyses of drug groups (for example, of new nonsteroidal anti-inflammatory drugs), prescribing advice, and drug price information.[14]

Supplementary bulletins are also published by the pharmacy staff. These contain information on such things as supply problems, sodium content of antibiotics or antacids, and changes in ordering procedures.

As was previously mentioned, the published formulary itself can act as a teaching document. The introductory material often describes the formulary system that restricts physician-prescribing to formulary items. The hospital by-laws authorizing the pharmacy to purchase and stock only medications from the selected supplier are also presented. The introduction may also outline pharmacy services and administrative details.

How well do the educational efforts of the pharmacy and therapeutics committee and formulary succeed? As in many aspects of the impact of the formulary system, there are almost no data on its educational effects. May, Stewart, and Cluff showed the ineffectiveness of their newsletter on altering prescribing at the Shands Teaching Hospital (University of Florida, Gainesville).[15] Although an extensive literature exists on the failure of lectures and other classical education techniques to alter physician behavior, no controlled studies have been done on the influence that the educational aspects of the formulary system may have on prescribing. What, for example, might have occurred without attempts at information transfer, guidance, or persuasion?

There are several new approaches to education for improved prescribing. One involves competitive presentations between PMRs and

---

[14] The price lists are believed to be important because it is thought that, inasmuch as physicians neither pay for nor consume the drugs they prescribe, they do not know the cost of medications. Unfortunately, uncritical publication of such lists creates the impression that drugs are an important factor in hospital costs and that simple substitution of the cheapest agent in a therapeutic class will not alter the outcome of the treatment. Drug costs make up a surprisingly low percentage of the hospital bill. At the University of Rochester Medical Center they made up only 1.7 percent of the hospital bill; pharmacy charges added another 1.8 percent, that is, slightly more than the cost of the drugs themselves. See M. Weintraub, "Drug Costs," *Drug Therapy* (September 1976).

[15] May, Stewart, and Cluff, "Drug Use," p. 835.

pharmacists. Another is presentation of information pertaining to drugs in the setting of their use—that is, on the wards or during participation in a clinical trial. A course on the analysis of the therapeutic literature might improve prescribing by making physicians familiar with primary data and increasing their ability to assess it critically. These techniques, although they do not directly involve the formulary, may be sponsored by the pharmacy and therapeutics committee as part of its educational function.

The Philosophic Basis for Formulary Control

The attempt to control drug utilization through the formulary on a scientific or theoretical basis rather than an economic one is often based on emotional views, with incomplete data, or no data at all, to support them. Statements such as: "Minor tranquilizers are no good and are overused," "Darvon is too expensive and it doesn't work," "Fixed ratio combinations are never the drug of choice," or "Surgeons overuse prophylactic antibiotics" exemplify the "philosophic" basis of utilization control. Such views may also be couched in scientific terms: "Not significantly different from placebo," "Impossible to prove the null hypothesis," "Physical dependence," or "Drugs have been shown to be a substitute for the time and effort needed to confront the patient's problems." Such apparently scientific statements aside, the actual basis for the institution of control is either economic or emotional.

Although data on the economic impact of controls are scarce and difficult to evaluate, there is some evidence that attempts to substitute the opinions of the pharmacy and therapeutics committee for those of fellow practitioners rarely succeed. At Strong Memorial Hospital, removal of Darvon (dextropropoxyphene) from the formulary was proposed to the medical staff. The committee received many letters and telephone calls supporting the drug and urging its retention in the formulary. The physicians writing these letters and making these calls perceived Darvon as necessary and would probably have continued to order it if the committee had decided not to retain it in the formulary. May, Stewart, and Cluff reported variable results of removing a drug from the formulary: pentazocine continued to be used despite its nonformulary status, but Darvon use declined when the drug was removed; the prescribing of such other minor analgesics as acetominophen and codeine increased, as would be expected, after

---

16 Ibid., p. 836.

the removal of Darvon.[16] The authors did not comment on the cost-benefit relationships, or on any other effects, of these changes.

Adverse effects from philosophically motivated controls on prescribing have been reported. Kaufman and Bickner, for example, in an attempt to improve medical care through the control of drug utilization, banned the use of minor tranquilizers in an American Indian health center.[17] Although the graphic data in their published paper are difficult to interpret, it appears that the use of minor tranquilizers decreased 50 percent. In discussing the Kaufman study, Blackwell raised the issue of increased prescribing of more powerful and dangerous drugs such as phenothiazines as replacement for minor tranquilizers, noting the absence of any discussion of this danger in the report.[18] In response, Kaufman and his colleagues reported that phenothiazine use did increase after the ban on mild tranquilizers, but they did not discuss the effects of their experiment on patient care.[19]

In South Carolina, Keeler and McCurdy found increased prescribing of barbiturates and phenothiazines when minor tranquilizers were banned from Medicaid payment schedules.[20] Some of the decrease in benzodiazepine prescribing, however, was not compensated for by increase in other agents, although increased use of alcohol or failure to keep follow-up appointments could explain the overall decrease in use of psychoactive medication. A possible six-year follow-up study of the longer-term effects of the plan has not been carried out.

Disturbingly little follow-up information has been obtained on experiments involving philosophically motivated formulary controls. What has become apparent is that physicians are not likely to change their prescribing habits if a major change in their therapeutic practice is required. Mundy and his colleagues, for example, found a high incidence of prescribing not sanctioned by FDA guidelines but believed to be valid by physicians.[21] In my opinion, similar situations probably exist with formulary proscriptions and other forms of regulation of drug utilization, although supporting data are not available.

[17] A. Kaufman and P. W. Bickner, "Tranquilizer Control," *Journal of the American Medical Association*, vol. 221 (1973), pp. 1504-6.

[18] B. Blackwell, "Tranquilizer Control," *Journal of the American Medical Association*, vol. 223 (1973), pp. 798-802.

[19] Kaufman and Bickner, "Tranquilizer Control," vol. 223 (1973), p. 803.

[20] M. H. Keeler and R. L. McCurdy, "Medical Practice without Anti-anxiety Drugs," *American Journal of Psychiatry*, vol. 132 (1975), pp. 654-55.

[21] G. R. Mundy, L. Fleckenstein, J. M. Mazzullo, P. R. Sundaresan, M. Weintraub, and L. Lasagna, "Current Medical Practice and the Food and Drug Administration," *Journal of the American Medical Association*, vol. 229 (1974), pp. 1744-48.

State Formularies

In an attempt to control drug costs, formularies have been devised for drug payment schemes in governmental health insurance systems. Hammel studied the effect of closed (restrictive) and open (unrestrictive) formularies on the drug expenditures of states in similar geographical regions.[22] His data were gathered in the late 1960s, just after the institution of Medicare and Medicaid. He found that per capita and per recipient drug expenditures were actually greater in southern states having closed formularies than in states having open prescribing programs. In one of the two states changing formulary status, a switch from closed to open formulary resulted in only a slight increase in expenditures, compatible with the previous growth trend. In the case of a change from an open to a closed formulary, when savings would theoretically be expected, a remarkable increase in drug expenditures occurred instead. These results indicate that formularies represent only one of the complex forces that determine drug expenditures through state payment plans. Although the data are neither new nor conclusive, they suggest that formulary regulation on a state level has little beneficial economic effect.

More recently, Tennessee instituted a partially controlled formulary system, whose purposes and effects have been described by Meyer, Bates, and Swift.[23] Tennessee's program includes computerized monitoring of prescriptions and bioavailability assessments of products accepted into the formulary. A primary reason for instituting computerized monitoring was to uncover abuses and errors. For example, patients filling multiple prescriptions at different pharmacies at close intervals, or from different physicians for the same medication, can easily be spotted. Also, prescribing vagaries (such as prescribing apparently illogical amounts of one drug or interacting drugs) become apparent. Finally, the program can reveal pharmacist fraud or error. In this aspect, Tennessee's program is similar to that of Paid Prescriptions of California (described by Morgan elsewhere in this volume). Price maximums have been set on various medications by the Tennessee system, and favored suppliers are selected on the basis of a state-run standards program for checking bioavailability, content uniformity, and so on. By not paying for over-the-counter, or non-

---

[22] R. W. Hammel, "Insights into Public Assistance Medical Expenditures," *Journal of the American Medical Association*, vol. 219 (1972), pp. 1740-44.

[23] M. C. Meyer, H. Bates, Jr., and R. G. Swift, "The Role of State Formularies," *Journal of the American Pharmaceutical Association*, vol. 14, New Series (1974), pp. 663-66.

prescription, medications (except insulin), anorectics, compounded medications, nonnarcotic analgesics, and some psychotherapeutic agents, the state has delineated philosophic as well as economic goals. Unfortunately the paper by Meyer and his colleagues does not contain information on the success of the program in controlling costs or affecting prescribing behavior, and there is no consideration of therapeutic outcome.

Data confirming the premise that restrictive (closed) state formularies do not necessarily result in monetary savings appear in Smith and Maclayton's article on Mississippi's attempt to control Medicaid drug expenditures through a state-wide formulary.[24]

In the random sample of 20 pharmacies (chosen from the 416 pharmacies in the state), Smith and Maclayton documented an average increase of $2,000 per pharmacy in analgesic expenditures over the anticipated sum even after allowing for increases due to inflation and changes in the population covered. This occurred in the first six months of the restricted formulary. Extrapolating from this sample (assuming it to be truly representative) would result in a $120,000 increase in the Mississippi Medicaid program's analgesic expenditures in the first year of its restricted formulary. This figure does not include any expenses arising from additional administrative costs required to implement the restricted formulary. By restricting analgesic choices, the state forced physicians to choose alternative drugs, some of which were more expensive and perhaps more dangerous than the ones that had been used. One possible explanation for the dramatic (26 percent) increase in analgesic prescriptions is that the alternative drugs available were less effective (or were perceived by patients and physicians as being less effective), thus necessitating higher doses or more potent drugs to achieve the therapeutic goal.

The apparent failure of restrictive formulary control to influence expenditures on a state-wide level has many explanations. The more heterogeneous the population served by a formulary jurisdiction, the more frequent will be valid exceptions to formulary regulations. These will add to the special administrative costs necessitated by a closed formulary—for example, the processing of claims and checking on compliance with regulation. The program must control pharmacist charges so that savings will be passed on to the customer, in this case the state government. The Maryland system has begun to do this, but the results of the program have not yet been reported. Of course,

[24] M. C. Smith and D. W. Maclayton, "The Effect of Closing a Medicaid Formulary on the Prescription of Analgesic Drugs," *Hospital Formulary* (January 1977), pp. 36-41.

manufacturers' prices can vary. Once a limit has been set on a multiple-source drug, prices may rise to that limit. A manufacturer may attempt to make up losses from price ceilings on one drug by raising prices on items for which he is the only supplier. For these reasons, rigidly controlled state-wide formularies may not produce the hoped-for benefits.

More economic impact studies of the type reported upon by Smith and Maclayton should be done—not only at the state-wide level but also at the hospital level. Only on the basis of such data can we make rational decisions about the economic and therapeutic desirability of the formulary system.

Formularies in Other Countries

Brown, Barrett, and Herxheimer have recently surveyed the structure, function, and development of hospital pharmacy committees in England.[25] The National Health Service reorganization of 1975 has forced a reevaluation of these committees, but their role in the system has not yet been well defined. English hospital pharmacy committees do not function in the same way as do their counterparts in the United States. Their memberships frequently have not included a physician or nurse. Since the government does most of the drug purchasing, the economic functions of the English committee are also fewer than they would be in the United States. Apparently these committees have not attempted to regulate prescribing through the formulary, through educational efforts, or through restrictions on physicians. However, Brown and his associates believe that the pharmacy and therapeutics committees can contribute to the rationality of drug prescribing in individual hospitals and through regional collaboration. They give as an example a recent Swedish symposium in which representatives of various committees exchanged ideas on their organization and work.

Few data are available on pharmacy committees in other countries, apart from those described elsewhere in this volume (for example, Czechoslovakia).

The Economic Effects of the Formulary System

Studies analyzing the outcome of economically oriented formulary decisions lack uniformity, and some are defective in various respects.

---

[25] A. W. Brown, C. W. Barrett, and A. Herxheimer, "Hospital Pharmacy Committees in England: Their Structure, Function and Development," *British Medical Journal*, vol. 1 (1975), pp. 323-25.

Thus the achievement of economic savings through the formulary remains difficult to prove. The few studies available suffer from the problems inherent in assuming either constancy of drug utilization from year to year or comparability between hospitals. The question of what to measure in such a study and the almost total lack of long-term follow-up data further complicate analysis of the results of formulary management decisions. Sometimes programs are described and their initial effects are documented and then no more is heard; either the program has ceased operating or the data are not being collected, as in the examples described below. Finally, in no study have the full costs of the system (including the personnel and all the activities of the committee) been incorporated in the economic analysis.

Nevertheless, optimistic claims about cost savings are some-times made. For example, a *New York Times* article of December 16, 1974, reporting on the cost-control program of the Long Island Jewish-Hillside Medical Center, claimed that $60,000 had been saved by switching from expensive antibiotics, such as cephalosporins, to cheaper ones such as tetracyclines or penicillins.[26] Moreover, accord-ing to the article, "the study showed that savings could be achieved without increasing the number of patient infections or the length of patient stays," and further grants had been provided to continue the investigation. However, by May 1976 not only had the program been suspended, but also several of the participants had left the institution and indeed the whole character of the institution (its patient popula-tion and type of illness treated) had changed. One of those who worked on the study said he knew of no publications on the results of the program, except for a progress report soon after its inception, and was unaware of a follow-on investigation on infections or the length of hospital stays. Yet the *Times* article projected a savings of $117 million for the United States as a whole on the basis of this program!

Some more carefully documented information on savings achieved by hospital formularies are available, however. One of the earlier studies of the economic impact of the hospital formulary used data collected in 1956 and published by Franke and his colleagues in 1964 in their book *Mirror to Hospital Pharmacy*.[27] Hospitals using the formulary system, the report stated, had less product duplication and hence lower drug inventories than other hospitals; they also spent

---

[26] M. H. Siegel, "L.I. Hospital Saved $60,000 by Using Fewer Costly Drugs," *New York Times*, December 16, 1974.

[27] D. E. Franke, W. Latolais, and G. N. Franke, *Mirror to Hospital Pharmacy* (Washington, D.C.: American Society of Hospital Pharmacists, 1964), pp. 19-21, 95-98, 139-55, 181-83.

less per year for drugs. Although the variation in spending for drugs between hospitals of the same size was high, the mean differences in annual expenditure between formulary and nonformulary hospitals were statistically significant. Part of the savings can be attributed to the more frequent use of bid pricing by the hospitals having the formulary system. Not all sizes of hospitals achieved savings, but no data were given on the use of bid pricing by those failing to decrease expenditures (the 300-400 bed hospitals) or the between-hospital variation in the two groups. Still, these pre-Medicare data are valuable, and it is unfortunate that in later surveys the economic issues were not analyzed in this same way and that the costs of running and revising the formulary were not included.[28]

In 1966 Rosner studied the financial performance of hospital pharmacies in twenty-four nonteaching, short-term hospitals of middle size (216-417 beds).[29] His main measures were cost of drugs per inpatient-day and inventory turnover rate. Neither of these measures was discussed in *Mirror to Hospital Pharmacy*, unfortunately, but the cost of drugs per day may reflect the same factors as those influencing total hospital expenditures. As the restrictiveness of the formulary increased, financial performance, as measured by Rosner's criteria, deteriorated. *Increased* drug cost per patient-day occurred concomitantly with *decreased* inventory turnover rate.

Rosner also grouped the hospitals according to the method by which physicians consent to pharmacists' dispensing a brand other than the one ordered. He then reanalyzed the data and showed that formalizing such agreements as part of the medical staff by-laws did decrease per-day drug costs. Also, as the number of inventory drug items decreased, drug costs decreased. Rosner's twin ideals of decreased cost per day and increased inventory turnover seem mutually unobtainable, at least in the size of the hospitals he studied. However, they may not be valid goals. In fact, the contention that higher inventory turnover rate implies better utilization of pharmacy investment may not be true. To achieve savings from volume purchases, pharmacies may need to tie up funds and thus decrease turnover. Although Rosner's data are helpful and provocative, neither he nor others have undertaken comparable studies to test the validity of his results or the probable outcome of his recommendations.

---

[28] See D. E. Franke, "Guiding Principles of Formulary System," *American Journal of Hospital Pharmacy*, vol. 17 (October 1960), p. 3, and P. P. Lamy and H. L. Flack, "Report on Current Status of Hospital Formularies," *American Journal of Hospital Pharmacy*, vol. 23 (1966), pp. 663-72.

[29] M. M. Rosner, "The Financial Effects of Formularies in Hospitals," *American Journal of Hospital Pharmacy*, vol. 23 (1966), pp. 673-75.

Muller and Krasner made an extensive survey of formulary practices, purchasing policies, and prices actually paid for six important therapeutic drugs in southern New York counties.[30] Unfortunately, these data do not help in measuring the impact of the formulary system on drug costs because they did not relate these costs to the presence of written formularies or to the restrictiveness of existing formularies. Perhaps the former would not have been of much value, since 88 percent of the hospitals surveyed had written formularies (66 percent of them current). However, in 43 percent of the hospitals, physicians were not restricted to prescribing from the formulary. It would thus have been possible to correlate formulary restrictiveness with the markedly different prices paid by some hospitals for the various drugs surveyed (for example, $17.50 against $44.40 for 1,000 tetracycline capsules, or $7.20 against $14.00 for 1,000 prednisone tablets). Muller and Krasner's study also provided data on the potential savings achievable from "better" (bid) purchasing practices. However, savings from bid-purchasing programs are dependent on assurances of both chemical and therapeutic equivalence—assurances which are not easily obtained at this time.

The data needed to analyze the influence of the type of formulary restriction on the cost of sixteen medications were collected by Gillies and Winship in a survey of 149 hospitals in the Rocky Mountain states.[31] Their interests, however, were in the effect of hospital size, acquisition costs, and the role of pharmacy services on drug costs, with no analysis of the effect of formulary type on drug cost. In a personal communication, Gillies stated that the small number of strict formulary hospitals (thirteen) precluded such an analysis. I offered to compare costs in the hospitals having unrestricted formularies, brand-selection formularies,[32] and restrictive formularies, but was not provided with the data.

Other difficulties involved in studying the economic impact of formulary control are illustrated in the report of Swift and Ryan.[33]

---

[30] C. Muller and M. Krasner, "Pharmacy Purchasing, Formularies, and Prices Paid for Drugs: A Survey of Hospitals in Southern New York," *American Journal of Hospital Pharmacy*, vol. 30 (1973), pp. 781-89.

[31] R. W. Gillies and R. W. Winship III, "The Differences in Costs to Hospitals and Prices to Patients for Pharmaceutical Products and Services," *Hospital Formulary* (April 1976), pp. 189-98.

[32] These are formularies in which all medications are available but the supplier and hence the brand of multiple source drugs are to be selected by the pharmacy on the basis of bid price.

[33] R. G. Swift, Jr., and M. R. Ryan, "Potential Economic Effects of a Brand Standardization Policy in a 1000 Bed Hospital," *American Journal of Hospital Pharmacy*, vol. 32 (1975), pp. 1242-50.

They calculated the potential savings evolving from the institution of a brand-standardization program in a 1,000-bed hospital without a formulary. As previously noted, under such a system all single-source drugs are available to the physician, but trade-name products of identical nonproprietary (multisource) drugs are restricted. Using computer simulation of utilization and costs, they projected a statistically significant savings of $35,000 on drug-usage costs and $9,000 on inventory costs through a brand-standardization policy involving fifty nonproprietary drugs. The ability to control inventory size, to use bid purchasing, and to reduce duplication all contributed to the potential savings.

There are, however, drawbacks to this study. It is a simulation that has not been tested and implies stable utilization and preference patterns despite brand changes. For example, such projections cannot include switching to a more expensive drug (for example, a cephalosporin) when a particular brand of a therapeutically similar but not identical drug (for example, ampicillin) is discontinued. Physicians might also think it necessary to prescribe a larger dose of an alternative agent to replace their first choice of medication, thus reducing or eliminating possible savings. Despite these problems, evidence for potential savings from even a mildly restrictive formulary is present in Swift and Ryan's study. However, these savings must be offset by the costs of implementing the formulary and its controls. (The paper also contains an excellent review of the literature, as well as the just-described innovative approach to a difficult problem.)

Madden devised and carried out an excellent program to control antibiotic-resistant bacteria and to improve antibiotic use through pharmacy educational programs.[34] The Brookhaven Memorial Hospital pharmacy and infectious disease committees publish charts showing trends in antibiotic sensitivity, with prescription recommendations. They have been able to document decreased use of cephalosporin and indicated a monetary saving, but have not said how much money was saved nor how much the program cost. Furthermore, no data on therapeutic outcome were obtained; the duration of hospital stay or development of other infections were not ascertained. Ignoring the administrative costs of the program, it has apparently saved the hospital money through decreased cephalosporin costs ($38,000 reported in six months in 1975 and $30,000 in six months in 1976). Although the effects of this well-devised program on length of hospital

---

[34] R. W. Madden, "Monitoring the Effectiveness of Antimicrobial Agents in a General Hospital," *American Journal of Hospital Pharmacy*, vol. 32 (1975), pp. 654-55.

stay or incidence of infections have not been quantified, the present head of the program (Mr. R. Dougherty) believes that the "clinical impression" is that no adverse influence on patient treatment has occurred.

The most recent report of an attempt to measure the effect of formulary control on drug costs comes from the Shands Teaching Hospital of the University of Florida.[35] The formulary committee there attempted not only to control costs but also to promote more "rational" prescribing. The committee made a survey of parenteral (intravenous and intramuscular) cephalosporin use and, on the basis of the data collected, recommended the following change: cefazolin was to become the only parenteral cephalosporin for general use, and cephalothin was to be included in the formulary only for rare use in ophthalmology or for patients with renal impairment. At the same time, the committee undertook an educational program on the use of cefazolin, since it had found that physicians had been prescribing unnecessarily high doses at too frequent intervals. Bids were let out to the two competing manufacturers of cefazolin. Once the bids were in, projections of potential savings were made by computer, using various dosing schedules and dose sizes. At the dose and interval most often indicated for cefazolin, 500 milligrams every eight hours, a savings of $14,000 per year could be expected. On the other hand, the regimen commonly used at the Shands Teaching Hospital of 1 gram every six hours would have resulted in a loss of $12,000. It could not be ascertained whether the program actually achieved the projected savings because the removal of cephalothin from the formulary had not been fully enforced and no comparisons could be made. The program was to be reinstituted with strict control of cephalothin use and an educational program on cefazolin prescribing, but with no plans to collect data on the effects of the treatment or on costs of implementation.

This program, like the one on Long Island, has not fulfilled its initial promise, and has contributed only partial data (and speculation) to our knowledge about the economic impact of controls. I believe that formulary control can bring financial benefits. However, this will not be known for certain until we have results from carefully done and continuing studies.

---

[35] W. A. Simon, L. Thompson, S. Campbell, and R. L. Lantos, "Drug Usage Review and Inventory Analysis in Promoting Rational Parenteral Cephalosporin Therapy," *American Journal of Hospital Pharmacy*, vol. 32 (1975), pp. 1116-20.

Challenges for the Formulary System

Regulation of prescribing through the formulary system has serious flaws. Too many decisions must be made on the basis of poor or misinterpreted data, or no data at all. The information necessary to answer the important questions of comparative efficacy and toxicity, the applicability of a medication to particular patient groups, the value of a drug in prophylaxis, the meaning of protein binding, and similar matters is being gathered—but slowly. Pharmacy committees are giving consideration to compliance and patient convenience as well as economic and scientific data when deciding to include medications in the formulary. The broad issues—knowledge of the good effects of drugs and of the harm from adverse reactions—depend on obtaining data on therapeutic outcomes, such as the duration of hospitalization and decreased work loss as well as the incidence and impact of adverse drug reactions. These data are not available. We also need information on the narrower issues, not only for making the best formulary committee decisions but also for making valid prescribing decisions.

As Paton indicated, therapeutics is a derivative discipline. Frequently therapeutic advances are not made until progress occurs in understanding of disease, in physiology, in basic pharmacology, in chemistry, and in other disciplines. The 1960s and 1970s have seen an increase in such knowledge, with commensurate increases in therapeutic sophistication. For example, physicians no longer think of hypertension as a unitary phenomenon and its treatment as standardized, but rather direct their therapy at various aspects of the complex condition characterized by increased blood pressure. This change is being reflected in hospital formularies, which now must contain multiple antihypertensives, some of which may appear redundant. Similarly, as subgroups of a population are seen to respond differently to compounds of the same therapeutic (and even chemical) class, the need for what might be considered "me-too" drugs becomes apparent. These developments have naturally increased the difficulty of deciding to include or exclude "therapeutic equivalents" (different members of a chemical class of compounds resulting in a similar therapeutic outcome). The proliferation of cephalosporin antibiotics is an example of this problem. The question raised is how to distinguish between those offering significant advantages and those so marginally different that no alteration in clinical outcome or adverse effects can be detected. If data were available, it would be possible to make a rational choice, thereby simplifying the formulary and creating the possibility of economic benefits for the hospital and ultimately for patients and third-party payers also. Without such data, we are currently working, to a large extent, in the dark.

Stifling Therapeutic Innovation and Stereotyping Prescribing

The total absence of a drug from the formulary can stifle therapeutic innovation. Physicians with real therapeutic challenges cannot determine whether a nonformulary drug would be of benefit to the patient. Unknown properties of a medication cannot be discovered if it is not available for use. This is rarely considered during pharmacy and therapeutics committee discussions, even at teaching and research institutions where such new knowledge should be developed. At the time of a total formulary revision, when housecleaning of unused medications occurs, potentially important medications or even whole chemical classes may be removed from the formulary. Occasionally, committees will err and exclude a needed agent, perhaps perceived by most physicians as excess baggage, or a truly valuable but unused agent that could at some time assume an important role. The advent and overwhelming acceptance of benzodiazepine hypnotics by physicians would have resulted in the removal of all barbiturate hypnotics from the formulary at Strong Memorial Hospital if the utilization criteria for formulary status had been strictly enforced. But, realizing that no barbiturate hypnotic would remain in the formulary, the committee decided to retain at least one (secobarbital) despite its decreased use. Similarly, "therapeutic faddism" caused removal of all but a few of the older anti-Parkinsonian drugs, which had been supplanted by L-dopa, amantadine, and three of the most popular anticholinergics. These last are effective, but few comparative data exist on whether the older drugs, especially anticholinergics, still have a valid place in the treatment of Parkinson's disease or at least would be valuable for a subgroup of patients. The cost-benefit question (monetary cost in this case) of retaining less used but perhaps valuable agents in the formulary has not been well studied. When formularies contain only the most important or "hottest" drug in a therapeutic class, there is a loss of the knowledge that arises from serendipitous discoveries (for example, amantadine in Parkinsonism), different uses for old drugs, the possibility of better results with older drugs at different doses or in combinations, and the response of subgroups of patients. For example, at our hospital recently, a patient's seizures were found to respond best to bromides, which had been removed from the formulary as outmoded. Fortunately, the drug was still being manufactured and was made available to the patient after the newer ("better"?) agents had failed. This example illustrates how decisions made for the majority of patients—as most formulary decisions are—can be detrimental to individual patients.

Another restrictive aspect of the formulary system has already been mentioned—the pharmacy and therapeutics committee's rules regarding PMR visits to physicians. These rules may deprive house staff physicians of an important source of drug information and keep them from developing a critical sense they will later need in evaluating PMR presentations. Controlled or supervised contact with PMRs should be part of house staff training.

Utilization recommendations may also be restrictive. The closer the printed formulary comes to providing "acceptable usage" criteria, the more stereotyped prescribing will become. Physicians may fear exceeding or falling short of the recommended doses. Patients will then lose the benefits of having the dose tailored to their individual needs. Too little study is made of exploration of individual dose-effect relationships, and if recommended doses come to be sanctioned by pharmacy and therapeutics committees and published in the formulary, therapeutic practices could become even more rigid.

Since data do not exist on the true economic outcome of formulary management, we may be making serious mistakes in believing that savings will accrue from restricting or including medications on either economic or theoretical grounds. Moreover, we have no data on the effect that any formulary changes have on therapeutic outcome. Obtaining such data may be the most important task of today's pharmacy and therapeutics committees.

Summary and Conclusions

The regulation of drug utilization through the formulary system has several purposes. Some seem quite rational—achieving economic benefits through bid pricing and prevention of wasteful inventory duplication, developing educational programs, promoting better prescribing, acting as a break on excesses, and considering the patient, the physician, and the institution as a unitary whole in assessing the impact of medication utilization. Even the simple costs of implementing a formulary have not been incorporated into any "savings" arguments yet presented. The system can discourage innovation by limiting drug availability or by stereotyped prescribing controls. Conversely, formulary restrictions can promote innovation. Physicians may find that a medication contained in the formulary is an excellent substitute or has unusual benefits at a different dose from that recommended or when combined with other medications.

No clear-cut data on the ultimate therapeutic outcome of formulary controls are available at present. The formulary system may place undue emphasis on the economic aspects of therapeutics and thereby harm patients.

The keystone of the system is the pharmacy and therapeutics committee. Its members must be knowledgeable and interested in therapeutics. Its actions should be carefully considered, with "trial balloons" and constituency feedback obtained before policy changes are made. These trials and feedback will decrease the necessity of backing down from unenforceable regulations and will permit adequate assessment of outcome. The system must also remain flexible and dynamic. New drugs of value to the patient population served by the institution should be rapidly introduced and unneeded agents frequently culled out. Some pharmacy and therapeutics committees have succeeded in including the whole medical staff in the regulatory process, making the formulary more reflective of patient care needs.[36]

Education alone has not been the answer to the problem of improving drug utilization, even in conjunction with the formulary system. Apparently, physicians do not change their behavior without both "structure and stricture." The complete restrictive formulary system provides both of these, while making valid attempts at education. But the effects have not been measured.

An important future task of the pharmacy and therapeutics committees will be research on utilization and therapeutics at their institutions. The newly trained doctors of pharmacy, oriented toward research, will be valuable adjuncts to this aspect of the work as they enter the practice of hospital pharmacy.

The formulary system regulates drug utilization on many levels. This regulation has potential for both good and bad therapeutic outcomes. Some research has been done on the result of such regulation, but unfortunately data do not exist which tell us what the system is doing or how to improve it. As in so many other areas of drug utilization control, more and better research is required before improvements can be devised or needed changes implemented.

---

[36] D. Zilz, "Total Medical Staff Participation in Formulary Revision," *Drug Intelligence and Clinical Pharmacy*, vol. 9 (1975), pp. 596-99.

2

THE UNITED STATES: DRUG USE REVIEW

John P. Morgan

It is surprising that extensive surveys of physicians' prescriptions have only recently become a reality. As a succinct, formal document of the physician/patient encounter, the prescription has no peer. According to the degree of thoroughness in the monitoring process, something may be learned of the behavior of all three principal parties: prescriber, consumer, and pharmacist.

Extensive collection of prescriptions from a large (or a well-documented smaller) group of prescribers and analysis of their practices could yield hitherto unknown characteristics of usual prescribing and prescription filling. If one physician prescribes narcotic analgesics for 17 percent of his patients, while his colleagues prescribe them for only 4 percent, a close study of that physician's habits and clientele would be appropriate. If an individual rate of prescription of antihypertensives is very low, information to this effect might be useful if the monitoring mechanism includes feedback to the prescriber. The existence of a deviant prescriber, on the other hand, might alert monitors to the possibility that unusual habits of prescription may in fact represent the best treatment, and this appropriate information could be supplied to the errant majority.

Watching and Reporting Prescriptions

Monitoring of prescribing is now an important reality in the United States. Monitors operate with different powers, skills, and—most important—goals. This paper analyzes some monitoring processes and concentrates on one particular monitor—Paid Prescriptions of Burlingame, California.[1]

---

[1] *Paid Prescriptions Basic Drug Program* (Burlingame, California: Paid Prescriptions) (undated).

IMS America. The earliest comprehensive description of prescribing habits sprang from commercial goals. IMS America Ltd. now acts as the principal overseer of most prescription auditing designed to yield product data to pharmaceutical firms. Cooperating physicians and pharmacists supply data to IMS. The most widely distributed of these reports is the *National Prescription Audit,* an annual tabulated report generated from monitoring of community pharmacies.[2] The more detailed and important data, however, are sold to drug manufacturers on an annual contract basis—contracts whose cost may exceed $36,000.[3] IMS has nonindustrial clients, such as the Social Security Administration, but its principal activities center on the drug industry.

Fiscal Intermediaries. The dramatic growth in prescription monitoring is tied principally to the growth of prepaid health insurance plans to the degree that these include drug expenses. Drug benefits may be included in established medical prepayment plans such as the Health Insurance Plan of Greater New York and the Kaiser Foundation Health Plan.[4] More important to the monitoring issue are plans designed solely to cover drugs, and most important among these are those in which the coverage includes a service plan wherein the pharmacist's claim is paid directly by the third party, rather than an indemnity plan in which the drug consumer is reimbursed. Service plans include the tasks of receiving and reviewing pharmacist claims.[5]

Those acting as fiscal intermediaries include the traditional payers of medical care costs in the United States, Blue Cross and Blue Shield, and, since 1958, a number of operations that act largely or solely to service drug benefits through insurance plans. Both Blue Cross and Blue Shield programs now often include prepayment for out-of-hospital drug costs (they have provided in-hospital drug costs for a longer time). This coverage has grown rapidly as labor negotiations have resulted in the inclusion of outpatient drug payment as a benefit. In 1973 the Blue Cross Association announced that Blue Cross plans

---

[2] *The National Prescription Audit Annual Report, 1974* (Ambler, Pennsylvania: IMS America, 1974).

[3] Personal communication with F. W. Stanton, vice president, IMS America, April 1974.

[4] Kenneth M. McCaffree and Harold F. Newman, "Prepayment of Drug Costs under a Group Practice Prepayment Plan," *American Journal of Public Health,* vol. 58, no. 7 (1968), pp. 1212-18.

[5] David A. Knapp, "Paying for Outpatient Prescription Drugs and Related Services in Third-Party Programs," *Medical Care Review,* August 28, 1971, pp. 826-59.

will offer outpatient prescription drug benefits to all subscribers by 1980.[6]

Along with Blue Cross/Blue Shield (BC/BS), a few private insurance companies (Aetna, Travelers) have begun to finance prescription programs.[7] More commonly, however, the stickers that share space on pharmacy doors with those for Master Charge and BankAmericard say PAID (Paid Prescriptions), P.P.P. (Paid Prescription Plans), and P.C.S. (Pharmaceutical Card System)—all plans that have recently come into existence solely to service prepayment of outpatient prescription benefits and to act as intermediaries between the pharmacist vendor and the private insurer or the governmental payer.

The first such plan was P.S.I. (Prescription Services, Incorporated) established in Windsor, Ontario, in 1958. It was sponsored by the pharmacists of Ontario themselves and offers to subscribers a prepayment plan. Other plans have followed, the most significant being Paid Prescriptions.[8]

Paid Prescriptions

Paid Prescriptions emerged in 1964 as California Pharmacy Service, Inc. Like P.S.I., it was established by pharmacists and is best viewed initially as a pharmacy "Blue Shield." It now operates nationally and acts as fiscal intermediary for a variety of insurers, private and governmental.

In 1965, PAID signed its first contract to pay prescription drug benefits under a medical plan for the Teamsters Union. The early years were not remarkably successful, and Marc Laventurier, vice president of PAID, recalls that some California pharmacists actually increased prescription costs if the client were a PAID subscriber, because of long payment delay.[9]

The number of covered individuals and plans grew rapidly. The evolution of prepayment plans helped shape the current format of PAID and other such services. The resolution of methodological details generally resulted in PAID's gaining greater influence over the pharmacist, rather than the other way around.

---

[6] H. G. Pearce, "The Economic Impact of Third Party Payment for Drugs," *Medical Marketing and Media*, vol. 4 (November 1969), pp. 25-28.

[7] *Pharmaceutical Payment Programs—An Overview* (Washington, D.C.: Pharmaceutical Manufacturers Association, 1972), p. 23.

[8] Ralph Engel, "Prepaid Prescriptions Now and Tomorrow," *Compensation Review*, vol. 3 (Third Quarter, 1971), pp. 16-25.

[9] Interview with Marc Laventurier, vice president of Paid Prescriptions, July 1974.

Service or Indemnity. PAID has increasingly moved to service contracts (in which the vendor is paid directly) rather than consumer reimbursement indemnity plans (where out-of-pocket costs initially came from the consumer). Indemnity plans have a lower claim rate than service contracts, but some subscribers may not obtain needed drugs at all because of initial outlay requirements. Service plans are more popular with clients and are sought by labor in labor/management negotiations. Because service programs require the vendor to deal directly with the intermediary, the latter is in a position to influence cost and provide quality incentives.[10] In many contracts, PAID will increase the level of reimbursement if the pharmacy maintains family profile records.

Usual and Customary Charges or Unilateralism. Until 1968, PAID contracts involved reimbursement under both service and indemnity contracts at the "usual and customary" fee. The prescription price was determined solely by the pharmacist, so that the intermediary had no hand in price determination. Such absence of price control occurs regularly in plans originating with pharmacists (for example, PAID and P.S.I.) and is readily endorsed by pharmacy trade associations. Under such arrangements, auditing to detect vendor abuse or to promote cost-consciousness on the part of the vendor is essentially impossible.

Unilateralism, an emotive term to pharmacists, means that a single fee is determined by the fiscal intermediary without the pharmacist's control. PAID, after 1968, determined the reimbursement fee and offered it to licensed area pharmacies. Such an offered fee must be high enough to attract pharmacists and must therefore be high enough to encompass costs and profit, but should not be so high that subscriber premiums become too expensive or a governmental payer considers the cost too high.[11] In a certain sense PAID does not "set" fees; the third-party payer does. However, such payers depend upon PAID's advice in this matter and others.

Antitrust, Legal Problems, and Corporate Restructuring. Legal considerations surround the question of a fixed fee. Pharmacists cannot band together in any fashion to discuss reimbursement levels with a third party, for such discussions violate federal antitrust laws. PAID or other intermediaries may gather information from pharmacy associations (and could negotiate with individual pharmacists), but the

---

[10] Engel, "Prepaid Prescriptions."
[11] Pearce, "The Economic Impact."

desire to control costs and the inability to negotiate a fixed fee with pharmacists as a group lead to the previously described "take it or leave it" unilateralism.

PAID could not remain a pharmacist-controlled plan once the decision was made to cease usual and customary payment. Pharmacist-controlled prepayment plans must operate only through usual and customary payment schedules because of the antitrust provisions noted.[12] The early history of PAID thus ends with the decision for unilateralism: this required severing the controlling ties with retail pharmacists. In 1969, PAID became a nonprofit fiscal intermediary, unaffiliated with retail pharmacists: corporate restructuring was extensive and PAID became associated with Health Application Systems (HAS), a profit-taking entity whose functions include methodologic developments for the monitoring process and expansion into other health-related fields. HAS/PAID is under the corporate structure of Bergen Brunswick, initially a drug wholesaler.[13]

Capitation and Risk Acceptance. The conflicts and resolutions cited above have led to increasing control of pharmacy pricing and provided mechanisms for pharmacist auditing. One remaining development is capitation as a method of payment. Two payment plans might be used. Insurance payment plans may be actuarial—that is, the insurer absorbs the cost and cost overrun of the plan. Under such an arrangement, PAID periodically submits requests for payment to the insurer and recoups prescription costs and administrative expenses. If the insurer and intermediary administer a capitation prepayment program, the intermediary may agree to accept a fixed fee per client, and must hold costs within that fee or suffer loss.

In certain programs, potential pharmacist participants may be offered a choice of risk or no-risk payment plans. Under a no-risk plan, the pharmacist is offered a set fee for filling prescriptions and will accept that fee if it is likely to provide him with a fair profit. Under risk-acceptance, a lower fee may be offered initially, so that if costs to the plan remain low, a share of any residual capitation money may be paid to the pharmacist—which provides him with an incentive to keep costs low.

This maneuver makes sense in a "professional fee" setting. The fixed fee discussed above constitutes a payment to the pharmacist for filling the prescription and is added to his wholesale drug cost: this differs from the more common retail situation in which a markup

---

[12] Engel, "Prepaid Prescriptions."

[13] *Paid Prescriptions* (Burlingame, California: Paid Prescriptions) (undated).

based on wholesale cost determines the prescription price. Under a professional fee system a risk-acceptance can lead to greater cost responsibility because the pharmacist may work to find lower-cost wholesale drugs or to increase efficiency in order to provide him with a profit at the lower risk-acceptance fee. Under many of PAID's programs entailing pharmacy monitoring, an average wholesale price range is recalculated at intervals and a lower fee may be paid if the pharmacist has exceeded the upper range. Obviously, no rejection occurs if the pharmacist is significantly below the average wholesale price.

Capitation is also a method by which incentives may potentially be extended to alter physician prescribing practices.[14] Drug coverage could be offered under capitation as a benefit in a prepaid group practice plan. Physicians in such plans might be easily encouraged to remember that excessive prescription writing may lower practice income, since the plan subscriber (or insurer) makes a single per capita payment to cover benefits. (The capitation concept may curtail other costly medical interventions, such as surgery, diagnostic radiation, and laboratory testing.)

Interaction with Governmental Payers. Under Medicaid (Title XIX), individual states administer medical programs for a variety of health customers. Most state programs include some form of outpatient drug coverage. In 1970, it was estimated that Medicaid programs represented 80 percent of the third-party prescriptions dispensed in the nation's pharmacies.[15] BC/BS organizations have often acted as fiscal intermediaries in such state programs.

If PAID had remained only a fiscal intermediary for labor/management contract plans and for voluntary prepayment plans administered through prepaid group practice, it is unlikely that it would have gained national attention. But it has gained national attention— through the provision of administration and data-processing services for prepaid out-of-hospital prescription services under Medicaid. In the process, PAID became the fiscal intermediary for a new insurer— the state agency.

PAID and the San Joaquin Medical Foundation. In August 1970, PAID contracted to administer the drug payment service under the Medi-Cal Title XIX program for the San Joaquin Foundation for Medical Care. This service covered more than 50,000 eligible recipients.

---

[14] Knapp, "Paying for Outpatient Prescription Drugs."

[15] Pearce, "The Economic Impact."

The San Joaquin prepaid group practice is a foundation health maintenance organization (HMO).[16] In foundation plans, a group of physicians functioning in separate offices constitute themselves as a group practice "without walls," and accept prepayment for patient subscribers who enter the plan. Usually, the plan is comprehensive, although some benefits may be excluded (psychiatric care or obstetrical benefits, for example). Most foundation plans accept a variety of clients: individual payers, those whose prepayment is made by employer or insurer, and often those covered under state/federal plans such as Medicare and Medicaid. The San Joaquin Foundation, in a pilot program, agreed to provide care to patients whose prepayment fee comes from the state of California under Medi-Cal. This is important for our purposes because, in California, the benefits provided include outpatient drugs. PAID agreed to administer these costs and submitted a bid to cover them.[17]

The PAID/San Joaquin experience deserves consideration in some detail, especially because PAID's successful experience there led to its assumption of Title XIX drug services for North Carolina, Arkansas, Florida, and another California program, the Four County Medicaid Drug Program (San Bernadino, Riverside, Contra Costa, and Alameda). As of 1973, PAID administered Medicaid and other drug benefit plans for more than 2 million clients and had 30,000 participating pharmacists.

The San Joaquin project represents a culmination of all the previously mentioned factors leading to major controls on the practice of pharmacy. These include service contracts with direct payment to the vendor, unilateral determination of fees, and a capitation payment, including assumption of risk (the source of capitation being a governmental agency). Further, the administration includes frequent prescription audits, with automated rejection of certain claims, and a pharmacy surveillance mechanism, which includes on-site investigation of pharmacies whose behavior has come into question. These constitute profound interventions into professional behavior and might alone raise far-reaching questions about the effects of increasing controls in this and other health fields. A pharmacist may not wish to allow someone else to decide his fee without regard to his unique operation. His prescription volume might be lower than that of those chain stores in his location that can easily make a profit at the uni-

---

[16] Richard H. Egdahl, "Foundations for Medical Care," *New England Journal of Medicine*, vol. 288, no. 9 (1973), pp. 491-98.

[17] *1970-1971 Report on Administration of the Medi-Cal Drug Program for the San Joaquin Foundation for Medical Care on a Prepayment Basis* (San Mateo, California: Paid Prescriptions, 1972).

laterally determined fee. He may not wish to have his records inspected at the wish of PAID or other plans. Yet he may not be able to stay out—many of his customers may be Medicaid recipients or may come from a large factory where a prepayment plan is in effect. Economic pressure already dictates some of his behavior, but these plans may herald a time when economic pressure defines what is and what is not professional pharmacy.[18]

The issue has become broader than it might have appeared initially. PAID has instituted surveillance of physician prescribing habits—principally in Medicaid plans—and has described, both in its in-house and promotional literature and in a variety of other publications, the idea of drug utilization review.

Drug Utilization Review. Many, if not all, of the hitherto recognized administrative functions of fiscal intermediaries might be described as pecuniary in nature. The intermediary pays the bills of eligible participants. As Rucker states: "the focus of management activity is directed toward apprehending participants who are defrauding the program."[19] Theoretically, drug utilization review clearly represents something quite different:

> The patient health approach, on the other hand, is significantly different in that it establishes new priorities. . . . While acknowledging that the insurance administrator should undertake all necessary procedures for catching crooks and conserving funds, the patient health view adds a new dimension to program operations. It asserts that the primary purpose of third party drug coverage is to aid those patients who need drugs by evaluating the quality of care so that health status may benefit from the most scientific application of contemporary knowledge.[20]

Rucker apparently means that the insurance administrator should critically assess quality of physicians' prescribing in the program with the intent of evaluating it, identifying bad prescribers, and communicating this information to the prescriber along with a suggestion for improvement. If the prescriber does not conform, pressure might be brought to bear to the point of excluding a defiant prescriber from the program.

---

[18] Arthur W. Sackler, "1974 or 1984?" *Medical Tribune*, July 3, 1974, p. 11.
[19] Donald T. Rucker, "The Need for Drug Utilization Review," *American Journal of Hospital Pharmacy*, vol. 27, no. 8 (1970), pp. 654-58.
[20] Ibid.

I will not deal here with the difficulty of identifying poor prescribing, except to say that it is clear the experts seldom agree on how to measure the quality of prescribing even in the widest sense. The task of drug utilization review is difficult.[21]

The first PAID Drug Utilization Review Committee (DURC) was formed in conjunction with the San Joaquin program in August 1970.[22] A series of publications in the pharmacy literature describe the DURC first in San Joaquin and then its extension to other programs. The review process is pertinent to both pharmacists and physicians and embodies the following philosophy:

> A selected group of local practicing health professionals review patterns of drug utilization in a program in which they participate, establish parameters of current practice based on computer reports, determine variances from accepted local standards which should be researched, and from this study prepare guidelines of proper drug utilization. By a constant process of review and study, the Committee assumes as its prime objective the achievement of high standards of patient care through the promotion of rational drug therapy.[23]

In the San Joaquin DURC four local pharmacists and one local physician participate in the process, making use of the administrative services of PAID. They evaluate prescriptions automatically rejected by the computer for meeting (or exceeding) certain criteria. They assess potential abuses by patients, physicians, and pharmacists and notify by letter those involved. This process, particularly the criteria which determine and select who is to be reviewed, will be examined below, but I will give my overall conclusions first.

Despite the admirable goals, what this program has achieved is stunningly mundane. The process of selecting patient records and the

---

[21] Donald C. Brodie and William E. Smith, "Constructing a Conceptual Model of Drug Utilization Review," *Hospitals, J.A.H.A.*, vol. 50 (March 16, 1976), pp. 143-49; Donald C. Brodie, *Drug Utilization and Drug Utilization Review and Control*, DNEW Publication No. (HSM) 72-3002 (Rockville, Maryland: National Center for Health Services Research and Development, Health Services and Mental Health Administration); D. A. Knapp and D. E. Knapp, "Drug Utilization Review with On-Line Computer Capability: Selected Methodology and Findings from a Demonstration" (review article), *International Journal of Health Services*, vol. 4, no. 1, (1974), pp. 201-3; Robert F. Maronde, *Drug Utilization Review with On-Line Computer Capability*, DHEW Publication No. (SSA) 73-11853 (Washington, D.C.: Department of Health, Education, and Welfare, May 1972).

[22] Marc Laventurier, "Guidelines of Drug Utilization Review of the San Joaquin Pharmaceutical Society," *California Pharmacist*, vol. 18 (1971), pp. 8-15.

[23] Marc Laventurier, "Utilization and Peer Review by Pharmacists," *Journal of the American Pharmaceutical Association*, vol. 12 (1972), pp. 166-70.

method of intervention are nearly all based on the traditional function of the fiscal intermediary: all are carried out principally to save money. The DURC at San Joaquin and elsewhere has engaged in nothing that should be described as research. The paucity of archival scientific publications from the immense data base is striking. The most disturbing feature of PAID, however, lies in the fact that its officers and some associated with them have been seduced by the massive unexploited data base into believing that they can make important statements about prescribing and its effects on patients. Such undocumented statements have been widely publicized and have become part of a drug mythology which has done no good and may have done harm.

Saving Money. PAID has saved the state of California money and has almost certainly saved money for its commercial program payers, insurance companies, union trusts, self-insured employers, and others. Although admirable, this is scarcely surprising. It is safe to say that easily trimmed money has always existed in the retail prescription drug market. The artificial price structuring (based principally on the prohibition of advertising by pharmacies) has allowed multiple small independent stores even in the same block to generate profits even when they are underutilized. The simple process of a fixed fee computed by PAID's staff and enforced on pharmacists is sufficient explanation for savings. A PAID brochure cites 20 percent savings in program costs during the first year in the San Joaquin project (costs compared with the previous year's Medicaid drug bill for that area). Most of the savings resulted from efficient computer-based auditing that excluded duplicate payments to pharmacists. (In previous years pharmacists, angered at long waits for payment from Medi-Cal, had resubmitted bills and sometimes received payments for both claims; for a time the check-generating computer produced duplicate checks as a result of programming errors and inadequate auditing.) Furthermore, before PAID, the Medi-Cal drug formulary had imposed a quantity limit on certain drugs. Often when a physician wrote a prescription for more than the limit, the pharmacist had simply split the prescription and collected two fees.[24]

---

[24] California State Auditor General's Office, *Medi-Cal Program: Report on Investigation of Payment of Claims of Pharmacists*, Assembly Concurrent Resolution No. 249 (Sacramento, California: Office of the Auditor General of the State of California, 1969); John Preston and Victor R. Boisseree, *Medi-Cal California Medicaid: A Management and Utilization Study* (Sacramento, California: State of California Human Relations Agency, Department of Health Care Services, December 1970).

Other Stimuli. Following are other stimuli for computer-generated automatic review:[25]

(1) *The costly consumer.* Regardless of drug, patient, or pharmacist, a prescription that costs more than seventeen dollars is reviewed by the DURC. The set fee determined by PAID is a professional filling fee for pharmacists and is added to the pharmacist's drug costs. If the pharmacist paid a very high price for the drug or is escalating his wholesale fee, a letter from the DURC will arrive. A similar query to pharmacist or physician or both will be generated if a patient has drug costs greater than thirty dollars in one month, or fills twelve or more prescriptions, or uses four drugs in a single therapeutic class.

(2) *Multiple prescriptions from different prescribers.* A patient who visits several prescribers and obtains the same prescription is automatically reviewed. This detection of patient abuse is centered on sedative-hypnotic or narcotic drugs. A shopper who buys at more than one pharmacy, regardless of prescribing source, will also be identified.

(3) *The too-frequently refilled prescription.* Utilizing dates and volumes dispensed, the computer will reject automatic payment when thirty capsules should still be available from a previous prescription. The converse warning has not been implemented: there is no similar notification when the prescription for a chronic medication is not refilled or not refilled soon enough. One might note that this converse notification, which should improve medical care, would not save money.

(4) *The too-small volume prescription.* When a chronically used medication is refilled in monthly or less-than-monthly intervals, notice is given to the prescriber that money can be saved by prescribing larger volumes so that recurrent dispensing fees can be avoided. This maneuver constitutes the only *documented* saving in a published paper from PAID.[26] (One could point out that large-volume prescribing occasionally results in adverse results, providing availability for accidental or purposeful overdosage, or accumulation of time-expired drugs in the patient's home. Letters from the DURC resulted in a yearly saving of $1,111.20 in San Joaquin.)

---

[25] Charlotte Muller, "Drug Benefits in Health Insurance," *International Journal of Health Services,* vol. 4 (Winter 1974), pp. 157-70.

[26] Frank F. Yarborough and Marc F. Laventurier, "Peer Review Works via a Committee of 7: 6 Pharmacists Plus One Physician," *Pharmacy Times,* March 1974, pp. 58-63.

Each of these DURC maneuvers can be described as pecuniary and hardly adventurous. The computer could have accomplished them without any DURC functions at all. I do not mean to imply that some of these corrections are not in the direction of better drug therapy— they are. But they are designed essentially to save money and scarcely represent the development of dramatic therapeutic guidelines.

As was noted above, the massive data base has not been used to increase knowledge of prescribing to any appreciable degree, much less to generate guidelines. The assumption of the proud mantle of drug utilization review clearly should be tied to the responsibility of documenting its achievements, preferably in the archival scientific literature. Most PAID publications discuss the methodology of the review process and extol the system's virtues: in other words, they are essentially public relations statements. Two papers emanating from PAID are, however, more ambitious; one of them represents the only attempt to utilize the existing data base.

Drug Interactions. A paper entitled "The Incidence of Drug-Drug Interactions in a Medi-Cal Population," was presented before the American College of Physicians in Atlantic City in April 1972, and later published in the *California Pharmacist*.[27] The provocative title is deceptive because the paper does not describe drug-drug interactions at all. Since PAID has no post-prescribing clinical follow-up data, this is not surprising. Instead, the paper describes the *potential* for drug interactions in prescriptions given to the cited population. This point was made in the text of the paper.

After selecting some important categories of interaction, the study identified patients who received two or more interacting drugs, generally within a sixty-day interval. The study calculated the percentage of those subjects who receive potentially interacting drugs in addition to the principal drug. For example, 148 patients of the 42,000 patients surveyed received coumarin anticoagulants. Seventy-nine of these also received one of a lengthy list of potential interactors: clofibrate, chloral hydrate, aspirin, and so on. No clinical assessment of the possible *appropriateness* of these combinations was mentioned. (A physician might prescribe the combination of coumarin and chloral hydrate, knowing that the potential interaction was likely to be of no clinical significance.[28]) Studies of this type have a potential for

---

[27] Marc F. Laventurier and Robert B. Talley, "The Incidence of Drug-Drug Inter-actions in a Medi-Cal Population," *California Pharmacist*, November 1972, pp. 18-20, 22.

[28] Paul F. Griner, Lawrence G. Raisz, Frederick R. Rickles, Paul J. Weisner, and Charles L. Odoroff, "Chloral Hydrate and Warfarin Interaction: Clinical Signifi-cance?" *Annals of Internal Medicine*, vol. 74, no. 4 (1971), pp. 540-43.

producing useful information, but only if the clinical follow-up is carried out. Nothing of a similar explorative nature has been published since 1972, and no follow-up to this specific paper has appeared.

The paper did, however, have high visibility for political purposes. It was used by Senator Kennedy to point out, inaccurately, the high incidence of drug interactions in the U.S.

The Georgia Sea Island Paper. In 1972, a paper entitled "Drug Utilization and Peer Review in San Joaquin" was read before the American Association of Foundations for Medical Care at Sea Island, Georgia.[29] In that paper the authors estimated that 30,000 deaths had been caused by adverse drug reactions in the previous year in the United States. The derivation of this figure had no relationship to the PAID data base, which, as we have already discussed, contains no post-prescribing clinical data. The figure was again picked up by Senator Kennedy during congressional hearings and was widely publicized and repeatedly mentioned by the press and other witnesses before the hearing. Later, the figure was revised upward to 60,000 to 140,000 per year in a letter in the *Journal of the American Medical Association* by the authors of the paper.[30] Karch and Lasagna have critically reviewed the extrapolations that generated these figures and point out that the extent of this serious problem is simply unknown.[31] The Sea Island paper must be viewed as tentative hypothesis, poorly carried out. It has never been published in the archival scientific literature, although photoreproduced copies of the manuscript have been widely circulated.

Drug utilization review is an idea whose time has come for consideration, if not implementation. It has been proposed as a potential method for Professional Standards Review Organization evaluation.[32] The Bureau of Quality Assessment of the National Professional

---

[29] Robert B. Talley and Marc F. Laventurier, "Drug Utilization and Peer Review in San Joaquin," read before the American Association of Foundations for Medical Care, Sea Island, Georgia, August 28, 1972.

[30] Robert B. Talley and Marc F. Laventurier, "Drug Induced Illness," *Journal of the American Medical Association*, vol. 229, no. 8 (1974), p. 1043.

[31] Fred E. Karch and Louis Lasagna, *Adverse Drug Reactions in the United States: An Analysis of the Scope of the Problem and Recommendations for Future Approaches* (Washington, D.C.: Medicine in the Public Interest) (undated); Fred E. Karch and Louis Lasagna, "Adverse Drug Reactions," *Journal of the American Medical Association*, vol. 234, no. 12 (1975), pp. 1236-41.

[32] Editorial, "Peer Review Spurs Monitoring of Physician Prescribing Habits," *Hospital Practice*, vol. 9, no. 9 (September 1974), pp. 195, 199, 201; George Provost, "The PSRO and Drug Utilization Review," *American Journal of Hospital Pharmacy*, vol. 30, no. 7 (July 1973), p. 583.

Standards Review Organization has awarded a contract to evaluate the utility of inpatient drug utilization review processes.[33]

Conventional wisdom has it that Americans are badly served by prescribing physicians. While no one would maintain that prescribing is optimal, the characterization of American prescribing and the real assessment of poor prescribing has not been approached, let alone begun. The fiscal intermediaries in their review of drug utilization have promised much but delivered little, and at least one has confused the issues. Pecuniary goals and insurance service may not constitute a framework for the evolution of assessments of drug utilization.

---

[33] Personal communication with David Olson, IMS America.

3

CANADA

Edward M. Sellers and Sirje Sellers

Introduction

In Canada, legal or regulatory control of drug availability and use is exercised by both the federal government and the ten provincial governments. Constitutionally, the provision of health care services is primarily a provincial responsibility, but the federal government entered the area of drug regulation in the late nineteenth and early twentieth centuries, using its jurisdiction over the criminal law to try to control the illicit drug market and to protect the public from unsafe, hazardous, and adulterated drugs. In 1972, the Health Protection Branch of the Department of National Health and Welfare was formed to coordinate the various federal programs designed to protect the public from unsafe products and fraudulent practices. Federal regulations currently govern over-the-counter (OTC) drugs, narcotics, and prescription drugs by a combination of the Proprietary or Patent Medicine Act, the Narcotic Control Act, and the Food and Drugs Act.[1] The Food and Drugs Act exerts the main influence since it is mainly concerned with prohibiting the sale of adulterated products, ensuring sanitary conditions of manufacture and storage, and requir-

We thank the many individuals across Canada who completed questionnaires and provided information for inclusion in this paper. In particular, we thank Dr. R. C. B. Graham, assistant director, Bureau of Drugs, Health Protection Branch, who kindly supplied the information in Table 1, and Ms. M. Stewart for assistance in preparation of the manuscript. The study was supported in part by the intramural funding program of the Addiction Research Foundation of Ontario. The literature review for this paper was completed in June 1975. In January 1976, the Health Disciplines Act came into effect in Ontario, Canada, bringing under one statute the legislation affecting the professions of medicine, nursing, and pharmacy.

[1] Proprietary or Patent Medicine Act, R. S. C. 1970, c. P-25; Narcotic Control Act, R. S. C. 1970, c. N-1; Food and Drugs Act, R. S. C. 1970, c. F-27.

ing that advertising, labeling, and packaging not be misleading or deceptive. In addition, regulations under the act control the access of new drugs to the market by requiring that these drugs meet standards of safety and efficacy, permit ethical drugs to be sold to the public only on prescription, and restrict the use of certain drugs to the treatment of specifically named diseases.

Provincial pharmacy acts are generally concerned with regulating the sale of drug products, record keeping, and the licensing of pharmacists. Most of the provincial acts also include a schedule of prescription drugs; it is generally conceded that these provincial schedules may add to the federal schedule of prescription drugs, but not subtract from it.

A national Medicare system that does not cover drugs was introduced in 1968. Since its introduction, many provinces have shown an interest in some form of drug benefit plan. Presumably these provinces would also be concerned about problems associated with drug utilization. To obtain information about current provincial regulations on drugs and drug utilization controls, the authors sent questionnaires to the minister of health, the deans of faculties of pharmacy, and the presidents of the medical association and the pharmacy society in each province. The main questions concerned the following: (1) restrictions in the respondent's province, (2) the basis for postmarketing control, (3) additional controls, (4) surveillance procedures, and (5) an evaluation of the performance. Answers were received from the presidents of the ten provincial pharmacy societies, three deans of faculties of pharmacy, three presidents of provincial medical associations, and three ministries of health. The relatively poor return probably reflects the general low level of interest in the problem of drug utilization in the past and the fact that in most provinces in Canada, relatively few well-recognized—let alone unique—use control systems are currently operating. Indeed, the most complete answers were obtained from provinces with the most developed drug use control systems (for example, British Columbia, Alberta, Manitoba, Ontario, and Quebec).

In the following sections of this chapter, the information gained from the answers to this questionnaire is incorporated in the text. We have taken this approach, rather than tabulating the answers for each question, for four reasons. First, the federal regulations pervade much of the provincial programs: indeed many answers confused federal and provincial regulation. Second, in general, no province has clearly defined its aims nor the indexes to be used in evaluating program success or failure. Third, the question of use controls is contentious and filled with conflicts of interest involving professional role and function, economics, and political acceptability; hence respondents representing professional groups and government probably tended to be cautious, giving superficial answers. Fourth, important misconceptions and confusion appeared in some replies, negating the usefulness of the answers (as, for example, the differences between federal and provincial jurisdiction). Our impression is that, except for those branches of governments directly involved in the application of drug regulations and utilization control systems, knowledge about these systems was incomplete, and information from governments not readily available. Of course there were important exceptions to this impression, and we are particularly indebted to those individuals who took considerable care and time to provide us with specific information.

It seems reasonable to us that answers to the questionnaire should be available in a health care system that has de facto embarked on drug use control systems. In Canada at present, however, answers to questions dealing with postmarketing use control either do not exist or are not available, or possibly the questions have not been considered. The Canadian parliamentary system has not encouraged open committee review and inquiry concerning drug use.

Premarketing Regulations for New Drugs

Before a drug is released for sale in Canada, it passes three stages of federal regulatory control aimed at ensuring both safety and effectiveness for the uses claimed by the manufacturer (see Figure 1). These three stages correspond to preclinical testing (Phase I and early Phase II), clinical testing (late Phase II and Phase III) and, finally, submission of all gathered information for marketing approval as a new drug submission.[2]

Preclinical and Clinical Testing. Acute and chronic toxicity studies of the drug must first be completed in at least three mammalian species, and appropriate dosages determined for possible human use. The drug manufacturer may then apply to the Health Protection Branch, Department of National Health and Welfare, for permission to have a qualified investigator conduct a clinical pharmacology trial. These initial trials are usually conducted in normal and healthy volunteers and their purpose is only to indicate the general nontoxic dose range for the drug. Prison populations are seldom used. Often the initial drug metabolism studies in man are also conducted at this

---

[2] E. M. Sellers, "Clinical Pharmacology in Canada" in *Clinical Pharmacology and Therapeutics*, vol. 16, no. 3, part 2 (September 1974), pp. 554-64.

Figure 1

NEW DRUG DEVELOPMENT AND REGULATION IN CANADA

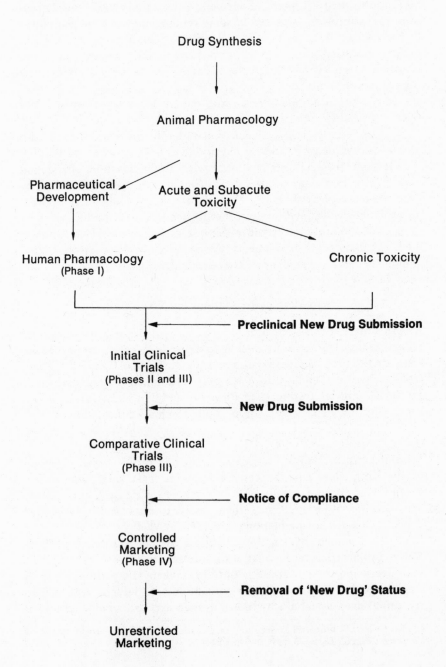

stage. After the initial studies in man have been conducted, the manufacturer files a preclinical new drug submission (PCNDS) with the Drug Advisory Bureau, Department of National Health and Welfare. This application is reviewed by the bureau and, if it is acceptable, the manufacturer may distribute the drug to qualified investigators for further clinical testing to determine if the drug is effective and safe for the treatment of the specific disease for which it has been developed.

The PCNDS presents all the evidence available on the new compound and indicates the following: the objectives of the proposed clinical testing; the identifying name or mark of the new drug; its chemical structure and source; the results of investigations made to support its clinical use (including data on toxicity, pharmacology, and biochemistry); the contraindications; the suggested treatment for overdose; the methods, equipment, plans, and controls used in the manufacture, processing, and packaging of the new drug; the tests applied to control its potency, purity, and safety; the names and qualifications of all investigators to whom the drug will be distributed; and the names of institutions where the clinical tests will be conducted.

New Drug Submissions. If, during the clinical efficacy studies, the new drug proves to be of value as a therapeutic agent, the manufacturer must file a new drug submission with the Drug Advisory Bureau prior to marketing. The new drug submission is more extensive than the PCNDS and includes all the human data from the preclinical studies, the results of any further animal studies carried out by the manufacturer, drafts of the product monograph, and samples of the finished form of the new drug. The new drug submission is reviewed by the Manufacturing Control Division and by the Medicine and Pharmacology Division of the Drug Advisory Bureau. The Manufacturing Control Division is concerned primarily with manufacturing processes and quality control, and the Medicine and Pharmacology Division reviews the animal investigations, the pharmacological studies, toxicity and teratologic studies, and the clinical trials of toxicity and efficacy. After these reviews are completed, this division reviews the wording of the product monograph. Often the manufacturer may be asked to conduct, and/or submit information on additional animal or clinical work to clarify questions of toxicity potential or of effectiveness in specific conditions. Once the review of the new drug submission is complete, and the submission is approved, then a notice of compliance is issued by the assistant deputy minister, Health Protection Branch.

Even though a notice of compliance has been issued, however, and marketing may take place, the drug may remain in the new drug status until sufficient additional information has been accumulated— as for example, information on long-term toxicity. This additional stage is known as Phase IV (see Figure 1). These requirements and the basis for such continued surveillance are not clearly defined: Phase IV offers the opportunity for some flexibility in permitting the early release of drugs that have important therapeutic benefit but for which toxicity studies in man are incomplete (an example would be cancer chemo-therapeutic agents).

One obvious consequence of the regulatory control of new drug testing in humans and the release of these drugs to the general market is the tremendous amount of paper work engendered. The number of pages of documentation required to satisfy the requirements for Ketamine was 67,128 in Canada and 72,200 in the United States. It was 120 in Mexico.[3]

In the United States, the average time between the first testing of a drug in a laboratory and its subsequent marketing is seven to nine years. In Canada, initial human testing of the drug may add at least three to four months to this period, since review of the PCNDS must be completed before actual testing can begin. During this time the proposed studies may already have been conducted in the United States or other countries, since the United States, for example, has only a thirty-day waiting period. If any adverse comment is made during review of the PCNDS, an additional three months may elapse before the studies begin. Thus, Canadian studies may begin five to eight months later than corresponding U.S. studies. Furthermore, since the compiling of the PCNDS is often dependent on information contained in the U.S. investigational new drug application (IND), Canadian applications may not even begin to be drawn up until the IND is processed by the U.S. Food and Drug Administration.

On the other hand, review of the new pharmaceutical agents receiving notices of compliance in Canada over the past four years indicates that, in general, slightly more new drugs have been released in Canada than in the United States.[4] (See Table 1 for list of drugs released in Canada between April 1, 1973, and March 31, 1974.)

[3] Ibid.
[4] Ibid.

Table 1

NEW PHARMACEUTICAL AGENTS RECEIVING NOTICE OF
COMPLIANCE FOR MARKETING, CANADA,
APRIL 1, 1973 TO MARCH 31, 1974

Proper Name	Brand Name	Manufacturer	Pharmaceutical Classification
Chlorazepate dipotassium	Tranxene	Abbott	Anxiolytic-sedative
Uracil mustard	Uracil Mustard	Upjohn	Antineoplastic
Calcium heparinate	Calciparine S.C.	Anglo-French	Anticoagulant
Benzylpenicilloyl-polylysine	Pre-Pen	Kremers-Urban	Skin test antigen
Antihemophilic factor (human)	Humafac	Parke, Davis	Antihemophilic
Trimethoprim + sulfamethoxazole	Bactrim Roche and Septra	Hoffmann-La Roche	Antibacterial
Clomipramine	Anafranil	Ciba-Geigy	Antidepressant, anxiolytic
Calusterone	Methosarb	Upjohn	Androgen
L-Asparaginase	Kidrolase	Poulenc	Antileukemic
Sodium cefazolin	Ancef	Smith, Kline and French	Antibiotic
Sodium cellulose phosphate	Calcisorb	ICN Canada Ltd.	Ion exchange agent
Metoclopramide	Maxeran	Nordic Bio-chemicals	Modifier of upper gastrointestinal tract motility
Amoxicillin	Amoxil	Ayerst	Antibiotic
BCNU	Carmustine	Bristol	Antineoplastic
Intrauterine copper contraceptive	CU-7 Gyne-T	Searle Ortho	Intrauterine contraceptive device
Enflurane	Ethrane	Ohio Medical Products	Inhalation anesthetic
Hydrotalcite	Altacite	Roussel	Antacid-antipepsin
Metolazone	Zaroxolyn	Pennwalt Corporation	Diuretic/saluretic/antihypertensive

Table 1 (Continued)

Proper Name	Brand Name	Manufacturer	Pharmaceutical Classification
Naproxen	Naprosyn	Syntex	Anti-inflammatory (non-steroidal)
Pivampicillin hydrochloride	Alphacillin	Frosst	Antibiotic
Carbenoxolone	Biogastrone	Merrell	Gastric ulcer
Poly (tetra- fluoroethylene)	Mentor	Ethicon	Surgical aid (vocal cord)
Cephradine	Velosef Anspor	Squibb Smith, Kline and French	Antibiotic
Dantrolene sodium	Dantrium	Eaton	Skeletal muscle relaxant
Cephapirin sodium	Cefadyl	Bristol	Antibiotic
Pimozide	ORAP	McNeil	Antipsychotic
Iocetamic acid	Cholebrine	Mallinckrodt	Cholecystographic X-ray contrast medium
Lactulose	Cephulac	Merrell- National	Colonic content acidifier
Mazindol	Sanorex	Sandoz	Anorexic
Dinoprost tromethamine	Prostin $F_{2\alpha}$	Upjohn	Induction of thera- peutic abortion
Miconazole nitrate	Monistat	Ortho	Antifungal, anti- bacterial

Source: List supplied by Dr. R. C. B. Graham, assistant director, Bureau of Drugs, Health Protection Branch.

Postmarketing Use Controls

Prescription Drugs. In Canada drugs which may be sold to the public only on prescription are listed in Schedule F of the Food and Drug Regulations. Importation of these drugs is prohibited, except by practitioners, drug manufacturers, wholesale druggists, registered pharmacists, and residents of a foreign country while visiting Canada. Provincial pharmacy acts also generally contain a schedule of prescription drugs but, as noted, these can only add to and not subtract from the federal list.

Federal regulations require that all prescriptions must be in writing, that written prescriptions must be retained by pharmacists for at least two years, and that the prescription may be refilled only on the direction of the practitioner (physician, dentist, or veterinary surgeon). Provincial legislation, which controls the licensing of health professionals, may be more stringent; in Ontario, for instance, pharmacists are required to retain records for six years.

The sale of prescription drugs contrary to regulations is a punishable offense under both federal and provincial legislation, and conviction under either may lead to cancellation or suspension of a pharmacist's license.

Narcotics and Controlled and Restricted Drugs. The Bureau of Dangerous Drugs of the Health Protection Branch of the Department of National Health and Welfare is responsible for administering the controls on the availability of narcotics and of controlled and restricted drugs for medical or scientific purposes. Narcotics are listed in a schedule to the Narcotic Control Act. Controlled and restricted drugs are listed in schedules to the Food and Drugs Act. Controlled drugs (Schedule G) are amphetamines and barbiturates and their salts (Table 2). Restricted drugs (Schedule H) are mainly hallucinogens, and include lysergic acid diethylamide (LSD), N,N-diethyltryptamine (DET), N,N-dimethyltryptamine (DMT) and their salts, various amphetamine derivatives and their salts, Harmaline, Harmalol, Psilocin and Psilocybin.

Restricted drugs are available only for investigational purposes and must be used in accordance with the protocol submitted when applying for authorization by the minister of national health and welfare. Controlled drugs and narcotics may be prescribed by a practitioner if the drug is required for the condition for which the patient is receiving treatment.[5] The practitioner must keep inventory records, as well as records of his administration of and prescriptions for these drugs.

Only licensed dealers are permitted to manufacture and distribute narcotics and controlled drugs. Pharmacists must keep separate records of all prescriptions filled for these drugs and may refill them only if the original prescription so directed and if it specified the intervals between refilling. Both dealers and pharmacists must keep records of inventories and all transactions in these drugs and make regular reports to the Bureau of Dangerous Drugs. Dealers are required to report monthly, pharmacists every two months. Records and inven-

---

[5] Food and Drug Regulations, G.04.001; Narcotic Control Regulations, s. 38.

Table 2

CONTROLLED DRUGS

(Schedule G, the Food and Drugs Act)

Amphetamine and its salts
Barbituric acid and its salts and derivatives
Benzphetamine and its salts
Methamphetamine and its salts
Methaqualone and its salts
Pentazocine and its salts
Phendimetrazine and its salts
Phenmetrazine and its salts

Source: Food and Drugs Act, R. S. C. 1970, Schedule G.

tories are also subject to unannounced inspection and audit by the bureau, whose policy it is to inspect all dealer and pharmaceutical outlets at least once a year. It is difficult to meet this objective, however, since Canada has approximately 200 licensed dealers in narcotics, 250 dealers in controlled drugs, and 4,700 pharmacies, and the bureau receives notices of over 3 million prescriptions a year. These are monitored by a special staff, but the monitoring system is not automated, and, although the staff has developed considerable skill and judgment in detecting abuse of the law, the system has serious limitations.

Unauthorized possession of any narcotic or controlled or restricted drug is a punishable offense. To prevent "double doctoring" in narcotics, the onus is on the patient to divulge to his doctor he is already receiving narcotics under treatment by another practitioner. Failure to do so results in loss of the defense of authorized possession if he is arrested for possessing a narcotic. A practioner has the onus of proving that any controlled drug or narcotic in his possession is for professional use, and that the drug was prescribed or administered in accordance with the regulations.

The Ontario Pharmacy Act also makes special provisions for amphetamines, barbituric acid, benzphetamine, and methamphetamine, four of the drugs listed as "controlled" in the federal act. Separate records must be kept of these drugs, and reports of sales and prescriptions made to the provincial minister of health. If it is found that unreasonable amounts of these drugs are being sold or prescribed, the minister may report the practitioner or pharmacist to the appropriate provincial disciplinary committee.

Special Regulations. There are special regulations involving so-called designated drugs and methadone.

"Designated drugs." These include amphetamines, phenmetrazine, and phendimetrazine. In Canada, as in other countries, there has been considerable concern about the indiscriminate use of amphetamines and other stimulants. In 1966, 1,040 kilograms of amphetamines (including methamphetamines) were medically available in Canada; in 1970, this quantity dropped to 309 kilograms; in 1971 it was slightly less than 300 kilograms.[6] Since evidence suggested the continuing abuse of legally prescribed amphetamines and related drugs (phenmetrazine and phendimetrazine), regulations were enacted, effective January 1, 1973, naming these controlled drugs as "designated drugs" and requiring that practitioners prescribe them only for certain specific medical conditions. These conditions, compiled by panels of nongovernmental medical experts, are shown in Table 3.

In their initial form, the regulations also required practitioners to notify the Health Protection Branch when a designated drug was prescribed and to obtain the opinion of a medical consultant if the drug was to be prescribed for more than thirty days. In the nine months after the regulation went into effect, the use of these drugs decreased by at least 90 percent.[7] The Health Protection Branch, therefore, modified the regulations by omitting the notification and consultation requirement. The designated conditions were, however, retained. Continued surveillance of the patterns of use of these agents is being made by the Health Protection Branch and the Bureau of Dangerous Drugs.

Methadone. About three-and-one-half years ago, it became apparent that large amounts of methadone were being diverted from the legal to the illicit markets in Canada. Surveillance by the Bureau of Dangerous Drugs showed many instances of forged prescriptions, "double doctoring," steadily escalating doses, "medical shopping," and permissive prescribing. As a result, regulations on methadone use were enacted effective June 1, 1972, whereby a practitioner could prescribe methadone only on authorization by the minister of national health and welfare. To receive this authorization, a practitioner is required to provide details of the way the drug will be prescribed in his medical practice or evidence of his association with a recognized

---

[6] A. B. Morrison, "Regulatory Control of the Canadian Government over the Manufacturing, Distribution and Prescribing of Psychotropic Drugs" in R. Cooperstock, ed., *Social Aspects of the Medical Use of Psychotropic Drugs* (Toronto: Addiction Research Foundation, 1974), pp. 9-19.

[7] Ibid.

Table 3

AUTHORIZED USES OF DESIGNATED DRUGS, CANADA

(amphetamines, phenmetrazine, and phendimetrazine)

In Humans

Narcolepsy

Hyperkinetic disorder in children

Mental retardation (minimal brain dysfunction)

Epilepsy

Parkinsonism

Hypotensive states associated with anaesthesia

In Animals

Depression of cardiac and respiratory centers

and approved drug treatment program. In addition, practitioners and institutions must report their use of the drug. This legislation has markedly decreased the earlier widespread abuses. Before enactment of the regulation, there were three structured methadone treatment programs in Canada; by the end of 1973, there were thirty accredited treatment units, with 132 affiliated physicians using methadone under acceptable protocols filed with the Health Protection Branch.[8]

Prohibition of Sale. After the thalidomide experience in 1962, a category of drugs whose sale was prohibited was established under the Food and Drugs Act. To date, only thalidomide is on the list; it is available only for research purposes under special permit.

Consultation among the Health Protection Branch, an expert advisory committee external to government, and a number of physicians connected with renal units in various provinces in Canada led to the assessment that excessive intake of analgesic mixtures containing both phenacetin and salicylates might be associated with renal damage. Therefore, as of May 1, 1973, under the Food and Drug Regulations, preparations containing phenacetin in combination with salicylates, including all salts and derivatives of salicylic acid, were prohibited from sale. Phenacetin and salicylates can still be sold separately.

Criteria Governing the Scheduling of Drugs. No attempt has been made to formulate and express clear criteria for the decisions to place drugs on schedules—decisions which must be made by the administra-

---

[8] Ibid.

tive authorities. Basically, such decisions appear to be guided by consideration of the drug's necessity, its usefulness for medical purposes, its potential for producing harm, and its actual and potential abuse for nonmedical purposes.

Other Legal Controls. In addition to the controls discussed above, there are postmarketing controls on advertising and distribution of drug samples.

Advertising. The Health Protection Branch regulates advertising of drugs under authority of the three federal acts relating to drugs. The Food and Drugs Act states as a general requirement that "no person shall label, package, treat, process, sell or advertise any drug in a manner that is false, misleading or deceptive or is likely to create an erroneous impression regarding its character, value, composition, merit or safety."[9]

Advertising to the public is prohibited for all prescription drugs, controlled drugs, narcotics, and any drug listed as a treatment, preventative, or cure for the forty-five diseases on a scheduled list. Drugs that supply a maximum daily dose of vitamins in excess of the limits stated in the regulations (in the case of Vitamin A, 10,000 international units) may not be advertised, nor may drugs intended for the treatment, mitigation, or prevention of a dietary deficiency in humans if the drugs are represented as containing minerals other than calcium, phosphorus, iron, fluorine, iodine, copper, or magnesium. A new drug may not be advertised to physicians or pharmacists until a notice of compliance has been issued, and final labels, package inserts, and brochures filed with the minister of national health and welfare.

Under authority of the Broadcasting Act, radio and television advertising of over-the-counter drugs must be approved by the Department of National Health and Welfare. OTCs are preparations used for medical purposes, whose name, definition, or composition is not found in a pharmacopeia or formulary approved by the federal minister of health. There is no jurisdiction for prior approval of OTC advertising in printed media although action may be taken subsequently upon infractions under the general provision of the Food and Drugs Act quoted above.

Distribution of drug samples. Unsolicited distribution of drug samples to physicians was first prohibited in 1962. On the advice of the Canadian Drug Advisory Committee and various trade and pro-

---

[9] Health Protection Branch, Department of National Health and Welfare, *Rx Bulletin*, vol. 5, no. 4 (September/October 1974), pp. 76-78.

fessional associations, this regulation was made more stringent in 1973. It now stipulates that a practitioner or pharmacist, registered and entitled to practice his profession in a province of Canada, must sign an order specifying the name and quantity of the drug sample ordered. This order may provide for refilling at specified intervals during any period not exceeding six months. Specifically excluded from distribution as drug samples are narcotics (as defined in the Narcotic Control Act), controlled drugs, or new drugs for which a notice of compliance has not yet been issued.[10]

Over-the-Counter Drugs. Over-the-counter drugs are subject to the general requirements of the Food and Drugs Act for packaging, labeling, advertising and sale, and sanitary conditions of manufacture and nonadulteration. Otherwise they are governed by the Proprietary or Patent Medicine Act. This act requires registration of all secret-formula nonpharmacopeial medicines with the Department of National Health and Welfare, as well as annual licensing of manufacturers. Use of certain drugs, including opium and its derivatives, is prohibited in the manufacture of OTCs. Drugs listed in the schedule to the act may be used in amounts approved by an advisory committee. Also prescribed by the committee are the maximum single and daily dose of such products. A bill to bring OTC medicines under the Food and Drugs Act and to require a quantitative list of ingredients on the labels of these products to improve the outdated secrecy aspect of the Proprietary or Patent Medicine Act became effective in 1976.

In-Hospital Drug Use Control. In 1958, the Canadian Council on Hospital Accreditation was incorporated under federal law, separating the Canadian organization from the Joint Commission on Accreditation of Hospitals in the United States. The guide to hospital accreditation in Canada spells out various standards which must be met for a hospital to be accredited including standards for pharmaceutical services.[11] Various aspects of these standards relate—some directly and some more obliquely—to the general question of drug use control. For instance, Standard 5 states that "Written policies and procedures that govern the safe administration of drugs shall be developed by the medical staff in co-operation with the pharmacist and with representatives of other disciplines as necessary."

Such policies, which are essential for the safe administration of drugs to patients, include at least the following requirements:

---

[10] Ibid., vol. 4, no. 8 (November/December 1973), p. 188.

[11] *Guide to Hospital Accreditation* (Toronto: Canadian Council on Hospital Accreditation, 1972).

(1) Drugs shall be administered only upon the order of the individual who has been assigned clinical privileges, or who is an authorized member of the house staff.

(2) All medication shall be administered by appropriately licensed personnel in accordance with any laws and regulations governing such acts.

(3) A reasonable stop-order procedure, appropriate to the type of treatment given in a hospital, shall be developed. It is desirable that narcotics, antibiotics, anticoagulants, sedatives, hypnotics, mood-affecting drugs, and any other appropriate drugs be considered for inclusion.

(4) Acceptable precautionary measures for the safe admixture of parenteral products will be developed.

(5) Each dose of medication administered shall be properly recorded in the patient's medical record.

(6) Medication errors and drug reactions shall be reported immediately to the practitioner who ordered the drug. The medication given and/or the drug reaction shall be properly recorded in the patient's medical record. Hospitals are encouraged to report any suspected or proven adverse drug reactions, major or minor, expected or unexpected, as well as the lack of effect of any drug, to the National Drug Adverse Reactions Reporting Program of the Food and Drug Directorate, Department of National Health and Welfare, and to the manufacturer.

(7) Policies shall be established on patient administration of their own drugs, or drugs brought to the hospital, and the appropriate labeling of investigational drugs.

Responsibility for drawing up policies on hospital drug distribution and safe administration are usually charged to a pharmacy committee or pharmacy and therapeutics committee, which typically reports to the medical advisory committee in the hospital.

Local hospital pharmacy and therapeutics committees have considerable latitude. The following are some forms of use controls known to us.

(1) Restriction of certain antibiotics—for example, gentamicin—to use by infectious disease specialists;

(2) Restriction of new drugs—for example, carbenoxelone—to use by one specialist group;

(3) Requirement for consultation before a drug—for example tobramycin—is dispensed;

(4) Removal of barbiturate and nonbarbiturate hypnotics—for example, secobarbital and glutethimide methyprylon, ethchlorvynol—from hospital stock;

(5) Limitation on size of prescriptions or interval of renewal—for example, chlordiazepoxide (one month)—for outpatient prescribing of minor tranquilizers;

(6) Central purchasing by groups of hospital pharmacies;

(7) Development of restrictive hospital formularies—for example, limitation of choice of tricyclic antidepressant or benzodiazepine to a single agent in each class;

(8) Establishment of an antibiotic utilization control committee; and

(9) Requirement that the indication for use of the drug and name of staff physician authorizing drug use—for example, with cephalosporins, clindamycin—be included with the drug order.

The value and extent of such use controls is highly variable and is dependent on individual chairmen of the committees, the interests of heads of hospital pharmacies, and the effectiveness of opposition of medical and surgical staff.

Quality and Price Assessment

Federal Assessment: the QUAD Program. In an effort to reduce the cost of drugs to the public, the Health Protection Branch instituted the Drug Quality Assessment Program (QUAD) in May 1971 to provide physicians and pharmacists with comparative information on the price and quality of drugs.[12] Drugs selected for inclusion in the QUAD program are single entity drugs manufactured or distributed by more than one company. Sustained release dosage forms are not included. Selection for QUAD is made on the basis of medical indication for use, precision of dose required, risk of contaminants, and the estimated dollar volume of drug sold.

The major components of the QUAD program are (1) *in vitro* analysis, (2) plant evaluation, (3) claims assessment on direction for use and bioavailability, and (4) publication of results and prices in the *QUAD Review*.

Chemical analysis makes use of four basic tests: identity, assay, weight variation, and the disintegration test of the Health Protection Branch. In addition, since April 1973, all tests required by the phar-

---

[12] Department of National Health and Welfare, *QUAD Review*, no. 2 (Ottawa: Information Canada, 1974).

macopeial or other standard named on the label of a product are performed, including tests for impurities, pH, and dissolution time. Samples for analysis are obtained under authority of the Food and Drugs Act, and all unsatisfactory results of analysis are published. Noncompliance with requirements of the labeled standard may lead to action by the Health Protection Branch, ranging from a simple warning to prosecution of the manufacturer, depending upon the potential health hazard.[13]

Plant evaluation. Until 1973, information on a pharmaceutical manufacturing company's capability to produce a specific drug was not available to prospective buyers or members of the health professions. Because the information was obtained during regulatory inspections under the Food and Drugs Act, it was considered privileged information. A clear distinction is now made between regulatory inspections and the QUAD evaluations. Companies voluntarily participate in the QUAD program and authorize the Health Protection Branch to publish results gathered during these evaluations, although the detailed information resulting from the evaluation is available only to federal departments and provincial departments of health and hospitals.

The QUAD standard is based upon the current requirements of the Food and Drug Regulations. Evaluation performed under this standard includes an intensive review of such indicators of manufacturing capability as master formula, manufacturing and packaging orders, standards and results of tests on raw materials, and finished products and stability data. The QUAD evaluation is unique inasmuch as the manufacturer is evaluated on his capability to manufacture, control, and distribute a *specified* drug product. The results of nearly 400 drug product evaluations, representing twenty-seven drug entities and manufactured by forty-one firms are published in *QUAD Review*, no. 2.[14]

Bioavailability. The Health Protection Branch obtains bioavailability information for the QUAD program either through its own studies, or through extramural studies carried out under contract. The 1974 criteria of acceptability for each drug category will probably be refined in the future, replacing the present guidelines of 80 percent content compared with a standard formulation. In particular, it is recognized that separate criteria must be used for different classes of drugs with differing margins of safety.

---

[13] Food and Drugs Act, s. 21; Food and Drug Regulations, A.01.050.

[14] Department of National Health and Welfare, *QUAD Review*, no. 2.

Drug monographs. When the QUAD program was instituted, the Health Protection Branch planned to prepare and publish directions for the use of products included in the program. This plan was modified to include all drugs of a particular pharmacologic or therapeutic class rather than only one or two drugs in any group. Plans call for publication as soon as the monographs for the majority of drugs in one group are prepared.

Price information. The *QUAD Review* includes prices ascertained, verified, and arranged in tabular form by the Department of Consumer and Corporate Affairs, prices representing the product cost to the retail pharmacist. The drugs are listed in order of price per single dosage, for quantities of 100; this allows comparison of relative prices of various products.

Provincial Assessment: Ontario PARCOST Program (Prescriptions at Reasonable Cost). The provincial government in Ontario publishes a drug formulary, the *Comparative Drug Index,*[15] which lists prescription products in comparative categories according to the nature, strength, and dosage form of the active therapeutic constituents. Unit price information is provided for each product. This index is compiled by the provincial Ministry of Health and its appointed advisory committee, the Drug Quality and Therapeutics Committee, composed of representatives from university departments of pharmacology and medicine, the faculty of pharmacy, the Ontario Medical Association, and the provincial government. It is distributed to practitioners, pharmacists, hospitals, and affiliated organizations associated with the manufacture, distribution, and use of pharmaceutical preparations.

The purpose of the *Comparative Drug Index* is to provide a ready reference (1) to practitioners in identifying quality products for prescribing, (2) to pharmacists in stocking comparable products for dispensing, (3) to professional committees in the selection of therapeutically effective pharmaceutical products recommended for use in hospitals, and (4) to anyone concerned with relative prices. In general, unless otherwise provided, the drugs are grouped in any one chart on the basis of similar therapeutic application (as, for example, diuretics). The products listed meet recognized standards of quality in the judgment of the Drug Quality and Therapeutics Committee, according to criteria set out in federal regulations and recommendations pertaining to drug manufacturing, in official compendia such as the British pharmacopeia and the United States pharmacopeia, and

[15] Ontario Ministry of Health, *PARCOST Comparative Drug Index,* no. 8 (Toronto: Queen's Printer, 1974).

according to similar criteria as defined by authorities in the World Health Organization (WHO), the United States, and Britain. The committee bases its decisions on a review of manufacturing facilities and procedures, on laboratory analysis of selected products, on exchange of information with the federal Department of National Health and Welfare and the U.S. Food and Drug Administration, on evaluation of selected documents pertaining to individual products, and on the knowledge and experience reported from drug usage at the clinical level.

The Ministry of Health in Ontario has gone to considerable lengths to indicate that the *Comparative Drug Index* is not intended to interfere with the practice of medicine, but rather to assist prescribers and pharmacists in selecting quality drugs. It is not intended to supersede the package insert, product monograph, or scientific and professional literature. Moreover, participation in the program by pharmacists is entirely voluntary. Those who do participate display a PARCOST symbol and agree to dispense only those drug products listed in the *Comparative Drug Index* if prescription is generic and the drug product is included in the index. The Provincial Pharmacy Act was amended in 1972 to permit pharmacists to dispense an interchangeable pharmaceutical product for a brand-name prescription if that product is lower in cost. The maximum price charged is to be the one listed in the index plus a negotiated dispensing fee (currently $2.75 per prescription). The listed cost is based on information supplied by the manufacturer or supplier, and is effective until the next index is distributed.

Provincial Third-Party Drug Payment Plans

Ontario. Since September 1974, Ontario has provided certain approved drugs, prescribed by a physician or dentist, free-of-charge to welfare recipients and old-age pensioners receiving provincial financial assistance.[16] By August 1975, this program included all persons aged sixty-five or over who receive the federal old-age pension or who have resided in Ontario for at least one year and are citizens or landed immigrants. Eligible persons receive a card which they deposit with the pharmacy of their choice; in this way they are restricted to only one pharmacy at any given time. (Although Ontario has no mechanism for maintaining patient profiles, it would presumably be easy to institute one under this system.)

---

[16] Ontario Ministry of Health, *Drug Benefit Formulary*, no. 2, January 1-June 30, 1974 (Toronto: Queen's Printer, 1974).

Approved drugs are listed in a drug benefit formulary, compiled and updated twice yearly by the Ontario Ministry of Health and the Drug Quality and Therapeutics Committee, with advice and assistance from the Ontario Medical Association Committee on Pharmacy and the Ontario Pharmacists' Association. The formulary is, in essence, a modification of the *Comparative Drug Index*, with the same requirements for therapeutic effectiveness and necessity in the diagnosis, prevention, and treatment of mental and physical disorders. Oral drugs that have more than one active ingredient and sustained, prolonged, or delayed-release dosage forms may be considered for listing only if they possess therapeutic advantages.

A signed prescription is required for all drugs dispensed under the plan, including the listed over-the-counter drugs. Prescriptions, including authorized refills, are usually valid for three months. For the following categories of drug products, however, the valid period is six months: antineoplastic agents, cardiovascular drugs, anticonvulsants, diagnostic agents, electrolytic, caloric and water balance drugs, gold compounds, hormones and substitutes, spasmolytics, vitamins, and minerals.

The normal quantity dispensed is limited to one month's supply, and over-the-counter drugs must be supplied in the package and size listed in the formulary, and are only for specific therapeutic purposes. In addition to drugs listed in the formulary, extemporaneous preparations, compounded in a pharmacy on the direction of a prescriber, are eligible for benefits if they do not duplicate a manufactured drug product already listed.

Pharmacists are reimbursed for drugs dispensed under the plan on the basis of the cost listed in the formulary. In the case of drugs listed as interchangeable in the PARCOST *Comparative Drug Index*, the cost is that of the lowest-cost product. Payment includes the negotiated dispensing fee or, in the case of OTC drugs, the pharmacist's usual markup. The physician may still specify a brand-name product listed in the formulary. However, for the pharmacist to be reimbursed for more than the lowest-cost interchangeable product, the prescriber must complete a special "no substitution form" for the pharmacist to submit along with a special pharmacy claim form. These forms are available on request by physicians and pharmacists. The simple requirement of completing a form probably is sufficient deterrent to the use of nonapproved drugs. The pharmacists usually phone the prescriber to change the prescription to the lowest-cost interchangeable drug when a nonapproval drug is ordered.

Manitoba. Manitoba has a government-sponsored drug plan which reimburses a family for 80 percent of the annual cost of its drugs in excess of fifty dollars. As of January 1, 1975, reimbursement is only for drugs on the province's Pharmacare List, which is not particularly restrictive. In addition, the Manitoba Drug Standards and Therapeutics Committee was appointed to prepare an interchangeable drug formulary.[17] In July 1974, the formulary listed seventeen individual drugs in the following five categories: antimicrobial agents, psychotherapeutic agents, corticosteroids, diuretics, and antiarthritic agents. In its choice of drugs, the committee relied to a great extent on information that had been obtained by the Ontario PARCOST program and the federal QUAD program and Canadian Government Specifications Board. The Manitoba Pharmaceutical Act has been amended to require that, unless the prescriber specifically directs otherwise, the pharmacist dispense the lowest cost interchangeable pharmaceutical product if it is listed in the formulary. The formulary also includes a brief therapeutic monograph on each category of drug, discussing the major indications for use, the significant side effects, and currently accepted information on clinical use.

Quebec. The Quebec Health Insurance Board published its *Drug List Manual* in January 1973, to assist physicians and dental surgeons in selecting drugs. It provides comparative drug prices and enables pharmacists to dispense insured drugs, currently available to Quebec's welfare population.[18] The drug list, drawn up by the minister of social affairs and following the recommendations of the Advisory Council on Pharmacology, is distributed to all physicians, dentists, and pharmacists registered with the Health Insurance Board. The manual is in loose-leaf style; updating is continuous and is subject to approval of all changes by the cabinet.

The drugs selected for this list must have therapeutic value and the approval of the federal Health Protection Branch and must be produced by firms complying with Canadian standards of manufacturing. For internal use, only single entity drugs are currently considered; oral forms with prolonged disintegration or sustained release are not considered. Only one package size is chosen. The list also contains a number of products which may be used to prepare "magistral" or extemporaneous mixtures on the direction of a prescriber. OTC drugs are not included in the list.

---

[17] Manitoba Department of Health and Social Development, *Manitoba Drug Standards and Therapeutics Formulary* (Winnipeg: Queen's Printer, 1974).

[18] Quebec Health Insurance Board, *Health Professionals' Manual* (Quebec Provincial Government, 1973).

Drugs are available free of charge to welfare patients, except for a deterrent charge of fifty cents per prescription imposed on tranquilizers, stimulants, sedatives, hypnotics, and vitamins.

Special Features of Provincial Drug Regulations

For the most part, few provincial regulatory controls are in effect for drugs. Reliance is primarily placed on federal regulations and on voluntary and ethical controls imposed by local hospital committees and the involved professions.

Patient profiles must be kept by pharmacists in Alberta through maintenance of family record cards. Three other provinces expect pharmacists to do this voluntarily. The usefulness of this requirement is limited inasmuch as members of a family may patronize more than one pharmacy, and there is as yet no central record-keeping mechanism. The use of a computerized monitoring system in Alberta has been discussed, but its cost has prevented implementation. One province, New Brunswick, does have a computerized surveillance system, but has no follow-up or review procedure for the information obtained.

Several provinces have enacted "product selection" clauses enabling pharmacists to dispense a generic product even when a brand-name drug has been prescribed. Under their drug benefit plans, Ontario and Manitoba require the dispensing of the lowest-cost interchangeable drug product. British Columbia has defined *dispense* so as to require the pharmacist to ensure the pharmaceutical and therapeutic suitability of the drug prescribed. In current practice, this formally acknowledges the previous, common informal arrangement where pharmacists occasionally checked drug dose, duration, and so on with the physician, if some aspect of a prescription was unusual. In the long run, some would view the new interpretation of "dispensing" as the thin edge of the wedge for pharmacists to become the "therapeuticians." The question whether pharmacists are qualified or necessary to decide if a drug is appropriately prescribed is an important issue.

Manitoba is the only province with a universal government drug insurance plan, but several others provide some sort of drug benefit plan to welfare patients and old-age pensioners. Three of the provinces charge a deterrent fee per prescription, and Manitoba provides only partial reimbursement. Most benefit plans also place restrictions on amounts of drug supplied and provide a formulary from which drugs must be selected.

No province places any restriction on new or expensive drugs, except for controls instituted by local hospital committees. Only one province, Manitoba, is currently providing information bulletins on drugs and therapeutics to its prescribers.

Drug Surveillance in Canada

Canada's Drug Adverse Reaction Reporting Program was established in 1965 at the request of the World Health Organization. Spontaneous reports were solicited from doctors, pharmacists, and hospitals, but participation in this program has been poor and there is little cooperation between clinical pharmacologists and the national program. Essential processing of the data is relatively unsophisticated and markedly slow. All the defects of a spontaneous reporting system are inherent in this program. No results have been published, and only recently has any form of feedback come to those who reported reactions.[19] Criticisms of the program and suggestions for improvement have been largely ignored.

Other surveillance projects of adverse drug reactions have been initiated in a number of hospitals. At the Montreal General Hospital, the Division of Clinical Pharmacology has conducted a number of studies to investigate adverse drug reactions. Two hospitals in London, Ontario, are part of the Boston Collaborative Drug Surveillance Program and receive partial financial support for this activity from the federal government. A number of Canadian hospitals have reasonably effective in-hospital reporting programs monitored by pharmacists. At the Toronto Western Hospital, an Adverse Drug Reaction Surveillance Program using nurse monitors is in operation. Studies have been completed investigating drug interactions with anticoagulants and adverse reactions associated with furosemide administration and with administration of ampicillin, cephalosporins, and gentamicin. At present, the hospital has a two-year project looking at the patterns and consequences of drug overdose in metropolitan Toronto.

---

[19] Edward Napke, "The Pharmacist's Role in Canada's Drug Adverse Reaction Program" in *Canadian Pharmaceutical Journal*, vol. 103, no. 2 (February 1970), pp. 44-45; Edward Napke and J. Bishop, "The Canadian Drug Adverse Reaction Reporting Program" in *Canadian Medical Association Journal*, vol. 95 (December 17, 1966), p. 1307-9.

Conclusions

The health care field in Canada is complicated by the fact that the provision of health care services, including the licensing and education of health care professionals, is the responsibility of the provinces, while the federal government is greatly involved in health care because of its spending power gained through control of tax revenues. Until recently, the provinces were content to leave drug regulation to the federal government, which, since 1963, has placed major emphasis on premarketing controls. By offering to pay for half the cost of a system of universal national medical care, the federal government was able to introduce such a system in 1968, although it has no legal jurisdiction in this area and there were strong objections by the two largest provinces, Ontario and Quebec. Medicare has several implications for the provinces in the area of drug regulation. First, the Medicare program only covers drugs used in hospitals, so there is strong political pressure for the introduction of government-sponsored drug insurance plans. One province already has such a plan, three provinces provide drugs free of charge to welfare patients, and several other provinces are in the process of introducing such a plan. Second, the cost of the Medicare system has proved to be exceedingly high and is escalating rapidly, so that governments have been forced to become extremely cost-conscious in their approach to health care. Although the federal government has recognized a need to provide information on drugs to physicians, and has embarked on a quality-testing program with publication of results and prices, it shows no interest in contributing to a drug insurance plan.

Several provinces have compiled their own formularies, listing therapeutically effective and interchangeable drugs. Therapeutic interchangeability involves two aspects: substitution among approved manufacturers' generic drug products, solely on the basis of cost, and interchange of one drug (say, one thiazide diuretic) for another. While interchange is not permitted, substitution is approved in Ontario and Manitoba. The method of placing drugs on the various lists assumes that bioequivalence will result in therapeutic equivalence. Provinces that provide some form of drug benefit plan strongly encourage prescription of the lowest-cost product, or charge a deterrent fee, or both. Although the development of a national drug formulary is only being considered at present,[20] postmarketing drug use controls seem to be inevitable since health care costs are becoming a major concern at

---

[20] "Editorial Comment" in *Ontario Medical Review*, vol. 24, no. 6 (June 1975), p. 307.

both levels of government. Unfortunately there is a danger that future decisions influencing drug use probably will have economy—and not necessarily quality or optimal care—as their basis.

Canadian systems of drug use control consist of a complex network of federal and provincial regulations. There are no valid systems to monitor patterns of drug use or postmarketing drug toxicity. Computerization is contemplated, but will probably be impractical because of the high cost and poorly defined objectives.

We believe the emphasis on regulatory control in Canada obfuscates the issue in the control of drug use. Superficially one might conclude that because of the extensive regulations, Canada has few problems with prescription drugs. However, even the most restrictive formularies and regulations cannot guarantee appropriate drug use. The development of a national formulary, as has been proposed, would be a pointless and expensive exercise. Canadian medical school students receive relatively little specific training in therapeutics and clinical pharmacology, and practicing physicians receive most of their continuing education about drugs from detail men and drug advertisements in journals. The suggestion that the pharmacist assume the role of therapeutic advisor and monitor on drugs would be unnecessary if the obvious and simpler step of increasing the physicians' drug education were taken.

The diversion of a small fraction of the money being spent by federal and provincial governments in drug regulatory activities to the development and support of undergraduate and continuing education in clinical pharmacology would, we expect, pay important economic dividends by ensuring that the "right drug in the right amounts is given to the right patient at the right time."[21]

---

[21] M. Silverman and P. R. Lee, *Pills, Profits and Politics* (Berkeley: University of California Press, 1974), p. 282.

PART TWO

SYSTEMS IN WESTERN EUROPE AND THE COMMONWEALTH

4

THE UNITED KINGDOM

M. F. Cuthbert, J. P. Griffin, and W. H. W. Inman

Historical Aspects of Control of Therapeutic Substances

The first act that had any bearing on the quality of medicinal products in England was passed in the reign of Henry VIII in 1540: the act empowered the College of Physicians of London to appoint four inspectors of "Apothecary Wares, Drugs and Stuffs." From the early seventeenth century these inspectors were joined in their activity by representatives of the Society of Apothecaries. Over the succeeding centuries legislation grew and like the first act was directed largely at the quality of the medicinal product. These were statutory provisions made in 1858 for the publication of the British pharmacopeia, laying down standards for quality control in its successive additions and addenda. In 1875 the Food and Drugs Act laid down penalties for the adulteration of drugs, and in 1925 the initial Therapeutic Substances Act established control of biologicals.

The Therapeutic Substances Act of 1925 was the first act passed to provide for the licensing of medicines. It controlled the manufacture and import for sale or supply of substances "the purity or potency of which cannot be adequately tested by chemical means." These substances are referred to as "biologicals," and include such products as vaccines, toxins, antigens, serums, enzymes, hormones, antibiotics, dextrans, and blood products. (The main powers of the Therapeutic Substances Act were subsumed in the Medicines Act of 1968. The U.K. government intends that the Therapeutic Substances Act be repealed and these substances be controlled under the Medicines Act.) Licenses were issued under the Therapeutic Substances Act (1956) to authorize manufacture, importation, or research by companies, individuals, or other organizations. The licenses provided in some cases that products should not be released to the market without the prior authorization of the Licensing Authority. In these cases release certificates were issued on the advice of the National Institute for Biological Standards and Control. License holders had to submit protocols for the manufacture of a product (and sometimes samples) before the product could be released for sale.

Other acts gave their attention to the regulation of sale and supply of medicinal agents. These extended from the Gin Act of the eighteenth century to the Pharmacy and Poisons Act of 1935 and its subsequent amendments and the Dangerous Drugs acts introduced between 1920 and 1967, to the Misuse of Drugs Act, which is the most recent legislation in this field. In this conglomeration of legislation only the Cancer and Venereal Diseases Act of 1917 was concerned with efficacy. It served to prevent the public advertisement and promotion of medicine for the conditions named in the title, and to protect the sufferers from inadequate and unsuitable treatment and from fraudulent claims.

Attempts to measure and assess the ill effects of drug therapy are recent and as yet can hardly be considered a discipline, yet it was in 1877 at a meeting in Manchester that the British Medical Association initiated the first collaborative study of adverse reaction to a drug. The committee was set up to investigate the sudden, unexpected deaths which sometimes occurred during the induction of chloroform anaesthesia.[1] Even before this time there had been concern among doctors about adverse reaction to drugs and about reaction to smallpox vaccine, and these fears had at various times been fanned to great emotional heights by anti-vaccinationists and others. At the end of World War I an epidemic of jaundice and fatal hepatic necrosis among soldiers treated for syphilis with organic arsenicals was so serious that it was the subject of a special report by the Medical Research Committee, which was the predecessor to the present Medical Research Council.[2] It is interesting to reflect how close medical and public opinion was, both in 1880 and in 1922, to the concept of setting up an independent body to assess the safety of drugs.

In the 1920s it was noticed that fatal jaundice could be caused by cinchophen, a remedy used in the treatment of gout,[3] and agranulocytosis by the analgesic drug amidopyrine (aminophenazone;

---

[1] J. G. McKendrick, J. Coats, and D. Newman, *British Medical Journal*, vol. 2 (1880), p. 957.

[2] Medical Research Council, *Special Report. Series of the Medical Research Council*, no. 66 (London: Her Majesty's Stationery Office, 1922).

[3] C. Worster-Drought, *British Medical Journal*, vol. 1 (1923), p. 148; C. L. Short and W. Bauer, *Annals of Internal Medicine*, vol. 6 (1933), p. 1449.

aminopyrine; Pyramidon).[4] The introduction of sulfonamides to medicine in the 1930s brought to all doctors familiarity with adverse reactions, but penicillin, streptomycin, and the corticosteroids led to such advances in the efficacy of medical treatment that adverse reactions, though recognized, caused no great anxiety. A degree of concern similar to that existing for chloroform in the 1880s and arsenicals in the 1920s did not arise. Although everything pointed to the need to consolidate the legislation on medicines, the old machinery seemed to work and for decades no great problem had arisen. The task of preparing consolidating legislation was formidable, and disentangling the complex legalities was a daunting venture. Lulled into the security by the quiet years, both public and government were unprepared for the tragedy of thalidomide that in 1961 left its mark not only on the unfortunate children but also on the medical profession, the pharmaceutical industry, the public, and on governments. It was now clear that some comprehensive legislation would have to be introduced.

Committee on Safety of Drugs—A Voluntary System

Following the thalidomide disaster, a joint subcommittee of the English and Scottish Standing Medical Advisory subcommittees recommended the establishment of an expert committee to review the evidence on new drugs and to offer advice on their toxicity. The Committee on Safety of Drugs, chaired by Sir Derrick Dunlop, was set up in 1963 by the health ministers in consultation with the medical and pharmaceutical professions and the pharmaceutical industry. The Committee on Safety of Drugs had no legal powers but worked within the voluntary agreement of the Association of the British Pharmaceutical Industry and Proprietary Association of Great Britain. These two organizations promised that none of their members would put on clinical trial or release for marketing any new drug against the committee's advice, which they undertook to seek in all cases. The terms of reference of the Committee on Safety of Drugs were as follows:

(1) to invite from the manufacturer or other persons developing or proposing to market a drug in the United Kingdom any report they may think fit on the toxicity tests carried out on it; to consider whether any further tests should be made and whether

---

[4] P. R. Kracke and F. P. Parker, *Journal of Laboratory and Clinical Medicine*, vol. 19 (1934), p. 799.

the drug should be submitted to clinical trials; and to convey their advice to those who submitted the reports.

(2) to obtain reports of clinical trials of drugs submitted thereto.

(3) taking into account the safety and efficacy of each drug and the purposes to which it is to be used, to consider whether it may be released for marketing, with or without precautions or restrictions on its use; and to convey their advice to those who submitted the reports.

(4) to give to manufacturers and others concerned any general advice they may think fit.

(5) to assemble and assess reports about adverse reactions to drugs in use and prepare information thereon which may be brought to the notice of doctors and others concerned.

(6) to advise the appointing ministers on any of the above matters.[5]

The Committee on Safety of Drugs (CSD) therefore attempted to provide a voluntary registration system covering (1) scrutiny before clinical trial, (2) scrutiny before marketing, and (3) surveillance of each drug after marketing so that adverse reactions could be adequately monitored and documented and if necessary to issue suitable precautions to the professions. The CSD set up a subcommittee structure drawing in a wide variety of expertise that could not be contained within the single committee of workable size. Subcommittees were first formed to advise on toxicity and clinical trials and on adverse reactions. Later it became necessary to form an advisory group of experts on vaccines and biological agents.

Under the voluntary system introduced by the Committee on Safety of Drugs some 600 companies (mainly members of the Proprietary Association of Great Britain and the Association of the British Pharmaceutical Industry, but including other companies not members of either) submitted their products for scrutiny before conducting clinical trials or marketing. The relations between industry and the Committee on Safety of Drugs and the professional staff serving the committee were good. The staff was always prepared to advise firms informally. Because there was not the present degree of formal documentation, and because it operated with simple machinery, the voluntary system was able to deal rapidly with submissions made to it.

---

[5] See J. P. Griffin, *Ulster Medical Journal*, vol. 41 (1972), for terms of reference of the Committee on Safety of Drugs.

The Committee on Safety of Drugs and the voluntary system did set the pattern of informality of approach and good relationships with the industry that the Committee on Safety of Medicines and the Licensing Authority have striven to maintain. This "approachability" and flexibility of the British licensing system, which is much appreciated both by industry and by the medical profession and is admired throughout the world, is largely due to the attitudes engendered by the Committee on Safety of Drugs during its period of operation from 1964 to September 1971.

The Committee on Safety of Drugs operated the adverse reaction reporting system in which doctors reported details of adverse reactions to drugs directly to the committee using reply-paid "yellow cards." The system provided machinery by which adverse reactions to marketed drugs could be detected and the profession alerted. The system to provide warnings to doctors operated through the "Adverse Reaction Series" of leaflets. During its history, the committee issued nine such leaflets to every registered medical practitioner in the United Kingdom.

This Adverse Reaction Series was used for the first warnings to medical practitioners of the (1) risk of sudden death in young asthmatics using pressurized aerosols containing sympathomimetic amines,[6] and (2) the problem of thromboembolic episodes in women on estrogen-containing oral contraceptives, particularly those containing a daily intake of more than fifty micrograms.[7] Another warning given to the profession in this way concerned adverse reactions to monamine oxidase inhibitors involving hypertensive episodes with sympathomimetic amines and foods containing tyramine.[8] The problem of drug-induced blood dyscrasias with phenylbutazone and chloramphenicol were also dealt with in other leaflets in this series.[9]

One number of the Adverse Reaction Series set a precedent by dealing with efficacy rather than safety; the warning given to the profession was that "sequential oral contraceptives appeared to have a higher failure rate than the combined regime."[10]

The disadvantage of the voluntary system was that firms were not legally obliged to submit their products to scrutiny before marketing. The magnitude of this problem can be seen by the fact that

---

[6] Committee on Safety of Drugs, *Adverse Reactions Series*, no. 5 (London: Her Majesty's Stationery Office, 1967).

[7] Ibid., no. 9 (1969).

[8] Ibid., no. 1 (1964).

[9] Ibid., no. 3 (1965), and no. 4 (1967).

[10] Ibid., no. 8 (1969).

when compulsory licensing of medicinal products was introduced in September 1971 (the date when the Medicines Act of 1968 was implemented), the number of pharmaceutical companies with products subject to licensing as medicinal products increased from about 600 to 3,600. Another shortcoming of the voluntary system was that there was no machinery for licensing the premises of the manufacturers of medicinal products and for regular inspection. The exception to this was that firms manufacturing substances subject to the Therapeutic Substance Act regulations did have to have their premises inspected.

During the last year of its operation the Committee on Safety of Drugs considered 170 applications for clinical trial and 589 applications for marketing of new medicinal products.[11]

The Medicines Act of 1968—The Statutory System

The Joint Subcommittee of the English and Scottish Standing Medical Advisory committees, which recommended the establishment of the Committee on Safety of Drugs to review the evidence on new drugs and offer advice on their safety, also made recommendations for future legislation. This joint subcommittee also recommended that there should be new legislation covering many aspects of drug safety, and, after a review and consultation, the White Paper *Forthcoming Legislation on the Safety, Quality and Description of Drugs and Medicines* was published in September 1967. The Medicines Act based on these proposals received the Royal Assent in October 1968. The act is a comprehensive measure that replaces most of the previous legislation on the control of medicines for human use and for veterinary use. It is administered by the health and agriculture ministers of the United Kingdom acting together (or in some cases separately as the health minister or the agriculture minister for human and veterinary medicines respectively). The main provisions introduced by the act are as follows: (1) a medicines commission appointed by ministers to give them advice generally relating to the execution of the act, and (2) the establishment of a number of expert committees with specific advisory functions appointed by ministers after considering the recommendations of the commission, as proposed in Section 4 of the Medicines Act.

---

[11] *Annual Report of the Committee on Safety of Medicines for 1971* (London: Her Majesty's Stationery Office, 1972).

Expert Committees. On the advice of the Medicines Commission, standing committees of independent experts were appointed by ministers. One of these, the British Pharmacopoeia Commission, was given the responsibility of preparing future editions of the British pharmacopeia, in succession to the former (nonstatutory) body of the same name that had carried out this task under direction of the General Medical Council.

The other committees have the main task of advising the Licensing Authority. These committees are the Committee on Safety of Medicines, the Veterinary Products Committee, and the Dental and Surgical Material Committee. The last will initially deal with a limited range of materials including intrauterine contraceptive devices, contact lenses, contact lens fluids, and absorbable suture materials.

A fourth committee, the Committee on the Review of Medicines, was established in 1975 to review all medicinal products on the British market, whether supplied by medical practitioners on prescription, through registered pharmacists over the counter, or on general sale to the public without restriction.

The Committee on Safety of Medicines, constituted under Section 4 of the Medicines Act of 1968, was established in 1970 for the following purposes: (1) to give advice on safety, quality, and efficacy for human use, of any substance or article (not being an instrument, apparatus, or appliance) to which any provision of the act is applicable, and (2) to promote the collection and investigation of information on adverse reactions, for the purpose of enabling such advice to be given.

The terms of reference of the Subcommittee on Adverse Reactions were reviewed and revised as follows: (1) to promote and assemble reports about the possible adverse effects of medicinal products administered to man, (2) to assess the meaning of such reports, (3) to recommend to the committee any special or extended investigations which it considers desirable, (4) to keep under review the methods by which adverse reactions are monitored, (5) to make recommendations to the committee, based on the subcommittee's assessment of any action it considers should be taken, and (6) to advise the committee on communications with the professions relating to the work of the subcommittee.[12] The titles of the subcommittees that advise the Committee on Safety of Medicines are shown in Figure 1.

---

[12] Medicines (Committee on Safety of Medicines) Order (SI 1970/1257) (London: Her Majesty's Stationery Office, 1970).

Figure 1

COMMITTEE ON SAFETY OF MEDICINES
AND ITS SUBCOMMITTEES

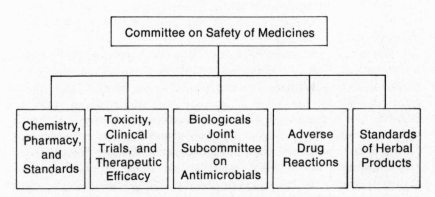

The overall aim of both the Committee on Safety of Drugs and the Committee on Safety of Medicines, is threefold: (1) scrutiny before clinical trial (clinical trial certificate), (2) scrutiny before marketing (product license), and (3) scrutiny after marketing (adverse reactions monitoring).

The Committee on Safety of Medicines is in effect a continuation of the former Committee on Safety of Drugs and it advises the Licensing Authority on questions of the safety, quality, and efficacy of medicines for human use. It is also responsible for collecting and investigating reports on adverse reactions to medicines already on the market and it may issue warnings about newly identified hazards, or, where appropriate, reminders about those hazards already recognized. The committee has at present seventeen members, who include professors of internal medicine, pediatrics, pathology, clinical pharmacology, biochemistry, anaesthetics, psychiatry, obstetrics and gynecology, pharmacy, and medical statistics, together with a general medical practitioner, a consultant physician, and an expert in pharmaceutical quality control.

There are six subcommittees from which the committee receives specialist advice. These are (1) Toxicity, Clinical Trials, and Therapeutic Efficacy, (2) Chemistry, Pharmacy, and Standards, (3) Biological Substances, (4) Adverse Reactions, and (5) Standards of Herbal Products, along with the Joint Subcommittee on Antimicrobial Substances, which the committee, acting jointly with the Veterinary Products Committee, set up to advise on the whole field of use of antibiotics and related substances in man and animals, for food preservation, and for other purposes. The Committee on Safety of Medicines and its subcommittee advise the Licensing Authority on the quality, safety, and efficacy of human medicines.

Classification of Medicines. The Medicines Act of 1968 makes provision for controls and regulation relating to the sale and supply of medicines. The broad effect of these powers has been that medicinal products are classified into three groups:

(1) Products which may be sold or supplied only on the prescription of a medical practitioner. In 1970 the Medicines Commission established a committee to propose a list of medicinal substances the sale of which should be restricted to sale by prescription only. This has been recommended where the medicinal product contains substances to which at least one of the following applies: toxicity hazard, production of physical or psychological dependence, or hazard to the community if used without proper safeguard. Such drugs are specified in the Prescription Only Medicines List.

(2) Medicinal products from which the hazard to health, the risk of misuse, or the need to take special precautions in handling is small and where wide sale would be a convenience to the purchaser. These prepacked products are available for retail sale in shops other than pharmacies. Some are to be specified as suitable for sale from automatic machines or for general sale from drugstores, mail order companies, and other outlets. Such drugs as are suitable for supply in this way have been specified in the General Sales List.

(3) Those drugs not specified as suitable for general sale and not included in the Prescription Only Medicines List, which may be sold only by or under the supervision of a pharmacist from a registered pharmacy.

The supply of dangerous and addictive drugs has been subject to a series of complex legislation in addition to that applying to medicines in general, the legislation being principally the Dangerous Drugs Act of 1925 and (more recently) the Misuse of Drugs Act of 1971. The administration of these acts is the concern of the Home Office; details of the operation of these acts have recently been reviewed by Cahal.[13]

---

[13] D. A. Cahal, "Misuse of Drug Act 1971," *British Medical Journal*, vol. 1 (1974), p. 70; "Misuse of Drug Regulations 1973," *British Medical Journal*, vol. 1 (1974), p. 73.

Figure 2

STRUCTURE OF THE DRUG REGULATORY BODY

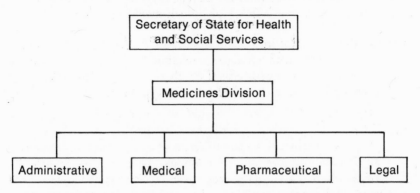

Operation of the Act. The day-to-day operation of the Medicines Act, as it affects medicinal products for human use, is the responsibility of the Medicines Division of the Department of Health and Social Security. The Medicines Division is involved in the licensing of medicinal products at every stage. The division provides both professional and administrative staff to service the advisory committees set up under Section 4 of the Medicines Act. All applications for product licenses and clinical trial certificates are examined in their pharmaceutical and medical aspects. The available data are evaluated with reference to the criteria of safety, quality, and efficacy, and the recommendations of the secretariat are put before the relevant subcommittees or committee to assist the members in formulating their advice to the Licensing Authority.

The division includes doctors, pharmacists, administrators, clerical staff, lawyers, and a dentist, and the various professions work closely together. There is integration both in particular projects and in the development of general policies. While the administration and the various professional groups have their own hierarchies and report to their own seniors, the head of the division is the senior principal medical officer. He acts as administrative head of the division, coordinating the professional staff, and as medical assessor to the Medicines Commission. In June 1976 the total full-time complement of the Medicines Division was 251, of whom 20 were doctors, 50 pharmacists, and 17 scientific staff (members of the scientific secretariat and laboratory of the British Pharmacopoeia Commission). Twenty were professionally qualified medicines inspectors, and 19 were senior administrative and executive staff. In addition 4 lawyers

Figure 3

FUNCTION OF THE DRUG REGULATORY BODY

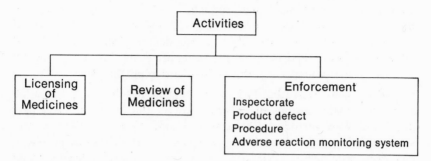

are engaged full-time in work relating to the Medicines Act. The main functions of the division are to act (1) as licensing authority, (2) as enforcement authority, and (3) as adverse reactions monitor.

(1) As licensing authority, the Medicines Division is involved in the licensing of medicinal products at every stage. Applications for product licenses and clinical trial certificates are assessed jointly by a doctor and pharmacist. The available data are evaluated with reference to the criteria of safety, quality, and efficacy, and recommendations are made to the Committee on Safety of Medicines to assist the members in formulating their advice to the Licensing Authority. The division provides both the professional and the administrative secretariat for these committees. Applications for manufacturer's and wholesale dealer's licenses are evaluated with advice from the Medicines Inspectorate to ensure that the premises are suitable for the proposed operations, and to check whether appropriately qualified expert staff are employed. The division ensures that applications comply with the relevant regulations and the relevant provisions of the act. Since licenses are legal documents, considerable care must be taken to ensure their accuracy. The division is responsible for the drafting, the authorization, and the issue of these on behalf of the Licensing Authority.

(2) As enforcement authority, the Medicines Division is also responsible for ensuring the enforcement of the act. The Medicines Inspectorate, which is an integral part of the division, inspects pharmaceutical manufacturers in this country and overseas, wholesalers, and hospital manufacturing units. Other enforcement activities are undertaken by the Pharmaceutical Society of Great Britain and the local food and drugs authorities under delegated powers.

(3) In adverse reactions monitoring, the division provides staff, who work under the direction of the Committee on Safety of Medicines and in particular its Adverse Reactions Subcommittee to monitor adverse reactions to medicinal products. Four doctors are engaged on this work full time, assisted by almost 100 doctors distributed around the country working part time. These doctors follow up selected adverse reaction reports from those reported to the committee by medical practitioners using the yellow-card reporting system.

The Licensing Authority in operating the Medicines Act of 1968 issues five major groups of licenses. Under the Medicines Act new provisions were introduced to control manufacture, distribution, and storage of drugs. To cover these provisions the Medicines Inspectorate has been established. Manufacturers and wholesale dealers must hold appropriate licenses.

(1) Licenses of right comprise two types. Product licenses of right are applicable to a product already on sale on September 1, 1971. These licenses will be converted to full product licenses after scrutiny by the Committee on Review of Medicines, who must be satisfied that the product is safe and efficacious for the proposed clinical use and that its quality is satisfactory. Clinical trial certificates of right are applicable to drugs already undergoing clinical trial with the approval of the Committee on Safety of Drugs on the duly appointed day. The existence of these certificates is self-limiting (that is, they will cease to exist as evaluation of these agents is completed).

(2) Clinical trial certificates are valid for a period of two years for drugs approved by the Committee on Safety of Medicines for Clinical Trial.

(3) Product licenses are valid for a period of five years on drugs approved for marketing by the Committee on Safety of Medicines.

(4) Manufacturer's licenses are granted only after the licensing authority considers the suitability of the premises and equipment and the completence of the personnel for the operations to be carried out under the license. The Department of Health and Social Security has a staff of twenty inspectors (most of whom are pharmacists) who inspect manufacturers' premises and advise on the granting of licenses and the conditions to be applied to such licenses.

(5) Wholesale dealers licenses are granted after consideration of the adequacy of the premises and arrangements for the turnover of stock.

Applications for Clinical Trial Certificate or Product License

Applications for clinical trial certificates or product licenses must be made to the Licensing Authority in accordance with the *Notes for Guidance on Application for Clinical Trial Certificates and Product Licenses* issued by the Licensing Authority.

Application for Clinical Trial Certificate. The clinical trial certificate application is usually made by the drug manufacturer. The application should clearly state the number of patients to be treated, the indications for which they are to be treated, the maximum daily dosage to be employed, and the duration for which dosage is to continue. In addition, details of trial design and safety monitoring through hematological and serum biochemical studies and urinalysis and frequency of clinical examination of the patients are expected.

The attitude usually taken toward the application for a clinical trial certificate of a new drug is that clinical trials should initially be limited to a few (usually not more than three) centers. If the drug looks promising in the initial studies, the evaluation of the drug may then be extended to other centers. (If the drug is for the treatment of such a rare condition that this limited number of centers would be unlikely to see enough cases for the drug to be adequately evaluated, then the situation would be judged accordingly.)

The application for the clinical trial certificate should be accompanied by experimental data. The pharmacological studies should demonstrate the mode of action of the drug substance by the proposed clinical route of administration. These studies should give sufficient promise of therapeutic potential to justify the study. In addition, details of the metabolism of the drug in animals and man—absorption, plasma half-life, rate of urinary and fecal elimination, and (ideally) identification of urinary metabolites of the drug—should be available. This is often the most difficult phase of the drug's evaluation in animals and man and may be technically impossible at the time the application for a clinical trial certificate is made.

Data from repeat dose toxicity studies in at least two animal species are normally required; the dosing should have been conducted by the proposed clinical route of administration and the duration of dosing should be appropriate to the proposed clinical use of the drug. These studies should be conducted with at least three dose levels. The lowest dose level should be in the therapeutic range, and the highest should have been selected after preliminary dose-ranging studies to reveal the target organ. The purpose of toxicity tests is to

111

demonstrate a pattern of toxicity to the clinical pharmacologist, not to provide a marketing organization with a testimonial establishing the safety of the product. Throughout the toxicity studies, repeated hematological and serum biochemical monitoring is essential, and at the completion of the study the animals should be autopsied and histopathological examinations of the major tissues performed.

The Committee on Safety of Medicines is loath to advise the Licensing Authority to release a drug for clinical trial until the results of adequate reproduction studies have been assessed, though exceptions may be made when therapeutic indications clearly preclude women of childbearing age. Using a comparable degree of precaution, many investigators prefer to exclude women of childbearing age from trials of all new drugs. They adopt the principle that a teratogenic hazard can never be entirely eliminated by animal studies and that it would be wrong to expose patients to this additional risk until the therapeutic potential of the drug has been established beyond reasonable doubt. The result of this very laudable caution, however, is that at the time the drug comes to be considered for marketing, it may never have been prescribed for a pregnant patient.

Finally, the pharmaceutical aspects of the formulation will be assessed. All too often we forget that what is being considered is not a simple drug but a formulation containing other ingredients such as antioxidants, preservatives, and solubilizing agents that is administered to the patient. Pharmaceutical assessment is broadly considered under the following main headings: (1) purity of the drug substance, the physical characteristics of the drug, and the nature of any impurities present; (2) stability of the drug substance itself, stability of the final formulation, and the nature of any decomposition products which may be formed; (3) the release characteristics of the drug from the final formulation. Although this section has been dealt with very briefly, it is highly important.

For example, teracyclines have a hepatotoxic breakdown product. In some cases, the bioavailability of the drug may greatly alter its therapeutic potential or toxic hazard—the latter having been seen recently with digoxin tablets, where a minor variation in the manufacturing procedure altered the bioavailability of the drug by 100 percent. Other drugs where bioavailability is a problem are the tetracyclines, where gross variation from one brand to another has been reported. Examples can be cited where clinical drug toxicity came from the excipients rather than the active principle; as with the cataract formation seen with preparations containing dimethyl sulfoxide (DMSO) as a solvent, or the renal toxicity reported with mephenesin injection containing propylene glycol as a solubilizing agent. (In the latter instance neither substance alone has ever been reported as causing renal damage, and so there may be an interaction between drug and excipient.) The excipient has also been shown to affect the bioavailability of the active drug, as with the effect of cyclamate or lincomycin syrup. Dietary circumstances can affect the bioavailability of the drug—as, for example, the inhibitory effect Fe^{++} on tetracycline absorption due to the formation of insoluble complexes, or the increased absorption of griseofulvin in the presence of fat. It is therefore desirable sometimes at the clinical trial stage and always by the marketing stage to ensure that the bioavailability and toxicity of the drug are not affected by formulation.

Aim of the clinical trial. If the Committee on Safety of Medicines is satisfied that a new drug is suitable for evaluation in the clinical situation (with judgment made according to the drug's potential therapeutic value and potential toxicity), it is not its function to decide whether the trial is in itself ethical. Monitoring procedures to assess the efficacy and safety may in themselves be the cause of ethical concern. For example, repeated liver biopsy or uterine biopsy have been proposed in protocols for monitoring drug actions. This problem is one that should be dealt with by an ethical committee (see below). Basically, the purpose of a clinical trial has been defined by Gray: "To obtain the maximum amount of unbiased information concerning the principal action and side effects of a drug or procedure, from the minimum number of patients in the shortest time, with the least potential hazard or inconvenience to them." [14] In essence, a trial that does not comply with these sentiments is not ethically justified.

Ethical considerations. The design and conduct of clinical investigation should be guided by a code of ethical practice,[15] and the Code of Ethics of the World Medical Association (Declaration of Helsinki) is accepted throughout the civilized world. The Medical Research Council has also issued a statement on "Responsibility in Investigations on Human Subjects" which has been reprinted in the *British Medical Journal.*[16] In this context the term "clinical investigation" was regarded by a Committee of the Royal College of Physicians of London in July 1967 as covering all forms of experiment on man,

---

[14] T. C. Gray, *British Journal of Anaesthesia*, vol. 39 (1967), p. 279.

[15] J. P. Griffin, *Proceedings of the Royal Society of Medicine*, vol. 67 (1974), p. 581.

[16] *Annual Report of the Medical Research Council for 1962-63* (London: Her Majesty's Stationery Office, 1963); *British Medical Journal*, vol. 2 (1964), p. 177.

there being broadly two kinds of investigational research. The first is the kind that has direct diagnostic or therapeutic relevance to the individual patient and therefore seldom poses serious ethical problems. "In the treatment of the sick person the doctor must be free to use a new therapeutic measure if in his judgment it offers hope of saving life, reestablishing health, or alleviating suffering. . . . The doctor, therefore, can combine clinical research with professional care, the objective being the acquisition of new medical knowledge, only to the extent that the clinical research is justified by its therapeutic value to the patient" (Declaration of Helsinki 1962).[17] The second kind of investigation or research is the kind that is carried out purely to advance knowledge and from which the subjects, be they patients or healthy volunteers, cannot expect benefits. This kind of investigation may benefit the community but may present difficult ethical problems as it affects the individual. In the latter category the individual has rights that must not be infringed and he must be a volunteer—that is, he must have consented freely, with a proper understanding of the nature and consequence of what is proposed.[18] The task of making the explanation and getting true informed and written consent to the patient's participation in an investigation must clearly be the responsibility of the doctor who is to conduct the investigation. The Committee of the Royal College of Physicians therefore recommended that the competent authority (for example, Board of Governors, Medical School Council, or Hospital Management Committee) has a responsibility to ensure that all clinical investigations carried out within its hospital or institution are ethical and conducted with optimum technical skill and precautions for safety.

In 1968 the Department of Health issued a document in which it was stated that the minister of health accepted the views of the Royal College of Physicians on the ethics of clinical investigations, and asked that the regional hospital authorities in the United Kingdom set up ethical committees.[19] It was envisioned that these groups would be informal advisory bodies rather than committees of hospital authorities. There seems to be confusion on the part of hospital ethical committees who seemed to believe that the Committee on Safety of Medicines considers the ethics of a trial, and that the committee's recommendation for a certificate from the Licensing Authority includes ethical approval. This is not so.

---

[17] Ibid.

[18] Ibid.

[19] Report on Supervision of the Ethics of Clinical Investigators 68 (33). *Hospital and Health Services Yearbook 1975.*

Patients and volunteers. In the selection of subjects, the Medicines Act of 1968 does not control the administration of a new drug to healthy consenting persons. The ethical responsibility for studies in these people is the responsibility of hospital ethical groups. On the other hand, the act does not recognize the existence of the patient/volunteer. If it is intended that a drug be administered to a sick patient as part of a clinical trial, or to a healthy person who might expect to obtain therapeutic benefit from the drug (for example, a vaccine or an oral contraceptive, which are usually administered to normal subjects), a clinical trial certificate must be held with respect to these studies either by the firm manufacturing the drug or by the responsible clinician.

Exemptions from the Need to Hold Clinical Trial Certificates or Product Licenses for Medical or Dental Practitioners. Under the act and exemption orders made under it, a license is not required for a medical or dental practitioner to prepare any medicine for a particular patient of his or for a pharmacist to dispense it to his prescription.

In the majority of cases clinical trials are promoted by the manufacturer of the drug substance to be evaluated. In some instances, however, a clinical trial may be initiated by a doctor who wishes to evaluate a new drug, or to evaluate an established drug in a new indication, or to administer the drug by a different route. For the last of these, the doctor may wish to obtain the preparation from a manufacturer: before he can do this he must either hold a clinical trial certificate for the trial or have obtained from the Licensing Authority exemption from the need to hold such a certificate. No doctor needs a clinical trial certificate to conduct a clinical trial on any established drugs used in the indications for which the drug was approved for marketing. Exemption from the need to hold a clinical trial certificate would, however, be required if he had approached the manufacturer to formulate identical capsules or tablets of one or more agents for the purpose of conducting a controlled double-blind study.

Somewhat different and more restrictive provisions apply to the preparation of medicinal products by or for a veterinary surgeon to an animal or a herd under his care, and no exemption system operates for the obtaining of medicinal products for which there is no full animal test certificate or product license.

Application for a Product License. Applications for product licenses are made to the Licensing Authority in accordance with the guidelines issued for the applicant. When application is made for a product license, it is expected that all the necessary pharmaceutical, pharmacological, metabolic, toxicological, and teratological studies will have been conducted that are required for the licensing of a product for the indications and method of use intended—that is, there is a considerable overlap in the kind of scrutiny given to a drug before clinical trial and before marketing as it relates to these aspects of quality and safety in preclinical studies.

Additional data required for a marketing application that may not be available at the time a clinical trial application is made include (1) long-term toxicity data if the indications and proposed method of use dictate the need for these studies, (2) data from clinical pharmacological and human metabolic studies, and (3) reports from clinical trials that demonstrate the drug's efficacy in the proposed indications and its safety when used in accordance with the proposed recommendations. In establishing the efficacy of a medicinal product it is expected that controlled studies will have been conducted and that evidence of efficacy will have been objectively measured. Extensive safety monitoring on patients treated during clinical trials is expected. The design of the trial to demonstrate efficacy and the nature of the monitoring to establish safety under the conditions of proposed clinical use will of course vary from product to product: no rigid requirements can be laid down in these respects. In the presentation of clinical data for a product license it is expected that during the clinical evaluation of the drug any interaction with other drugs with which the new agent is likely to be used concomitantly will have been investigated.

Advertising and Promotion. If a product license is granted, the Medicines Act of 1968 has controls that it can exert on the sale and promotion of the product. These are briefly as follows: (1) The Medicines Act of 1968, section 93, makes it an offense to issue advertisements or make oral representations such as to mislead or to constitute a false statement concerning the nature or quality of a medicinal product. Recommendations for use other than the uses specified by the product license are prohibited. Section 85 of the act makes it an offense to sell or supply a medicinal product of any description labeled in such a way as to describe the product falsely. (2) The Licensing Authority has powers to specify particular labeling requirements within the provisions of the product license for any individual product. (3) Before the promotion of any medicinal product to a practitioner, it has been necessary since 1973 to present the medical practitioner with a data sheet that contains an objective statement about the product and its uses, contraindications, and warnings. These data must be in accordance with the license.

Control of Veterinary Medicine. On the veterinary side, there were longstanding statutory controls on biological products, under the Diseases of Animals Legislation, and a voluntary veterinary product safety precaution scheme was introduced in 1964 to safeguard human beings, livestock, domestic animals, and wildlife against risk from veterinary products on direct sale to the farming industry. This scheme was set up following discussions between the health and agriculture departments and professional and commercial organizations. The Ministry of Agriculture and Fisheries and Food was the coordinating body advised by the Advisory Committee on Pesticides and other Toxic Chemicals and the Veterinary Products Committee.

Under the Medicines Act of 1968 scrutiny of veterinary products was made under the same principle as scrutiny of human medicines. The principles for assessment are on the basis of (1) quality, (2) efficacy for the animal treated, whether the drug is to be used as a growth promoter, a preventative medicine, or a therapeutic agent, and (3) safety of the drug for the animal treated, safety for the operator administering the drug, and safety in the residue of the drug or its metabolites in milk, eggs, or meat for the consumer.

The Licensing Authority issues licenses in the same way as on the human medicines—namely, animal test certificates of right, product licenses of right, animal test certificates, and product licenses. The Licensing Authority for veterinary medicines is advised through a subcommittee structure which operates in a somewhat different way from the subcommittee structure for human medicines. The Veterinary Products Committee is composed of appropriate experts and obtains its advice from the Pesticides and Toxic Chemical Advisory Committee and from the professional secretariat at a meeting attended by members of the Medicines Division of the Ministry of Agriculture, Food and Fisheries, Medicines Division of the Department of Health and Social Security, Environmental Health Division of the Department of Health and Social Security, and various outside experts making recommendations to the committee. On the use of antibiotics and antimicrobial substances, the Veterinary Products Committee is advised, like the Committee on Safety of Medicines, by the Joint Antimicrobial Subcommittee.

The Veterinary Products Committee considers applications for animal test certificates and product licenses for veterinary medicines made in accordance with the guidelines issued by the Licensing Authority. A large number of veterinary product licenses of right exist and these, like their human medicine counterparts, will be subjected to scrutiny in the future by a systematic review.

Postmarketing Surveillance

In parallel with the scheme for voluntary submission of laboratory and clinical trial data, the Committee on Safety of Drugs started a reporting scheme of suspected adverse drug reactions in 1964. This was passed on to its successor, the Committee on Safety of Medicines, at the time the Medicines Act became effective in 1971. The functions of the Adverse Reactions Subcommittee serving the Committee on Safety of Medicines have changed little since the passage of the act, the only appreciable difference being that manufacturers can be required by law to submit reports of any adverse effects brought to their attention. This has increased the proportion of reports originating from the industry from approximately 2 percent to approximately 20 percent of the total input.

Although the information obtained through the voluntary reporting system has proved to be invaluable in the detection of various new problems arising with medicinal products marketed after approval by the Committee on Safety of Medicines, and in the assessment of the hazards of some long-established products, the generally low reporting level has been responsible for a situation which is still far from satisfactory. In addition to our describing the subcommittee's current activities in monitoring the safety of marketed products, emphasis in this account will be placed on the reasons for underreporting of data and for the consequent delays in the detection of hazards.

The "Yellow Card" System. Over a period of thirteen years (1964–77), the number of reports submitted spontaneously in the form of reply-paid cards has remained remarkably constant. They account for between 60 percent and 75 percent of the total input of between 3,000 and 4,000 reports each year. The most important additional source of information has been material derived from other forms of correspondence with doctors and material derived from death certificates supplied by the Office of Population Censuses and Surveys (formerly the General Register Office). Other bodies such as the Royal College of General Practitioners, the Family Planning Association, and a number of hospital-based intensive monitoring schemes have also supplied valuable data. Approximately 50 percent of the reports are derived from the observations of general practitioners, approximately 35 percent from hospital consultants or other medical staff, and the remainder from groups such as coroners and dental surgeons.

The Committee on Safety of Medicines has asked doctors to report all serious or unusual reactions to all drugs and all reactions to recently introduced drugs. For the latter, this request has generally been interpreted as meaning all but the more trivial reactions. Before further considering the techniques used to detect and measure the hazards of drugs, we should examine some of the factors that may account for the relatively low level of reporting experienced by the committee.

Failure in the early detection of safety problems arises from an inability to recognize drug-induced effects or from a failure to take action and report effects that are recognized. The first depends on the degree of suspicion in the minds of individual doctors who witness adverse changes in their patients' conditions. Only by considering the possibility that some change may have been brought about by treatment, and by communicating with colleagues who may have seen similar events, or by referring to a central body such as the committee itself, can a physician determine that these changes are likely to have been drug-induced. Increasing awareness of the possibility that a serious, unusual, or even apparently unconnected event may have been caused by treatment might result from improvement in medical education and especially from improvement in the feedback of information about adverse reactions—either from the committee or from other bodies concerned with investigation of drug-safety problems.

Once the possibility of the connection between an adverse event and the treatment is recognized, there is perhaps an even greater problem in persuading the observer to report his suspicions. Among many reasons for the apparent reluctance on the part of the physicians to cooperate with the committee, at least seven seem to be of considerable importance: (1) complacency, resulting from the belief that only safe drugs are marketed, and failure to recognize that all effective drugs will cause damage to some patients: much of this may stem from promotional methods that advertise efficacy and minimize risks; (2) fear of involvement in litigation or investigation into prescribing costs by the Department of Health and failure to recognize the Committee on Safety of Medicines as a scientifically independent body that treats all reports in strict confidence and would not reveal the identity of a doctor or patient to any outsider or to divisions of the Department of Health responsible for matters other than drug safety; (3) guilt for having administered a treatment that may have harmed the patient; (4) ambition to be the first to collect and publish a personal series of cases; (5) ignorance of the committee's requirements for data collection; (6) diffidence about reporting mere suspicions or, alternatively, about reporting serious reactions that already are well-recognized; and (7) failure to recognize that once a drug has been

119

marketed, only the prescriber can play the part of clinical investigator, or advance knowledge of the benefits and dangers of the new product.

These seven factors are not arranged in any special order of importance, but experience has shown that publication of a small series of suspicious cases often triggers a large volume of retrospective reporting. By waiting until they are reasonably certain of a causal relationship, doctors may easily delay actions necessary to warn others of the risks their patients may be subjected to. On several occasions, physicians have been urged to publish their observations at a very early stage in recognition of the importance of their discovery and to encourage other doctors to report similar findings. The deterrent, and quite erroneous, image of the Committee on Safety of Medicines as a bureaucratic body seeking to control doctors' prescribing is difficult to overcome. The committee's true role is to advise the health departments and the professions in matters relating to drug safety; its principal objectives are not to "ban the drug" but merely to establish as far as possible the risks of drug treatment in relation to its benefits and to acquaint the professions with its findings. No doctor has become involved in litigation as a result of collaboration in the committee's work; on the contrary, it is probable that, in any dispute, his report would be seen as a responsible action aimed at helping towards a better understanding of the unmeasured and largely unknown risks of effective therapy.

In spite of the low reporting level, the yellow-card system has proved to be of considerable value. Much of its value is not obvious to the profession as a whole because on many occasions the action taken has been to modify a manufacturer's claims or to insert suitable warnings in the promotional literature. On several occasions drugs have been voluntarily removed from the market by the firm involved, on the advice of the committee: it has not so far been necessary to resort to legal powers to remove a drug from the market because of toxicity. Early reports of thromboembolism in women using oral contraceptives enabled the committee to exert pressure on other organizations to conduct further research, and the committee's own field study of fatal cases provided the first positive evidence of a cause-effect relationship between oral contraceptives and thromboembolic disease. A study of the voluntary reports also revealed the importance of the estrogen dose in determining the risk of thromboembolism.[20] Action to remind doctors of the risks of chloramphenicol was reflected

20 W. H. W. Inman, M. P. Vessey, B. Westerholm, and A. Englelund, "Thromboembolic Disease and the Steroidal Content of Oral Contraceptives: A Report to the Committee on Safety of Drugs," British Medical Journal, vol. 2 (1970), pp. 203-9.

in an immediate reduction in the number of reported deaths in the United Kingdom from an average of one report per month to zero, with the exception of a small number of fatal cases among patients who had been treated with chloramphenicol while traveling overseas.

The yellow-card system was not, unfortunately, the first to reveal the harmful effects of the beta-adrenergic blocking agent practolol. This drug was used in more than 250,000 patients before its tendency to produce serious ocular effects was recognized, a tendency often coupled with a skin reaction resembling psoriasis and sometimes by deafness or an unusual and potentially lethal form of sclerosing peritonitis. This recognition did not result from reporting to the committee, but from three independent publications in the medical journals. Up to that time only a single report of conjunctivitis had been received prior to these publications, but once the ocular effects were recognized, more than 200 cases with eye damage, some dating back nearly three years, were reported retrospectively.

Techniques for Monitoring by Spontaneous Reporting. The various stages in the recognition and assessment of drug hazard are summarized in Figure 4. Some problems are drawn to the attention of the monitoring staff as a result of inquiries from outside while others are "signaled" by the reports themselves. Each report is subjected to an elaborate coding procedure. Every active ingredient contained in the products that have been used is identified by clerical staff. Details of dosage, dates of starting and stopping treatment, information about rechallenge, and so on, are entered on a computer coding sheet. The clinical details are then assessed by a doctor, and further codes for adverse reactions are added. The system has the capacity for storage of information on up to twenty-four different pharmacologically active substances and up to ten distinct signs or symptoms of an associated adverse reaction affecting a single patient.

Each report entering the system is also discussed at twice-weekly meetings. Experience has shown the value of collective discussion of the reports as opposed to single-person scrutiny. At these meetings use is made of computer printout and file retrieval facilities. Moreover, in addition to the production of standardized tabulations listing the reactions that have been reported, a number of research programs are being developed that may result in computer-signaled warnings of the existence of problems not apparent to those conducting the initial scrutiny. These may be particularly useful for the detection of drug interactions. The principal use of the computer, however, is for the rapid retrieval of relevant case records. At present a batch-pro-

Figure 4

IDENTIFICATION, ASSESSMENT, AND ACTION ON REPORTS OF SUSPECTED ADVERSE REACTIONS TO DRUGS RECEIVED BY THE COMMITTEE ON SAFETY OF MEDICINES

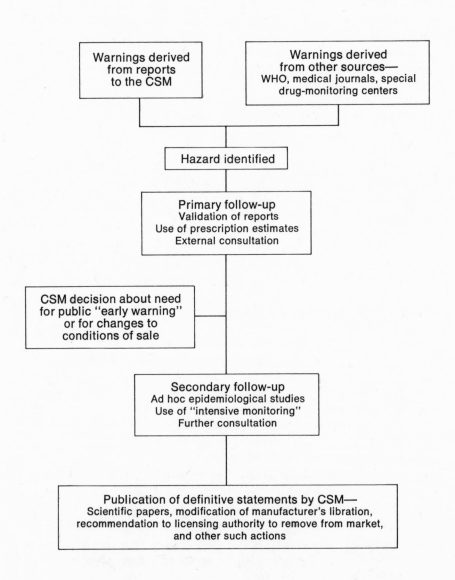

cessing mode is used but future enhancement of the system should provide for "on-line" interrogation of the data.

Once identified, a new problem is subjected to a follow-up procedure. First, individual reports are validated and additional data are obtained either by correspondence with the reporting physician or by interview with a member of the committee's team of about 100 part-time medical field workers. The reports are compared with the prescription estimates obtained from the National Health Service Pricing Bureau or with manufacturers' sales data. They are also considered carefully in comparison with reports for therapeutically related drugs. The examination of the pattern or "profile" of the reactions to the suspect drug, in comparison with the profiles for related drugs, may reveal an unexpectedly large proportion of one type of reaction. The possibility of biased reporting is considered, and also the possibilities of batch variation or interaction with other concurrently administered drugs. Outside experts may be consulted and a search may be made of data assembled by the World Health Organization International Drug Monitoring Agency in Geneva. Discussions may be held with the manufacturers or with other national drug regulatory authorities.

On completion of the primary follow-up procedure, the committee may decide that a warning should be published. A delicate balance must be struck between premature announcements that could damage the reputation of a valuable product and delayed announcements that would allow avoidable harm to continue.

Since many different problems may be under investigation simultaneously, difficult decisions must be made about the allocation of manpower and other resources. The importance of the hazard that has been demonstrated may require epidemiological studies aimed at measuring more precisely the incidence of the adverse reactions. An approach may be made to an outside body such as the Royal College of General Practitioners or the Medical Research Council in the hope that a survey may be started. The committee's team of field officers may be briefed to conduct a case-control study using as a starting point patients whose deaths had been recorded on certificates obtainable from the Office of Population Censuses and Surveys, or various registers such as the Cancer Register, or the Register of Congenital Abnormalities. Major studies have been conducted of fatalities from thromboembolic disease in relation to the use of oral contraceptives. An ongoing study of the drug histories of mothers of babies with congenital abnormalities is providing evidence that may confirm suspicions of teratogenicity or free certain drugs from existing suspicions.

The committee is mainly concerned with reaching decisions as to whether adverse reactions are occurring and with estimating the magnitude of these risks. It is not so much concerned with the mechanics by which the reactions occur. It has no facilities for conducting pharmacological or pathological studies, but wherever possible it seeks to interest physicians and scientists in academic institutions in the possibility of initiating sophisticated studies that might lead to a better understanding of the etiology of adverse reactions.

Communications with the Medical Profession. Communications are two directional; the output of information supplied by the committee is very much dependent on the input of information reaching it. As time passes and the data available for study increase, it is likely that output will accelerate.

During the past thirteen years, a total of fifteen pamphlets have been issued in the "Adverse Reaction Series." Some of these have taken the form of warnings about recently identified hazards, others have been reminders about known hazards or have drawn attention to the importance of collaborating with the committee in adverse reactions monitoring. The effect of these warnings has been variable. The highly beneficial effect of a warning on chloramphenicol has already been referred to, but on occasion warnings have been seized upon by the popular press, and unnecessary and undesirable fears have been aroused among the general public. The strength of the evidence on which these warnings have been based has varied from near certainty in the case of chloramphenicol to what was only strong suspicion in the case of a warning issued about the possible dangers of pressurized aerosols. This latter warning nevertheless was shown to have had a profound effect in bringing to an end a large-scale "epidemic" of sudden deaths of asthmatic patients.[21] No statement has so far had to be retracted or modified.

Other forms of communication have included letters to all doctors, letters to the editors of medical journals, and the publication of scientific papers by members of the committee or by its secretariat. Whereas the effects of direct mailings to doctors tend to be ephemeral, scientific publications become part of medical knowledge and are of long-lasting value. The fact that statements by the Committee on Safety of Medicines have to be authoritative undoubtedly tends to inhibit the frequency with which such statements are made. Some mechanism for publishing advanced warnings is required to allow release of information based on suspicion rather than proof of the

[21] W. H. W. Inman and A. M. Adelstein, *Lancet*, vol. 2 (1969), pp. 279-85.

existence of safety problems. It is possible that a mechanism could be established for publication of data derived from the Register of Adverse Reactions in such a way that it need not be interpreted as carrying the full weight of the opinions of members of the Committee on Safety of Medicines.[22]

A new experiment in the production of a "low-key" communication appears to have met with some success. The document, the first of a new series, is entitled *Current Problems* and contains information about problems which are of concern to the committee, but about which no firm conclusions could yet be reached.[23]

The Review of Medicines

Under the Medicines Act of 1968, a medicinal product may be marketed in the United Kingdom only if the promoter of the product holds a product license. Since 1971, product licenses have been granted for new products only after the safety, quality, and efficacy of the products have been assessed. The Committee on Safety of Medicines, established in 1971, provides expert independent advice on these matters. Some 36,000 products on the market before September 1971 were granted product licenses of right automatically without any assessment, apart from those considered essentially according to their safety aspects between 1964 and 1971, by the Committee on Safety of Drugs. The Committee on Safety of Drugs was replaced by the Committee on Safety of Medicines in 1971 with the implementation of the Medicines Act of 1968.[24] Hence standards which have been applied to new drugs since the establishment of the Committee on Safety of Medicines have not been applied to those marketed prior to 1971. This is the reason why the review of medicines is being undertaken and for the establishment of the Committee on the Review of Medicines in 1975.

Scope of the Review. The review will cover all drugs presently on the market. Although the bulk of the work will concern those drugs which at present hold product licenses of right, those drugs with full product licenses will be included. This may well be important in the

---

[22] Data derived from the Register of Adverse Reactions reported to the Committee on Safety of Medicines (1964-73), distributed free to regional pharmacists, university departments, postgraduate medical centers, et cetera.

[23] Committee on Safety of Medicines, *Current Problems*, no. 1 and no. 2 (London: Her Majesty's Stationery Office, 1975 and 1976).

[24] Medicines (Committee on the Review of Medicines) Order (SI 1006) (London: Her Majesty's Stationery Office, 1975).

broad consideration of groups of products in the standardization of recommended indications. Those products marketed before 1964 were given a product license of right automatically. Those marketed between 1964 and 1971 were considered from safety aspects by the Committee on Safety of Drugs, and they are also the subjects of product licenses of right. Those drugs marketed since September 1971 have been processed through the Committee on Safety of Medicines in which case considerable preclinical and clinical data have been accumulated; these have full product licenses. The review will therefore cover a total of approximately 36,000 licenses, of which 34,000 are product licenses of right and 2,000 are full product licenses. These 36,000 products contain a total of some 6,000 active ingredients.

The total figure of 36,000 product licenses is a fair estimate but needs to be interpreted with care since separate licenses have been issued for each dosage form. Hence some six to eight product licenses may exist for a single ingredient manufactured by one pharmaceutical company. Many products are standard remedies sold under various trade names. Since the definition of a medicinal product is wide, it includes a number of borderline substances such as dandruff shampoos, toothpaste, breathing gases, and so on; however, the number of such borderline substances licensed is not large.

The Products. These include proprietary prescription items, brand-name remedies, prescription fillers, herbals, and homeopathics.

Proprietary prescription items. These are essentially items which are found in MIMS (*Monthly Index of Medical Specialities*) and represent some 4,000 to 5,000 products, many promoted directly to medical practitioners.

Branded home remedies. These are proprietary products advertised directly to the public. There are some 1,500 sold on a national scale, along with a number of brands made by a few firms and labeled with the name of the druggists that sell them.

Prescription fillers. These are generic products—that is, products sold under the name of an active ingredient without any indications for use. There are some 12,000 of these although probably only some 2,500 different ingredients are involved.

Herbals. These include some 10,000 products essentially of plant origin, many of them containing synthetic ingredients in addition. They may be sold directly to the public or to herbal practitioners. A small proportion have no indications but many have wide and largely unacceptable indications. Simple herbal preparations, such as those prepared by crushing, comminution, or infusion are exempt from licensing, but the remainder are treated in exactly the same way as other products.

Homeopathics. The figures here are very misleading since there are many dilutions and different pharmaceutical forms. Some 4,000 of these products exist, many sold only to homeopathic practitioners without indications, but there is a proportion sold direct to the public.

Therapeutic Categories. For the purpose of the review of medicines in the United Kingdom is that the whole range of products, whether sold by prescription only or directly to the public through pharmacists or general sale, will be divided into broad therapeutic categories *according to the indications for which they are promoted.* These categories will be considered in turn. The basis for the selection of the major groups has been (1) the volume of usage and (2) the reported incidence of associated adverse reactions. The first groups selected on this basis are shown in Table 1.

For example, in the antirheumatic group, some 3,500 adverse reaction reports were received between 1964 and 1972; this represents 12.5 percent of the total adverse reaction reports. In 1973 there were 12 million prescriptions for this type of drug, at a cost of £11 million to the National Health Service. This group was selected as the first for review since its products are in widespread use for essentially nonfatal conditions and also for trivial indications and there is a high percentage of serious adverse reactions. The analgesic category contributed 3,000 (approximately 9 percent) of the adverse reaction reports, with 371 million prescriptions in 1973 at a cost of £7.8 million to the National Health Service. There is, of course, a large over-the-counter sale which is not included in these cost figures.

Psychotropics contributed 5,000 adverse reaction reports (17 percent). There were 33 million prescriptions in 1973 at a cost of £20 million to the National Health Service. Extensive use and a possibility of drug abuse were reasons for the selection of this category.

Antibiotics contributed 4,000 reports (14 percent). There were 40 million prescriptions in 1973 at a cost of £26 million to the National Health Service. As a result of their extensive use for both serious and trivial conditions, this was also considered an important group for review.

Basic information on all the products has been installed on a computer which acts as an index (or rather as several indexes) to the files. Information can be retrieved by product name, active con-

Table 1
THERAPEUTIC CATEGORIES

	Products	Ingredients
Non-steroidal antirheumatics	489	411
Analgesics	567	385
Psychotropics	825	463
Antibiotics	78	46
Anabolic steroids	34	19
Anorectic agents	139	177
Immunologicals	133	64

Source: M. F. Cuthbert, unpublished observations, 1975.

stituent, therapeutic code, and route of the administration. Information is also included on methods of marketing, name of manufacturer, and number of license or certificate.

Important additional information is now also on the computer; this includes dosage, indications, contraindications or warnings, nonactive ingredients, and information on review action.

Sources of Information. Reports summarizing all the available data are prepared by the professional staff on the individual ingredients and put to the relevant subcommittee and the Committee on the Review of Medicines for their consideration. Important sources of information include applications for product licenses or clinical trial certificates, adverse reaction reports, prescription data, medical and pharmaceutical literature, professional organizations, and individual license holders.

Applications for product licenses or clinical trial certificates. Since licensing started in 1971, applicants have been required to provide extensive supporting data on animal toxicity, teratology, pharmacology and pharmacokinetics, clinical pharmacology, and clinical trials. In total there is clinical data on 300 to 400 compounds and information on toxicity on approximately 560 to 700 compounds.

Adverse reaction reports. Since 1964 reports of suspected adverse reaction associated with drugs have been collated by the Committee on Safety of Medicines. A breakdown of the reports associated with a particular ingredient will indicate the main areas in which adverse reactions occur. Difficulties in interpretation arise from underreporting but this data represents a most important source.

Prescription data. This provides a denominator for studies involving prescribed medicines and is provided by the NHS Pricing Bureau which derives its data from a large sample of prescriptions issued by general medical practitioners.

Medical and pharmaceutical literature. Literature searches can be made for selected products. The review staff also has the advantages of a Medline terminal of which computerized searches of recent medical literature can be carried out. The Royal Botanic Gardens have also offered access to information on herbal products.

Professional organizations. Both the Association of the British Pharmaceutical Industry and the Proprietary Association of Great Britain have set up their own review teams and have offered to collate information on specific ingredients. This will be particularly valuable for groups of products and for those widely prescribed, for example, in the consideration of aspirin and related salicylates.

Individual license holders. Data on chemistry and pharmacy for all products have been requested. Data on safety and efficacy of drugs falling into the first and second review categories (non-steroidal antirheumatics and analgesics) have been requested also on immunological agents.

As the review proceeds, individual license holders will be approached and asked to provide data. Initially this will not involve any new work; the review staff will only request data which is already available. At a later stage, after the subcommittee has considered the ingredient, specific requests for further information may be made.

Procedure for the Review. In December 1974 consultation on the broad aspects of the review was undertaken. At the first meeting of the Committee on the Review of Medicines in October 1975 the procedure was agreed in principle and the following reflects the approach of the Licensing Authority as advised by the Committee on the Review of Medicines.

Establishment of subcommittees. The antirheumatic, analgesic, and immunologicals subcommittees have now been set up and discussion has taken place on the constitution of members for both the analgesics subcommittee and the subcommittee on psychotropic agents.

Ingredient-based review. It has been agreed that the review of each comparative category will begin with consideration of active ingredients rather than individual products. To ensure consistency, ingredients used for similar indications or of related chemical structures will be considered together as far as practical.

Grouping of ingredients. As a working arrangement the ingredients in each category have been grouped as follows: Group A ingredients are those which have an established or well-documented activity relevant to therapeutic category under review. Group B ingredients are those which have no apparent activity relevant to the therapeutic category or where evidence of such activity is not well documented. Within the group, B1 ingredients are those which are single ingredient products while B2 ingredients are those contained in multi-ingredient products. Many of the latter may be present coincidentally since the product may have claims other than of the therapeutic category under consideration.

Procedure regarding Group A ingredients. The secretariat will prepare reports based on the literature, information on product files, and information from license holders and the trade associations, which will include all available information (including information on quality, the need for bio-availability and stability data, toxicology, teratology, pharmacology, and clinical evidence). The revelant subcommittee of the Committee on the Review of Medicines will be asked to agree on acceptable indications, contraindications, and warnings for a particular ingredient. This will form the provisional recommendation.

Procedure regarding Group B ingredients. For B1 ingredients, a brief summary related to individual products will be prepared and the subcommittee invited to consider the indications in the light of available evidence. B2 ingredients will be examined for potential toxicity and established activity or use in a brief report of the available evidence put to the subcommittee. These reports will be on groups of products or on multi-ingredient products as far as is practicable. The relevant subcommittee will be asked to provide general guidance on the acceptability of the components for the claimed indication.

In all cases the provisional recommendations will be communicated to the trade associations and license holders and their comments invited before the Committee on the Review of Medicines comes to its final recommendations. Only after this stage will licensing action be considered.

Progress. The Committee on the Review of Medicines has undertaken a formidable task in attempting to review the quality, safety, and efficacy of some 36,000 products. The review does depend on

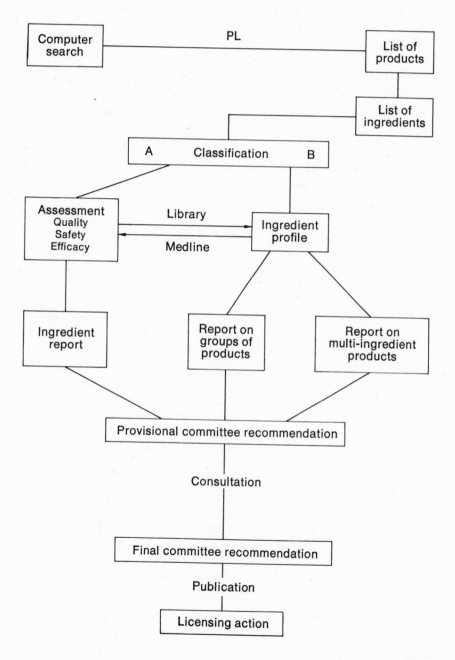

Figure 5

REVIEW PROCEDURE

the cooperation of the pharmaceutical industry and on its cooperation with the appropriate trade associations so that all the relevant information can be put to the review committees and that many minor points can be resolved at any early stage. As the review proceeds, those product licenses of right deemed to be satisfactory will be converted to full product licenses. Since the review commenced in 1975, some 12,000 product licenses have been withdrawn voluntarily by manufacturers largely as a result of enquiries on the quality of products.[25] Considerable inroads have also been made in the review of the major drugs used in the treatment of rheumatic disease.

The overall aim of the review is to ensure that drugs available in the United Kingdom are of adequate quality and are safe and efficacious for their recommended indications. This will inevitably lead to the more rational use of the remedies available to the prescriber and to the general public who purchase remedies in pharmacies or through general sales outlets.

Summary and Conclusions

The implementation of the Medicines Act in 1971 and the establishment of the Committee on Safety of Medicines means that all medicines in the United Kingdom are now licensed. A clinical trial certificate or a product license is now mandatory before a new drug can undergo clinical trial or be marketed. All drugs on the market in September 1971 were granted product licenses of right, but all these are subject to a systematic review according to their therapeutic claims.

The United Kingdom does not issue detailed requirements (regulations) regarding the content of applications, but issues guidelines in collaboration with the pharmaceutical industry. In general, the United Kingdom adopts a flexible approach, and the adequacy of submitted data will usually depend on the intended clinical usage. In applications for clinical trial certificates, great emphasis is placed on the clinical trial protocol and the monitoring facilities. In applications for marketing, it has not usually proved necessary to insist that individual patient data from the clinical trials be submitted.

The United Kingdom fully supports the concept of international collaboration in drug testing and actively encourages the inclusion of such data in applications. There is no objection to the inclusion of toxicological and clinical studies performed outside the United

---

[25] *Annual Report of the Committee on the Review of Medicines for 1976* (London: Her Majesty's Stationery Office, 1977).

Kingdom provided that the work has been carried out to a high standard; that strains of animals have been used which are generally acceptable; and that dietary factors, environmental factors, and the design of the clinical trials are satisfactory.

The basic concept of the U.K. approach to drug regulation is that premarketing controls are not sufficient, since most serious adverse reactions are very rare events, unlikely to be detected in clinical trials involving a few hundred patients. In the U.K. view, extensive clinical trials are less useful than an effective postmarketing drug surveillance scheme.

The advertising and promotion of drugs in the United Kingdom must be in accordance with the terms of the product license, though a doctor is always free to prescribe a drug for any purpose he considers appropriate for the treatment of his patient, whether the indication is approved or not. In the latter instance, he acts without the approval of the regulatory authority but on the grounds that the use of the drug in a particular clinical situation is in the patient's best interest.

Advertising of drugs to the general public prohibits reference to cancer and venereal diseases, and this legislation will be extended considerably in due course. Drugs are also controlled by classification into those which are only available on prescription and those available to the general public either through registered pharmacies or on general sale.

Under the National Health Service (NHS), a doctor may prescribe without restriction any drug except those of addiction. The Medicines Division of the Department of Health and Social Security (DHSS) does not concern itself with the cost of drugs but only with their quality, safety, and efficacy. Other divisions of DHSS advise doctors on the costs of drugs and distribute comparative cost information.

There are no prescribing restrictions based on specific drug costs or formularies in the United Kingdom, but some drugs (particularly in the early stages after marketing) are restricted to hospital use. In addition, however, there is a mechanism for identifying those doctors or groups of doctors in general practice that have unusually high total prescribing costs. This mechanism consists of a sampling of all prescriptions written by every practitioner for one month each year. Such practitioners may be called upon to justify their high prescribing costs. Initially there is an informal approach by a doctor from the Regional Medical Service, who offers advice; this is usually sufficient to resolve the problem. If the initial approach proves ineffective, a senior doctor, with a wide experience of general practice, visits him formally and provides him with an analysis of his prescribing. If both these approaches fail, the situation is reported to the Local Medical Committee, which consists of elected representatives of the general practitioners in the same area. It may recommend that the Local Family Practitioner Committee (to which a doctor is under contract and which is responsible for providing the general medical services in the area under the NHS) withhold a portion of the doctor's remuneration. In this case the doctor has a right of appeal to the secretary of state for health and social services. It is very seldom indeed that recourse needs to be made either to the formal approach or to the Local Family Practitioner Committee. Despite the relative lack of restriction, prescribing costs in the United Kingdom compare very favorably with those of other developed countries, including those in which the patient pays for prescription medicines.

Drugs of addiction are subject to the Misuse of Drugs Act (1971) and Misuse of Drug Regulations (1973). A doctor may also, on his own responsibility, have a drug supplied, manufactured, or imported for the treatment of an individual patient under his care.

5
SWITZERLAND

Rudolf Preisig

Introduction

Three major factors have shaped the present system of drug control and utilization in Switzerland.

First is the existence of a system known as a free medical practice. Although over 90 percent of the population carry some form of health insurance, Switzerland lacks a national health service. As a consequence, the practicing physician usually deals with several health insurers, and thus may be exposed to several different policies on insurance. Throughout, the principle of freedom of choice of medical care (physician, hospital, pharmacy) is upheld.

Most of the health insurers are private companies. However, government subsidy—either directly to the insurance system, or indirectly by carrying the hospital deficits—has recently gained in importance. Moreover, in many states (that is, cantons) health insurance is obligatory for the low-income groups. But even in this category, the insurance is geared to major risks, while minor risks are carried largely by the patients.

Second is the fact that health care is organized on a regional basis. Thus, all aspects of health care (including licensing of health personnel, licensing of drugs, and so on) fall under the jurisdiction of the particular canton. In terms of drug utilization, the only exception is the control of narcotics, carried out by cantonal offices but supervised by a federal bureau.

Third is the existence of a pharmaceutical (and chemical) industry which plays a large role in the national economy. The close

I am grateful to Dr. P. Fischer, director of the Interkantonale Kontrollstelle für Heilmittel, Berne, for his advice and critical review of the manuscript.

interrelation between industry scientists and universities assures that pharmaceutical research is represented at all levels of health policy making. Conversely, appreciable support for academic research comes from the industry.

These three factors are important for an understanding of the system of drug control, which at first sight appears rather complex.

Historical Background and Present Drug Control

The present drug administration (called Interkantonale Kontrollstelle für Heilmittel, IKS) dates from the year 1900. At that time, the heads of government of five cantons agreed to set up an office for the licensing and quality control of drugs. By 1934 all twenty-five cantons had joined the agreement. Over the following decades, the IKS was enlarged in a stepwise fashion and the intercantonal convention adjusted to modern needs.[1] According to the updated agreement of June 3, 1971, the IKS must fulfill the following four major tasks:[2]

(1) *The quality control of marketed drugs.* In its own laboratories, the IKS analyzes drugs according to their active ingredients. Samples are obtained both at the time of submission for registration and at intervals following marketing. The importance of this task is emphasized by the fact that in 1973 some 16 percent of 1,730 samples analyzed had to be returned to the manufacturer for appropriate action.

(2) *The quality control of manufacturing.* Detailed requirements to assure the quality of the manufacturing of drugs have been issued. They are enforced by periodic inspections under the auspices of the IKS.[3]

(3) *The licensing of new drugs.* The full-time scientific staff of the IKS receives all documents submitted by the manufacturer and

---

[1] P. Fischer, "Interkantonale Kontrollstelle für Heilmittel Berne: Rechtliche Aspekte der Begutachtung: Organisation," *Bulletin der Schweizerischen Akademie der Medizinischen Wissenschaften*, vol. 29 (1973), pp. 43-53, and F. Wüst, "Die Interkantonale Vereinbarung über die Kontrolle der Heilmittel vom 16.6.54," *Europäische Hochschulschriften*, Series 2, *Rechtswissenschaft*, vol. 16 (Berne: Herbert Lang & Co. AG, 1969), also published separately by the author (Berne, 1969).

[2] Intercantonal Office for the Control of Medicaments, *Intercantonal Convention on the Control of Medicaments* (Berne, 1971).

[3] P. Fischer, "Rechtsgrundlagen und Bedeutung der Herstellungskontrolle in der Schweiz," *Pharmaceutica Acta Helvetiae*, vol. 47 (1972), pp. 629-36.

prepares a summary. The present guidelines (May 1972) require that efficacy, safety, and indications be judged by an independent board of university scientists (pharmacologists, clinical pharmacologists, and clinicians).[4]

(4) *Continuous review system.* Since a license is issued only for a duration of five years, marketed drugs are reviewed after this period by the same board. This review system guarantees permanent re-evaluation of the manufacturers' claims (package insert). It also assures silent elimination of obsolete preparations. In addition, the IKS may call for an extraordinary review of a drug at any time it deems such an action to be in the public interest.

Although—with the exception of permanent drug review—this system of controls over access of drugs to the market is quite comparable to that in other countries (Figure 1), there are some notable differences. The IKS is responsible only for assessment of drugs (and apparatus designed for medical therapy by the public—which is to say, medical devices); by contrast, the administration of food and cosmetics is handled by the Federal Office of Public Health.

It is obvious that the separation of drugs and devices from food and cosmetics has the advantage of better definition of tasks. On the other hand, it cannot be denied that drugs, cosmetics, and food-stuffs have a number of common denominators (such as the necessity for assessing safety of preservatives) that would seem to call for common regulations. Close cooperation among the various agencies is a prerequisite for the proper functioning of this system.

Switzerland also differs from other countries in its limited scientific manpower. Thus, the Swiss drug administration carries out its function with a full-time academic staff of only fifteen persons. It relies heavily on a board of seven university scientists (the Drug Evaluation Board), who—as a part-time activity—meet every two weeks. In addition, this board makes extensive use of outside specialists in various fields of pharmacy and medicine, calling on their expert help whenever needed. The "review time" between submission of documents and definitive decision on a new drug (a measure often cited to assess the functional capability of a drug administration) is on average six to eight months, and thus compares favorably with that in other countries. There is no doubt, however, that the IKS has reached the limits of its capacity. Consequently, any new task must

[4] Intercantonal Office for the Control of Medicaments, *Regulations for the Implementation of the Intercantonal Convention on the Control of Medicaments* (Berne, 1972).

137

Figure 1

FLOW CHART OF DRUG CONTROL IN SWITZERLAND

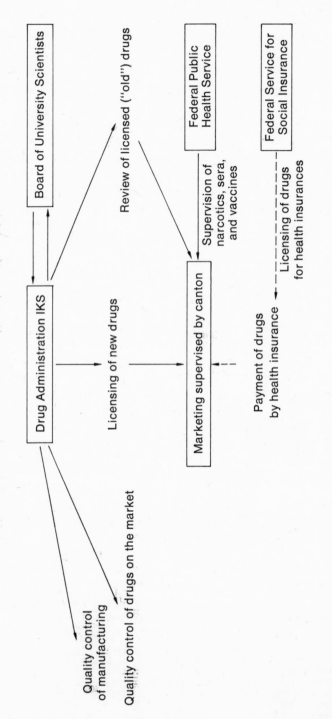

Note: Sales categories are: "A"—prescription, pharmacy (corresponds to "apotheke" run by a pharmacist (academic level); "B"—prescription, pharmacy; "C"—over-the-counter, pharmacy; "D"—over-the-counter, drugstore (corresponds to "drogerie" run by a druggist (nonacademic level); and "E"—over-the-counter, other stores.

be viewed with great reservations, since further expansion of this body may not be justifiable in view of the small size of the country. This is one major reason that the IKS has so far refrained from setting up an investigational new drug (IND) procedure. Instead, periodic statements are issued to physicians in hospitals and in practice and the physicians are urged to consult university experts before participating in new drug trials. Further, the increasing tendency to establish "committees for medical ethics" (peer review) in hospitals and the action of the Swiss Academy of Medicine in establishing guidelines for clinical investigation appear to offer a valid alternative to a central agency.[5] Finally, the establishment of clinical pharmacology divisions or departments at the five medical schools has undoubtedly contributed to an increased awareness of potential hazards, particularly in the use of investigational drugs.[6]

In this connection, it is also worth mentioning that all IKS-approved drugs carry on the package (and package insert) the IKS stamp (Figure 2) and the registration number. The physician (and also the public) may thus easily identify preparations that have not (or not yet) passed through legal channels. Apart from illicit traffic in narcotics, the "black market" in nonapproved drugs appears to be a minor problem.

With the exception of journals for the health professions (physicians and pharmacists), the advertisement of prescription drugs (groups "A" and "B" in Figure 1) and nonprescription pharmacy drugs (group "C") by any media is strictly forbidden. By contrast, advertisements for other OTC drugs (group "D") may be carried in journals available to the public, although the text of the advertisements is supervised by the IKS.

It is worth emphasizing that, in general, the relationship between the Drug Evaluation Board and the Swiss drug industry is marked by an atmosphere of mutual trust and respect and by flexibility. As a result, it has been possible to arrive at "gentlemen's agreements" on such items as self-discipline in professional advertising and restriction of the sales of phenacetin-containing OTC drugs. Unfortunately, foreign companies not familiar with the attitude of "reasonable com-

---

[5] Schweizerische Akademie der Medizinischen Wissenschaften, "Richtlinien für Forschungsuntersuchungen am Menschen," *Schweizerische Aerztezeitung*, vol. 52, no. 8 (1971), pp. 233-60.

[6] R. Preisig, "Begutachtung von Heilmittel: ihre Bedeutung für den praktizierenden Arzt," *Therapeutische Umschau*, vol. 31, no. 11 (1974), pp. 859-64.

Figure 2

IKS STAMPS FOR PHARMACEUTICAL SPECIALTIES

Sales Categories	Stamps
Class "A": Prescription—Pharmacy (restricted, e.g. narcotics)	
Class "B": Prescription—Pharmacy	
Class "C": Over-the-counter—Pharmacy	
Class "D": Over-the-counter—"Drugstore"	
Class "E": Over-the-counter—Other stores	

Source: "Interkantonale Kontrollstelle für Heilmittel," Berne/Switzerland.

promise" at times assume a position of fighting a (nonexistent) adversary.

According to the Intercantonal Convention, an IKS decision may be subject to reconsideration by an independent appeal board (called the *Rekurskommission* and composed of scientists and a judge) whenever the manufacturer (or his representative) calls for such a review.[7] The decision of this board is final. It is interesting to note that manufacturers only rarely use this channel: during the last five years, the number of appeals treated by this board has averaged six to ten cases per year.

---

[7] Intercantonal Office for the Control of Medicaments, *Regulations*.

Graduate and Postgraduate Education in Clinical Pharmacology and Therapeutics

Since the structure of hospital medicine and the organization of medical training in Switzerland has recently been described in some detail,[8] only a brief summary relevant to the teaching of therapeutics will be given here.

Basically as outlined above, medical care is organized on a regional basis. Thus, each canton has one or more medical centers. Although only five of these centers (those in Basle, Berne, Geneva, Lausanne, and Zurich) are university hospitals with corresponding medical schools, a number are university-affiliated teaching hospitals. The same holds true of some city hospitals in the cantons with universities. Affiliated or not, most of these regional medical centers (called *Kantonsspital*) operate full-fledged ancillary services, including diagnostic laboratories, radiology, and pathology.

At the graduate level, all five medical schools carry divisions or departments of clinical pharmacology. According to the present curriculum (which is under federal jurisdiction), all students must pass a written final examination in clinical pharmacology and therapeutics. A framework for teaching has been agreed upon by the chairmen responsible; a twice-yearly meeting serves to establish the country-wide examination and to discuss any changes in the curriculum deemed necessary. This relatively young specialty has already pioneered a remarkable *unité de doctrine*.

By contrast, the teaching of therapeutics at the postgraduate level is so far more or less rudimentary and heterogeneous. Even at the university hospitals it is not sufficiently emphasized. Here and there therapeutic rounds or conferences are being held, but the prevailing attitude of clinicians (who consider the problems of pharmacotherapy to be of second priority) is as yet characterized by a lack of interest.

Presumably, therefore, the major teaching of therapy at the postgraduate level is now achieved by publications such as the *Therapeutische Umschau* [Therapeutic review], an independent journal devoted exclusively to therapeutics. Some five years ago—with a new editorial board—the journal began its present policy of providing broad monthly reviews of therapeutic topics. Since then, the prac-

---

[8] R. Preisig and B. Cueni, "Medical Care, Research, and Education in Switzerland," *Medical Research Systems in Europe*, Ciba Foundation Symposium 21 (Amsterdam: Associated Scientific Publishers Elsevier-Excerpta-Medica-North Holland, 1973), pp. 223-31.

ticing physician's need for up-to-date information on therapy has been demonstrated by the increase in the number of the journal's subscriptions until it now reaches approximately 75 percent of all Swiss physicians.

Whereas the major medical specialties have defined their requirements to obtain board certification (issued by the Swiss Medical Association), there is as yet no official training program for clinical pharmacology. All that has been achieved so far is acceptance of a one-year period spent in a clinical pharmacology unit toward board certification in internal medicine or its subspecialties.

In the author's experience, one major problem in setting up a clinical pharmacology training program lies in the fact that in Swiss departments of pharmacology it is no longer possible to get experience with routine pharmacological or toxicological procedures. These tasks have been taken over by the pharmaceutical companies. In order to remedy this, the Department of Clinical Pharmacology at the University of Berne has had an agreement over the last five years with some of the Swiss pharmaceutical firms. Thus, our fellows were able to spend one year in divisions of pharmacology and toxicology in these companies. During this time they participated actively in the investigations of new compounds and had a chance to become familiar with the problems of the industry. The companies generously provided for the salaries of the fellows during this stay. Although our experience with this approach is as yet limited, so far there has been a favorable response on the part of the fellows.

Another problem which hinders the development of training in clinical pharmacology arises in the organization of clinical pharmacology units. At present, these units are either participating in patient care within a department of medicine, thus leaving little time for investigative work, or they are established as independent departments having restricted (or no) access to bedside medicine. Only a fundamental change in attitude of clinicians towards medical specialization and in particular towards the importance of rational therapeutics can pave the road for true interdisciplinary activity beyond the boundaries of internal medicine.

Controls over Drug Utilization

The use of narcotics represents the only strictly controlled aspect of drug utilization. Under the Federal Act on Narcotic Drugs of October 3, 1951, a control organization was established by each canton under the supervision of the Federal Office of Public Health. The latter coordinates the activities of the cantonal offices and supplies annual statistics to the Permanent Central Opium Board. It is empowered to carry out spot checks. Import and export of narcotics to or from Switzerland is under the direct control of the federal office. Details of the procedures have been published by Bertschinger and others.[9]

For nonnarcotic drugs, there is no general system of control over utilization. Three factors may, however, be considered to favorably influence drug usage by patients: the handling of prescription drugs, the direct dispensing of drugs by the physician, and the *List of Specialties.*

Since drugs in class "A" or "B" are only available in pharmacies on medical prescription, and since well-trained pharmacists are generally aware of their responsibilities, abuse of such drugs by the public is virtually unheard of. Furthermore, the long-established class "C" drugs, while available without prescription, are restricted to pharmacies. This procedure assures some—albeit limited—counselling and supervision by the pharmacist. Thus, pharmacists may be viewed as an important backbone of "control" over drug utilization.

Most physicians practicing in rural or mountain areas are also licensed to maintain a (limited) pharmacy for direct dispensing of drugs to patients. This system, which arose for practical reasons, provides the advantage of closer medical supervision of drug usage, since the patient is likely to obtain all medicines (prescription and OTC) from the same source. A broadening of this approach is not desirable, however, since it could hinder the existence of pharmacies necessary for public drug supply.

Like the system in New Zealand, the scheme of benefits for drugs paid by health insurances is based on a limited list, the *List of Specialties (Spezialitätenliste).*[10] Ordinarily, no drug may be prescribed at the cost of the health insurers unless it is on the list. A committee established under the auspices of the Federal Office for Social Insurance and made up of representatives of academic medicine, medical practice, and health insurers decides on admission of drugs to the list. Although any drug admitted by the IKS for marketing can be a

---

[9] J. P. Bertschinger et al., "Narcotics Control in Switzerland," *Bulletin on Narcotics,* vol. 16, no. 2 (1964), pp. 1-16.

[10] See W. M. Wardell, "Control of Drug Utilization in a National Health Service: The New Zealand System," *Clinical Pharmacology and Therapeutics,* vol. 14 (1973), esp. pp. 773-90, and the contribution by W. M. Wardell in this volume, "British Usage and American Awareness of Some New Therapeutic Drugs," pp. 1022-34.

candidate for the list at the request of the manufacturer, therapeutic need and cost are the most important criteria for selection.

Occasionally, a new drug not yet included in the list may be obtained under insurance benefits. In that case, the physician must apply to the insurer giving the reasons for his intention to prescribe the drug under the health insurance scheme. The physician may, of course, at any time prescribe any drug admitted for marketing, but not on the *List of Specialties*, provided his patient is willing to pay for it. In this context, it should also be pointed out that within the health insurance schemes some drugs are restricted to approved indications. Should the physician wish to use a preparation for a non-approved indication, he must apply to the insurance company for permission to do so. Otherwise his patient must pay for the medication himself.

In many cantons, review committees check the prescribing habits of physicians and other factors affecting the costs of medical practice. Such committees consist of representatives of the medical association and the health insurance company. Physicians constantly exceeding "average costs" for investigation and treatment of common ailments in that area may be investigated. Disciplinary measures consist of cutting the insurance company's payment to the physician to the amount considered justifiable.

Surveillance of Adverse Drug Reactions

A physician noting adverse reactions to a drug may report his findings either to the manufacturer, to the office of the Swiss Medical Association (SMA), or to the IKS. Although no data are available on reports to pharmaceutical companies, the situation is certainly unsatisfactory, since the reporting rate to IKS and SMA is exceedingly low. The revival of an adverse reaction register under the auspices of the SMA has been under discussion.

To obtain information concerning frequency and types of adverse reactions, prospective drug surveillance programs have been set up by some hospitals in Berne and elsewhere. The Berne program is run in conjunction with the World Health Organization and encompasses two hospitals.[11] They are viewed as a pilot study for Swiss hospitals. Within the next decade, surveillance of drug utilization may be extended to include all major hospitals in the country.

---

[11] U. Klein et al., "«Drug monitoring» in der medizinischen Abteilung eines Regionalspitals," *Schweizerische Medizinische Wochenschrift*, vol. 102, no. 31 (1972), pp. 1083-90.

6
WEST GERMANY

Hermann Kampffmeyer

Postgraduate Education in Clinical Pharmacology and Therapeutics

In the Federal Republic of Germany (as in other countries) there are in general three possible ways of influencing therapeutic drug use: by education, by controls over the access of drugs to the market, and by postmarketing surveillance. These possible approaches provide the framework for the discussion that follows, with brief attention to other topics.

In Germany, as in other central European countries, academic institutes of pharmacology are fully integrated within faculties of human or veterinary medicine, and most staff members hold the degree of M.D. Medical students are taught basic pharmacology, but there are no formal training programs leading to an academic degree in pharmacology.

Therapeutics is taught to medical students by members of the pharmacology department for about three hours per week during the second term of the six-term clinical curriculum; in addition, a few mandatory (and therefore poorly attended) lectures in therapeutics are offered by clinicians alone or together with pharmacologists during bedside teaching.

Since 1974 physicians who have completed five years of research in pharmacology at approved institutions (university or industry) may apply for a certificate issued by the state medical association granting the title of pharmacologist; two of these five years required can be spent in physiology or biochemistry and one year must be spent in clinical drug research. The lack of training programs in basic pharmacology has prompted universities as well as the pharmaceutical industry to appoint nonclinical scientists, in addition to M.D.s, as staff members. Since about 1960, chemists, biochemists, biologists, and pharmacists who are not eligible for certification by the medical association but who have training in pharmacology in the pharmaceutical industry may apply at a commission of the German Society of Pharmacology for the title of Fachpharmakologe (DPhG)—that is, expert in pharmacology, recognized by the German Society of Pharmacology. The guidelines set by the society require a person to be capable of filling a top position in industry. Currently, 10 percent of the individual members of the pharmacology society hold this title; data for the number of M.D.-pharmacologists have not yet been collected from the state medical associations.

Because postgraduate programs are not available, many doctors seek training in clinical pharmacology abroad. About three dozen foreign-trained clinicians have returned to academic posts during the last ten years after receiving one or two years' training in the United States, the United Kingdom, or Sweden. They have been supported mainly by the Paul Martini Foundation (a foundation supported by the five largest German pharmaceutical companies) or foundations supported by foreign companies. These former trainees have been trying to establish their own research units integrated with hospitals and basic pharmacology departments.

Several sources of information on the therapeutic use of drugs are offered to practicing physicians. The Federal Alliance of Practicing Physicians [Kassenärztliche Bundesvereinigung] which is a commission of the Federal Medical Association [Ausschuss der Bundesärztekammer], together with regular health insurance companies, jointly distribute to practicing physicians leaflets about the efficacy of old and new drugs. In addition, the Drug Commission of the Federal Medical Association has edited a pocket book which lists about 2,000 brand-name drugs arranged by their clinical indications. This book is published about every three years and can be bought in bookstores.[1] Recently, the same commission has been distributing leaflets four times a year to practicing physicians, these leaflets covering certain topics of drug treatment.

Over the past eight years, Der Arzneimittelbrief [The drug letter], an independent private publication,[2] has been published monthly and distributed to subscribers. The Arznei-Telegramm [Drug telegram],[3] published monthly for the past six years, attempts

---

[1] Arzneiverordnungen: Ratschläge für Ärzte und Studenten, 13. Auflage [Drug-prescriptions, advice for physicians and medical students, 13th edition] (Köln: Deutscher Ärzte-Verlag, 1976).

[2] Der Arzneimittelbrief [The drug letter], ed. H. Herxheimer, M. Schwab, and H.-W. Spier (Berlin: West Kreuz-Verlag).

[3] Arznei-Telegramm [Drug-telegram], ed. Dr. Ulrich Möbius (Berlin).

to serve the same purpose. The federal or state medical associations organize voluntary postgraduate medical education programs of three to five days duration. Usually some lessons on therapeutics are offered at about six meetings per year.

Controls over Access of Drugs to the Market

The first drug law effective in the Federal Republic of Germany was enacted in 1961,[4] though there had been several unsuccessful attempts between 1918 and 1939 to pass a German drug law. The law has been extended several times during the past years by amendments and additions.[5]

The Present Law. Under the present law, new brands of both allopathic and homeopathic drugs are subject to registration at the Federal Office of Health. The registration of brands expires automatically after five years if no application for renewal is submitted by the manufacturer.

A fundamental change was introduced in 1971, when the federal secretary of youth, family affairs, and health signed regulations requiring, for registration of a new drug, more detailed information on the drug's effects in several animal species, pharmacokinetic evaluation, and evidence of efficacy from controlled clinical trials, in addition to the information previously required about the drug's safety.[6] These national regulations are based on the draft recommendations for all countries of the European community (EEC). The physician administering an investigational drug to man is required to ask the pharmaceutical company for detailed information and to discuss that information with an expert pharmacologist or clinician (who can be an employee of the promoting company). Definitions of distinct phases of clinical evaluation are not provided in the regulations.

The regulations do not require an independent review committee to be involved in decisions as to what constitutes adequate preclinical data or in decisions on the first administration of the drug to man. However, a few university hospitals have installed ethics and drug

---

[4] "Gesetz über den Verkehr mit Arzneimitteln" [Law on drug circulation], *Bundesgesetzblatt I*, 1961, p. 533.

[5] "Zweites Gesetz zur Änderung des Arzneimittelgesetzes" [Second law for changing the drug law], *Bundesgesetzblatt I*, 1964, p. 365; "136. Bekanntmachung über die Eintragung von Arzneispezialitäten in das Spezialitätenregister" [136th notification about the registration of branded drugs], *Bundesanz.*, 1973, p. 333.

[6] "Bekanntmachung der Richtlinie über die Prüfung von Arzneimitteln" [Notification of the guidelines on drug investigation], *Bundesanz.*, 1973, p. 1.

147

review committees on their own initiative to decrease the number of premature drug trials within their own walls.

The New Drug Law. In August 1976 a new drug law was promulgated after passing the Federal Diet [Bundestag] and the Federal Council [Bundesrat] at the very end of the seventh session of the Diet and following six years of discussion among the various groups concerned.[7] Effective on January 1, 1978, the law requires all readymade allopathic drugs distributed by pharmaceutical companies to have a license from the Federal Health Office [Bundesgesundheitsamt] for admission to the market. Homeopathic preparations must be registered separately without tests for efficacy. In general, more stringent requirements on quality control are imposed on manufacturers; this, among other factors, mobilized the drug lobby to attempt to delay the law's effective date.

The application for a license must include complete pharmaceutical data and complete information on animal pharmacology and clinical pharmacology, and it must be accompanied by experts' reports. However, the word *efficacy* [Wirksamkeit] has not been employed in the law. New pharmaceutical formulations containing drugs of known pharmacological effect may not even need pharmacokinetic studies for admission. Foreign companies will be treated according to their domestic regulations but their standards cannot be below those of the German law. Prior to decisions about the admission of a given drug, the Federal Health Office must consult an independent expert commission composed of delegates from the medical association and the pharmaceutical industry. Regulatory guidelines for decisions about admission will be published by the federal secretary of the interior according to current scientific knowledge and following consultations with medical and pharmaceutical scientists. The drug's license must be renewed after five years and will expire after two years if the drug is abandoned commercially.

Registration of homeopathic preparations is designed to ensure that pharmaceutical standards are met and that the drug label does not indicate therapeutic effects.

For protection of human subjects during clinical investigation, the new drug law follows those principles outlined by the Declaration of Helsinki. The pharmaceutical company will still be responsible for drug development from synthesis to the registration of a new com-

---

[7] Gesetz zur Neuordnung des Arzneimittelrechts [Law about new arrangements of the drug law], *Bundesgesetzblatt I*, 1976, p. 2445; or *Deutsch. Apotheker Zeitung*, vol. 116 (1976), p. 1348.

pound. Complete data on animal pharmacology will have to be submitted to the federal office for the purpose of documentation, but no government office or independent advisory board will decide whether a pharmaceutical compound can be given to man for the first time. Drugs released on the market before 1971 will not be tested for efficacy in the foreseeable future. Drugs restricted to prescription use, and those subject to additional restrictions, will be announced by decree. All new compounds for medical use require prescription. Two years after marketing the drugs the pharmaceutical company must report to the Federal Health Office all of its experience with the drug.

Those drugs unlikely to harm anybody may be dispensed without prescription after three years of surveillance under prescription conditions. The Federal Health Office will be authorized by law to watch, to collect data, and to analyze the risks of all drugs on the market and to coordinate its activities with those of other domestic and foreign authorities. The secretary of the interior will be authorized to publish plans to react to undesirable drug effects that endanger patients or the population in general.

The new drug law also requires a minimum educational level for drug firm representatives, and provides legal grounds to introduce price margins by decree at the wholesale and retail levels. Probably unique in international legislation are the provisions on liability for drug injuries in man. The drug company must compensate for death or severe injury caused by a marketed drug if the accident occurred during proper use of the drug or as a result of improper labeling of the package. Such risks must be covered by a German insurance company or a German bank. Volunteers participating in clinical investigations must be insured for liability by a company operating in Germany.

Controls over Drug Utilization after Marketing

Drugs for patients covered by the National Health Insurance System are prescribed on forms different from those for patients covered by a private health insurer. All new drugs and those requiring a prescription may be legally dispensed only by pharmacists on prescriptions issued by physicians.[8] However, three years after registration a drug may be sold by pharmacists over the counter, free of prescription, if no adverse effect capable of endangering people during uncon-

---

[8] "Verordnung nach Paragraph 35 des Arzneimittelgesetzes über verschreibungspflichtige Arzneimittel" [Decree on prescription drugs after chapter no. 35 of the drug law], *Bundesgesetzblatt I*, 1971, p. 1991.

trolled use without medical supervision has been reported. A drug may be prescribed for any purpose, including those not mentioned on the package insert.

Narcotics and related drugs have been subject to additional restrictions since April 1974, permitting less narcotic per prescription.[9]

Apart from those restrictions on drug distribution described here, no government agency or health insurance company has any direct influence upon the physician's choice of drugs from among those available for treating a given medical condition. Generally, homeopathic or allopathic drug prescription for a given patient is paid for by the regular health insurance system.[10] The federal government has called for a commission to clarify what is required for economic and effective drug treatment.

The Federal Association of Pharmaceutical Industries. About 2,000 branded products account for 94 percent of total drug sales in the Federal Republic of Germany. Thus, approximately 6,000 of the 8,000 brands listed in the *Rote Liste* [11] and an additional 20,000 brands not listed in the *Rote Liste* have not been much used by practicing physicians. Previous issues of the *Rote Liste* were merely a list of brand names in alphabetical order, but since 1974 it has been divided into sections listing the brands by indication. Brands containing single drugs, drug combinations, and homeopathic preparations are placed in subsections with prices and some product information. Still, many claims for therapeutic effectiveness lack a scientific basis, and the physician may thus be able to exercise some judgment only in comparing price figures.

Universities and Large Community Hospitals. Recently, these organizations have been establishing their own drug committees to select the most effective drugs. This has come about because the money reimbursed to the hospital administration by the health insurance companies is calculated as an overall figure per hospitalized patient

9 "Verordnung über das Verschreiben, die Abgabe und den Nachweis des Verbleibs von Betäubungsmitteln" [Decree on prescription, distribution, and whereabouts of narcotics], *Bundesgesetzblatt*, 1974, p. 110.

10 "Richtlinien des Bundesausschusses der Ärzte und Krankenkassen über die Verordnung von Arzneimitteln in der kassenärztlichen Versorgung" [Guidelines of the Federal Association of Practicing Physicians and of the National Health Insurance Companies on drug prescription for the National Health Insurance System], *Sonderdruck zum Bundesanzeiger*, vol. 59 (March 26, 1975), p. 14.

11 *Rote Liste, Verzeichnis pharmazeutischer Spezialpräparate* [Physicians' desk reference, list of branded drugs] (Frankfurt: Bundesverband der pharmazeutischen Industrie, 1975).

per day, and must include items such as wages paid by the hospital as well as drug costs—which are increasing. On a tight budget, elimination of uneconomic drugs may save some money for other expenditures. The hospital pharmacist is provided by the hospital's drug committee with information on drug effectiveness and on the reputation of each drug firm so that he can deal with representatives of the competing firms and get the lowest possible price among comparable products. Such activities have created a reduction in the number of different package units in the pharmacy warehouse of one university hospital by 74 percent (to 1,300). Whether these local drug lists will reduce drug expenses within hospitals and influence drug treatment outside the hospital by example is debatable. The drug industry has put considerable pressure on members of such drug committees, because the brand names of those drugs used on the ward for the individual patient are transmitted to the private physicians, who do not use generic names.

The Regular Social Health Insurance System. This system which pays for prescribed drugs was founded in 1881, and the basic social security act [Reichsversicherungsordnung] was promulgated in 1911.[12] By law, every employee earning wages within a defined range is covered by the Social Insurance System [Sozialversicherung], which provides health insurance, accident insurance, unemployment pay, and a pension plan for more than 90 percent of the population.

Currently, about 16 percent of an employee's gross wages are earmarked for the social security package; an equal amount must be added by the employer. About 50 percent of the package is designated for health purposes, of which a subfraction of 18 percent pays for drugs. The state-sponsored health insurance companies, who pay the local association of private pharmacists, have no direct influence on the prescribing practices of the physicians. For instance, decisions in early lawsuits have prohibited the insurance companies from issuing lists of preferred drugs for economical treatment, arguing that such lists interfere with competition among drug companies.

In the past, physicians also opposed the idea of "recommended drug" lists because insurance companies might pay only for those drugs listed and thereby reduce freedom of choice in drug treatment. Today, private physicians are more inclined to accept the idea of "recommended" drugs because, in the context of ceiling limits for

---

[12] *Reichsversicherungsordnung mit Arbeiterrentenversicherung Neuregelungsgesetz* [German National Insurance System and law about new arrangements of the annuity insurance] (Munich: Deutscher Taschenbuch-Verlag, 1973).

health expenditure, the rising costs of drugs have eroded the increases in physician's remuneration. Furthermore, the health insurance companies monitor the prescription costs of each practicing physician. If the total cost of drugs prescribed by a physician exceeds the "average" by more than 40 percent, the health insurance companies make claim to that physician for restitution of the excess. The Federal Chamber of Practicing Physicians surveyed such claims in twelve out of eighteen districts for 1971. An application for inquiry on prescribing habits was filed by local offices of the Association of Practicing Physicians or by insurance companies against 11 percent of the 32,515 practicing physicians living in the twelve districts. Claims for reimbursement were made against 38 percent of the subjects initially investigated for their prescribing habits. About one-third of the claims were opposed at a social court (which settles cases arising among social security agencies, health insurance companies, and individuals). In the end, less than 2 percent of the physicians examined had to reimburse the social health insurance companies. The sum reimbursed amounted to less than 0.1 percent of the total drug expenses.

Expensive drug treatment (such as antibiotics, or vaccination against herpes simplex—the effectiveness of the latter being unproven) is paid by the health insurance company provided the patient's problem has been discussed between the physician and the health insurance company.

Side Effects. The side effects of marketed drugs are monitored by the office of the Federal Drug Commission founded by the German Medical Association. This drug commission serves several functions. It gives advice to all physicians and to health authorities in drug-related matters and it collects information on, and evaluates the side effects of, marketed drugs. At frequent intervals the office has issued appeals for information and has supplied reporting forms in the weekly journal of the German Medical Association, the *Deutsches Ärzteblatt*, which is distributed to all registered physicians.[13] In 1972, 749 adverse effects were reported, of which 42 had a fatal outcome; in 1973, 1974, and 1975, 1,000, 2,252, and 3,280 cases of adverse effects were collected respectively, of which 3 to 4 percent were fatal. When suspicion or reports of severe side effects of a certain drug or brand accumulate at the Federal Office of Health or at the Federal Drug Commission, procedures for the adequate collection of further data

---

[13] *Deutsches Ärzteblatt* [Journal of German physicians] (Köln: Bundesärztekammer und kassenärztliche Bundesvereinigung).

and appropriate safety measures are discussed jointly with the manufacturer by the office and the commission. Where there is profound suspicion or definite evidence of serious adverse drug effects, the Federal Office of Health initiates safety measures and publishes warnings in the medical press. These latter activities have usually led to changes of the package insert or the withdrawal of the drug from the market.

In five university hospitals, adverse drug effects are now being monitored in relation to total amount of drugs distributed by the hospital's pharmacy.

Advertisement of Drugs. Advertisement of prescription drugs is restricted by law to medical journals. Editors of these journals have almost no control over the publisher's choice of commercially oriented advertisements. Representatives of the drug companies are allowed by law to dispense drug samples and literature for promotional purposes to practicing physicians on request either personally or by mail.[14] In fact, many of these drug samples are then given to patients free of charge. The total drug costs of some physicians are thereby lowered by approximately 5 to 10 percent and many pharmacologically ineffective brands are kept on the market. Recently, the federal association of pharmaceutical companies has imposed some self-restraints on expenses and quality of advertisements. Although such self-restraint may have been necessitated by shrinking sales, it was explained to the public as an act of integrity and sincerity demonstrating that a tough drug law was not needed.

Summary

The pharmaceutical companies bear full responsibility and have freedom of decision within the guidelines of the drug law during all developmental stages of a new drug. An application for drug registration at the Federal Health Office must include evidence for the drug's safety and therapeutic efficacy in humans. Admission of the drug to the market is granted after consultation of an advisory board.

This should guarantee that the public will receive safe and effective drugs with minimum interference from federal agencies or other scientists during drug development. Whether the current picture will change much in future years will depend on the quality of the decrees that will be introduced according to the drug law; these

---

[14] "Gesetz über die Werbung auf dem Gebiete des Heilwesens" [Law on advertising of Remedies], *Bundesgesetzblatt*, 1965, p. 604.

will be enacted by the secretary of the interior or the secretary of health without need of passing the parliaments.

The efficacy of drugs registered before 1971 will not be reviewed within the next decade or so. The physician's choice among 30,000 branded drugs is in no way restricted. Information about the therapeutic application of both new and old drugs is spread most effectively among practicing physicians by written and verbal information from the pharmaceutical companies. The curriculum for graduate medical students does not favor thorough teaching of clinical pharmacology. Physicians are not yet obliged to participate in continuing postgraduate education programs; this could, however, be a point where unbiased information about effective and economic drug treatment might be spread. Objective information about drugs should be supplied on a much larger scale than at present and free of charge to every physician. Insurance companies should subsidize those tasks.

7

SWEDEN

L. E. Böttiger

It is interesting and symptomatic of the present situation in the field of pharmacotherapy that questions and discussions regarding drug control and drug utilization have arisen more or less simultaneously in many countries the world over. Governments and health authorities have for obvious reasons become more and more concerned about the safety and efficacy of drugs. The public, at least in the industrial countries, is becoming better informed about drugs—and also more concerned about drug safety. In Sweden this expanding public awareness has, among other things, led many to turn "back to nature," to put their trust in "safe" natural remedies (herbs, decoctions, et cetera), and to fight the strict rules of "scientific medicine" and its synthetic drugs. Natural remedies are not regarded as drugs in Sweden; they are not controlled by the government, they do not have to be registered, and they are not available on doctor's prescriptions— which means they do not qualify for price subsidies. These preparations are sold in health shops but, by law, they may not be advertised, whether by statements on packages or elsewhere, in ways that claim anything about disease or the cure of disease. There are outcries that the Swedish health authorities are depriving individuals of their rights to use whatever they want, and large pressure groups have been formed to alter the drug regulations so that natural remedies will be accepted as approved drugs. The pressure has been so strong that a governmental committee has been formed to investigate the problem.

Sweden, a small Scandinavian country of 8 million inhabitants with a homogeneous population and a high standard of living, has evolved a national health system that is financed through heavy taxation—indirect as well as direct. It provides hospital care free of charge and outpatient care for a nominal fee of twelve Swedish crowns (U.S.$3). The latter fee includes not only all laboratory workup, including x-ray examinations but also any necessary follow-up visits and treatment.

Until 1954 the patient paid the full price for all drugs bought in a pharmacy, regardless whether a doctor's prescription was presented. In 1955, the first type of subsidy was introduced, under which the government paid the first four Swedish crowns (U.S.$1) and half the remainder of the total cost of any prescription and the patient paid the rest. At the same time, the first list of free drugs was introduced, at first covering only a handful of indications.

The next step was taken in 1968 when the present system became effective. Under this system drugs bought outside hospitals on a doctor's prescription cost a maximum of fifteen Swedish crowns (U.S.$4) for any amount or any number of different drugs prescribed at the same time. Certain drugs are given to patients entirely free of charge. This is the case for chronic or lifelong treatment with well-established drugs, such as insulin for diabetes and vitamin B_{12} for pernicious anemia. An official list gives the specific indications and the drugs available on this basis (Table 1). A special prescription form, valid for one year, must be used. To date, no drugs have been taken off the list, while new drugs have been added at irregular intervals. Additions are made after requests—from physicians, patient organizations, or individuals—to the government or to the Department of Drugs. Such a request leads to a careful examination of the situation regarding the disease and the drug, often involving testimony from outstanding clinical specialists in the field. If the Department of Drugs finds that the therapy is medically well established, is used in chronic or lifelong cases, and is costly, it recommends that the government put the new drug on the free list.

All drugs for hospital inpatients have always been given entirely free of charge.

In 1972 the total public cost for health and medical services amounted to 16,045 million Swedish crowns (U.S.$4,000 million), which corresponds to 8 percent of the gross national product. The cost of drugs during the same year, paid for mainly by the government and only to a small extent by patients, amounted to 1,484 million Swedish crowns (U.S.$370 million) or 9 to 10 percent of the total cost for all health and medical services. The cost for the drugs on the free list amounts to 17 percent of the total drug cost.

Table 1
LIST OF DISEASES FOR WHICH SPECIFIED DRUGS MAY BE PRESCRIBED FREE OF CHARGE

Pernicious anemia
Diabetes insipidus
Diabetes mellitus
Hypothyroidism
Chronic adrenal insufficiency
specified as:
  Primary adrenocortical
    insufficiency
  Addison's disease or post
    adrenalectomy
  Secondary adrenocortical
    insufficiency due to anterior
    pituitary hypofunction or
    removal of the pituitary
  Congenital adrenogenital
    syndrome
Hypogonadism
Tetany in hypoparathyroidism
Malabsorption syndrome
Myasthenia gravis
Glaucoma
Epilepsy
Bronchial asthma
Chronic cardiac insufficiency

Tuberculosis
Specified forms of malignant
disease:
  Mammary carcinoma
  Ovarian carcinoma
  Prostatic carcinoma
  Testicular carcinoma
  Thyroid carcinoma
  Leukemias
  Lymphomas
  Multiple myeloma
Parkinsonism
Hypogammaglobulinemia
Gout
Cystic fibrosis of the pancreas
Systemic lupus erythematosus
Schizophrenia
Hemophilia A and B
Phenylketonuria
Cystinuria
Dermatitis herpetiformis
Hepatolenticular degeneration
  (Wilson's disease)

Note: For every disease on the list, only specified drugs may be prescribed free of charge. This means, among other things, that the patients are not entitled to get all drugs free, but only those that may be regarded as the main or basal treatment of their conditions. By the same token, the listed drugs are free only for the indications specified in the list. (It would be too space-consuming to print the entire free drug list.)

Education and Information

Training in Pharmacology. All medical schools in Sweden teach basic pharmacology, offering both lectures and experimental work, as part of a two-month course in pharmacology. This training takes part during the last half-year of the two years devoted to preclinical training.

Training in Clinical Pharmacology and Therapeutics. Clinical pharmacology in Sweden has developed along two lines. There are two departments of clinical pharmacology—one in Stockholm at the Huddinge Hospital and the other in Linköping at the Regional Hospital, each with a full professor of clinical pharmacology and laboratory facilities. Each department has a standing comparable to that of the departments of clinical physiology or clinical chemistry. The heads of the departments of clinical pharmacology are full academic professors and, at the same time, hold positions as chief physicians at the hospital. This means that, if they choose, they can take full clinical responsibility for patient care. However, since the clinical pharmacology departments in Sweden do not have any beds of their own, their personnel work mainly in close cooperation with departments of internal medicine, pediatrics, and psychiatry.

In addition to these two independent departments, there are clinical centers of clinical pharmacology in most other university hospitals. Each is headed by a physician with basic training in pharmacology and with some clinical education as well. This physician has a full-time hospital position but holds no formal academic position on the faculty. The position in the hospital organization varies from place to place, depending on local conditions. The important fact is that this physician produces clinical pharmacology, in the form of research and assistance, for clinical colleagues dealing with therapeutic problems.

Clinical pharmacology has not yet become a formally accepted specialty, primarily because of unrelated and complicated changes in the structure of Swedish medicine. My personal opinion is that it soon will be accorded such status—which in Sweden entails the establishment of a formal training program integrated into the Swedish medical curriculum.

For at least ten years, however, clinical pharmacology—or, rather, therapeutics—has been taught during the clinical portion of medical education, mainly in the form of therapy conferences during which clinicians and pharmacologists together discuss for the students therapeutic problems in a certain group of disorders (for example, infections), for a specific symptom (for example, pain), or with a certain group of drugs (for example, anticonvulsants).

Postgraduate Training and Information on Drug Problems. Formal postgraduate medical training has lagged in Sweden and is only now being organized. The need for better education in therapeutics is reflected by the fact that formal training programs are now being introduced which include, in short courses on pharmacotherapeutics, discussion of the basic facts of clinical pharmacology and the principles of therapeutics. These courses will gradually increase the physicians' knowledge of drugs and how to handle them, although it will take many years before a significant number of Swedish physicians benefit from such courses.

Other important sources of information on drugs are the *Pharmaceutical Specialties in Sweden (FASS)*, a yearly publication by the Swedish joint organization of national and international pharmaceutical industries, along with the Central Drug Information Committee and the drug committees in the various hospitals. Published since 1966, *FASS* corresponds to some extent to the U.S. *Physicians' Desk Reference (PDR)*. The latter contains drug labeling in the form of the wording of package inserts, which are the formal end-products of the control activities of the U.S. Food and Drug Administration (FDA). The package inserts, however, have legal implications, tend to be detailed, and therefore are difficult to read and use in everyday hospital work.

The final product of the Swedish drug control organization, the Department of Drugs, is an official protocol, legally kept secret from everyone except the manufacturer and therefore not usable as a basis for the *FASS* texts. The latter, prepared by the manufacturers according to a special format decided upon jointly by the Department of Drugs and the *FASS* editorial office, are written directly for the *FASS*. All texts are carefully scrutinized and modified by the Department of Drugs so that they state only basic facts without any advertising overtones. This work often leads to prolonged discussions between a manufacturer and the Department of Drugs before the department can accept the text and submit it to the Board of Drugs for final approval at the time of registration. (This means that the editorial office of the *FASS* manages all the technical aspects of the production of the book, but has no real influence on the content.) Cooperation between the editorial office and the Department of Drugs is good, as indicated by the existence of regular discussions between the two on how to improve the *FASS*.

The information in the *FASS* contains the following headings: declaration of the properties of active ingredients, indications and contraindications (if any), adverse reactions (if any), dosage, special warnings, special information on storage and stability, available packages, and prices. (Status of the indications is discussed later in this paper.) In a special index, all drugs are listed according to pharmacological groups—drugs for respiratory diseases, cardiovascular drugs, et cetera—an arrangement that enables the reader to search out drugs for a specific indication. Other cross-indexes make it possible to find information on a specific drug or brand of drug, and special chapters give the structural formulas for the drugs, deal with important interactions among certain drugs, and symptoms and treatments of overdosage.

FASS has rapidly proven to be valuable and is distributed free of charge to all physicians, hospitals, et cetera. It has had a definite impact on drug utilization in Sweden.

Central Drug Information Committee. In 1968 the National Board of Health and Welfare organized an independent committee, known as the Central Drug Information Committee. The main responsibility of this committee is to supply physicians, medical students, nurses, and other health professionals with objective and unbiased information on drugs. The committee is made up of four members—two clinical pharmacologists and two experienced clinicians (from internal medicine and general surgery)—all chosen and appointed by the National Board of Health and Welfare. The committee has fulfilled its task by publishing a series of eighteen booklets written by outstanding experts. These monographs have been published and distributed free of charge to all physicians in Sweden and Norway. (See the chapter on Norway for further information.) All follow the same pattern: Part I deals rather extensively with pharmacology and clinical problems; Part II contains a short summary of Part I and a description of the drugs available; the last part gives the committee's recommendations on which drugs or type of drugs are preferable for various indications. There is no special slant to the recommendations, which are kept as neutral as possible and are based on the extensive review in Part I. The recommendations have no legal or moral force.

Recently, an attempt was made to evaluate the impact of the recommendations. Results showed that many physicians found the information in the booklets too detailed and too difficult to read, although all booklets have short summaries at the end. Also, sales studies revealed that a number of drugs that had been described in the recommendations as badly documented and probably without effect continued to be sold and used to an amazingly high degree.

Hospital Drug Committees and Hospital Formularies. The first hospital drug committee was created at the Karolinska Hospital, the central university hospital in Stockholm, in 1960. It has been followed by similar committees in other hospitals, and today most major hospitals have such committees. Their main task is to work for better and safer drug therapy, and they do this by evaluating available drugs and by recommending one or a few from every group for routine use in the hospital. The physician can still use any drug he chooses for any patient without any special procedure or hindrance, except that drugs not on the recommended list may not be immediately available on the ward. The intent is that in *routine* everyday care the selection of drugs be limited to those recommended by the committee. This procedure is designed to facilitate the handling of drugs by the hospital pharmacy and by ward nurses and to help familiarize the physicians with the drugs. Most committees summarize their work in the form of drug lists (formularies) which, in some larger hospitals, take the form of printed booklets that the physicians can carry in their pockets.

There are great differences among the committees with regard to qualifications of members and committee composition. The ideal committee, existing only in a few larger hospitals, has three basic members: an experienced clinician (usually an internist), a clinical pharmacologist, and a pharmacist. Smaller committees generally have to work without the help of someone trained in clinical pharmacology, because the number of physicians with such training still is limited.

In more recent years, the committees in many centers have taken on new responsibilities. Many act as intermediaries between the pharmaceutical industry and the house staff, so that all sales representatives who want to "detail" the hospital physicians must first make their presentations to the committee. If the industry's representative has new drugs or developments worth discussing, a short meeting is arranged with members of the proper departments. Under this arrangement, individual visits from sales representatives to house officers are not permitted, and only essential information is accepted for presentation.

Other committees have taken it upon themselves to collect the local reports on adverse drug reactions, to help physicians examine and evaluate these reactions, and to formulate the necessary official report to the adverse drug committee.

Adverse Drug Reaction Committee. Since 1965 the Adverse Drug Reaction Committee has been active in Sweden. Physicians and dentists are asked to report all adverse drug reactions to this committee, which has a standing secretariat at the Department of Drugs. After additional information has been collected, all reports are evaluated in an effort to determine whether there was a causal relationship between drug intake and ensuing reaction. In severe cases, the additional information consists of the entire medical record from the hospital or physician. The evaluation is performed in three steps: (1) by the medical officer in charge, (2) by a working party of the committee, and finally (3) by the committee itself.

An important part of the committee's work is publication of lists of all adverse reactions that have been reported and evaluated. Such lists are sent to the pharmaceutical industries and, on request, to physicians. The lists contain only generic names of drugs and the reported adverse reactions, with information also on the cause-and-effect group into which the report has been put after evaluation by the committee. Such lists, without any patient identification or information, do not seem to create any medico-legal problems, at least not at present. (A new situation may arise when a proposed plan for general insurance against unexpected adverse drug reactions is put into effect in Sweden, which probably will occur within a year or two.)

A short report from the committee is published at least twice yearly in the weekly issue of the journal of the Swedish Medical Association, and is also mailed to all physicians in the country. These reports contain short comments on important drug reactions, sometimes with definite warnings against the use of specific drugs.

It has been demonstrated that the work of the committee may influence drug utilization to a great extent. The case of Dipyrone (metamizol, noramidopyrine) is an example. This drug, which is chemically similar to amidopyrine, was introduced many years ago as an analgesic/antipyretic. It soon became evident that it caused agranulocytosis to the same extent as the parent compound, amidopyrine—a drug that has been on prescription for a long time, but has now virtually disappeared from the Swedish market, mainly because of publicity and teaching regarding its dangers. The committee issued warnings against the indiscriminate use of Dipyrone. Although the warning had to be repeated, there was a remarkable drop in the sales figures, accompanied by a similar drop in the number of reported cases of agranulocytosis (Figure 1). Later, the sales figures and the agranulocytosis cases increased slowly and, at the direction of the Department of Drugs, the drug was withdrawn from the market in early 1974.

The Legal Situation

As early as 1913, those substances were defined that were to be regarded as drugs, and to be made available only in pharmacies (*Apotek* in Swedish), which sell drugs only. In 1934, it became compulsory to "register" (the Swedish term for *approved*) a drug at the National Board of Health and Welfare before that drug could be sold—still only through pharmacies. It was stated even then that the safety and the efficacy of the drug should be proven. The actual wording of the law was that the authorities should investigate "whether the composition was suitable and whether the drug had been

Figure 1

DIPYRONE TABLET SALES BEFORE AND AFTER WARNINGS AND CORRESPONDING INCIDENCE OF DIPYRONE-INDUCED AGRANULOCYTOSIS

(1965 = 100)

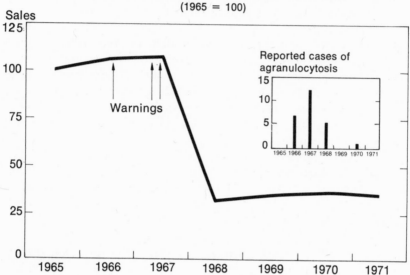

Source: L.E. Böttiger and B. Westerholm, "Drug-induced cytopenias in Sweden," *British Medical Journal*, vol. 3 (1973), p. 339.

shown to be able to prevent, cure, or alleviate disease or disease symptoms in man or animal." In 1964 a new law, the present Drug Ordinance, was passed. In essence, it has the same meaning as the old one, although a number of definitions and regulations are much more specific.

The important statements in the 1964 Drug Ordinance are that a drug, in order to be registered, (1) must be of good quality, (2) must have proven efficacy (the Swedish wording literally means that the drug should be "medically suitable," which includes somewhat more than pure efficacy), and (3) must not, during normal use, cause adverse reactions out of proportion to the intended effect. Such are the bare legal specifications. It is up to the Board of Drugs (see below) to interpret the demands of the law.

Registration is predominantly, but not entirely, a matter of proven efficacy. For example, a narcotic drug might have proven efficacy in alleviation of pain, but if the tendency for abuse has been demonstrated to be great, such a drug could be denied registration

163

on the ground that it would not be "medically suitable." All generic versions of a drug must be registered and require proper documentation.

To help the manufacturers, the Department of Drugs publishes a booklet titled *Registration of Pharmaceutical Specialties, Instructions for the Application et cetera* (also available in English).

The Department of Drugs. An application for registration is evaluated by the Department of Drugs, which is a part of the National Board of Health and Welfare. (The Swedish Department of Drugs corresponds closely to the Bureau of Drugs of the U.S. Food and Drug Administration and, in fact, the two organizations cooperate on many things.) The task of evaluating an application, which is performed mostly on the basis of written documentation submitted by the drug manufacturer to various divisions of the department (pharmaceutical, pharmacological and toxicological, and pharmacotherapeutical), ends in a written protocol that is put before the Board of Drugs.

The Board of Drugs. The Board of Drugs is a separate body, not connected with the Department of Drugs. Its ten members are appointed by the crown and represent such basic specialties as pharmacy and pharmacology and such clinical specialties as internal medicine, psychiatry, infectious diseases, and clinical pharmacology. Other specialists may be called in, if necessary. The chairman is a judge from the Supreme Administrative Court.

The Board of Drugs decides whether a drug should be registered, acting upon all the documentation submitted by the manufacturer, but mainly upon the protocols produced by the Department of Drugs. Separating the Board of Drugs from the Department of Drugs was done in order to put the decision-making power on registration in hands other than those that perform the actual scrutiny and evaluation of the documentation. This means that the Department of Drugs undertakes a strict, matter-of-fact evaluation of the submitted documentation, stating whether it is sufficient in amount and quality. The Board of Drugs, on the other hand, has to make the final decision on whether the documentation fulfills the demands of the law. The Board of Drugs, by its decisions, actually has a strong impact upon how the legal text should be interpreted because complaints against its decisions have to be filed with the Administrative Court of Appeal.

Local clinical trials are not a necessary part of the required documentation. The guidelines refer to "well-presented and controlled investigations of therapeutic properties" as the basis for the evaluation, and add that "no weight as evidence can be attached to undocumented claims and testimonials or to speciously reasoned assertions." Nothing is stated about the origin of the controlled clinical trials; the important factor is their quality. The decision of the Board of Drugs includes the indications to be allowed for the use of the drug, the contraindications that should be stated, and the complete text to be published in the *FASS*.

Only those indications for which effectiveness has been specifically proven are approved. No advertising is permitted for non-approved indications. Regarding the status of the approved indications, it may be said that if a general practitioner follows the approved indications *and* the recommended dosage given in the *FASS*, and if untoward reactions occur, a malpractice action against him would probably not be successful. On the other hand, a specialist in active research and teaching may feel free to try new indications as well as an increased dosage, without any formal hindrance. It is important to realize, however, that the legal status of the approved indications has not yet been tested in Sweden.

The state pays for all prescribed drugs (in the way described above), whether or not they are prescribed for approved or non-approved indications. As the physicians' prescriptions do not contain any information on the indication for the drug, there are no practical ways to check for the indication for which a specific drug has been prescribed.

Drugs already registered are being controlled on a regular basis; a continuous review procedure exists, although the resources for such controls have been insufficient for some time. Such controls deal with pharmaceutical quality as well as therapeutic efficacy, and a manufacturer may be asked to present up-to-date documentation to prove the efficacy of a drug. If such documentation cannot be presented, the registration may be withdrawn.

If a serious complication arises, the drug can be withdrawn from the market immediately. Procedures are available that make it possible to take a drug away from all pharmacies and hospital wards within twenty-four hours, and all physicians are notified by mail about the withdrawal.

The Price of Drugs

Since 1971 price negotiations with manufacturers, which used to be conducted by the Department of Drugs, have been handled entirely by the government-owned Apoteksbolaget (National Corporation of

Pharmacies). The Department of Drugs enters into price negotiations only after it has decided what indications are to be recommended for approval and thus, only when the use of the drug can be foreseen. Negotiations must be concluded before registration. If agreement on price cannot be reached, the Board of Drugs will refuse to register the drug. Special legal procedures are then followed in an attempt to reach a final agreement, if at all possible.

No really new drug has been admitted directly to the list of free drugs, since only well-established drugs are admitted to that list. Thus, in practice, price negotiations looking to admission to the free list occur only for different preparations of the same drug, including the generic versions. In this case, the negotiations generally are easy for the Apoteksbolaget because the manufacturer offers a price lower than the prices for drugs already on the market. The difficult negotiations have been those for new drugs for which the manufacturer claims a high price as a reward for his innovation.

Drug Availability in Sweden

Registered Drugs. Once a drug is registered, the manufacturer is free to sell it through the pharmacies. Since 1971, all 630 pharmacies in Sweden have been owned by the Apoteksbolaget, a company in which 75 percent of the shares are owned by the government and 25 percent by the Association of Pharmacies (which represents the former private owners).

Unregistered Drugs. Unregistered drugs may be sold only under special conditions. The main stipulation is that a physician must apply to the Department of Drugs for a license to obtain a specific amount of the drug for an individual patient. Once the license is granted, the general principles for economic subsidy apply. The three main categories of licenses for unregistered drugs are as follows:

(1) Drugs withdrawn from the market by the manufacturer because of uneconomically low sales.

(2) Drugs pending registration when international experience may warrant limited use under strict supervision. In all instances preliminary data must be available on toxicity, et cetera.

(3) Special narcotics, for example, amphetamines and related substances that are forbidden in Sweden. Because of the great abuse problems encountered in Sweden during the 1940s and 1950s, the greatest restriction is applied to granting licenses for

these drugs. The Department of Drugs uses independent medical consultants in psychiatry and/or neurology for each case and grants licenses mainly for narcolepsy and, in a limited number of cases, for general central stimulation.

Unregistered drugs may also be used for clinical trials. Permission for such trials is granted by the Department of Drugs upon application jointly signed by the manufacturer and the clinical investigator. Applications must be filed with the department for a new drug as well as for new indications for an already registered drug, and detailed instructions are available on what information an application should include. The difference between licensed use and clinical trial use is that the former is valid for individual cases and for therapeutic purposes that do not have any investigational aspect. The latter, of course, constitutes a scientific trial involving a group of patients, a carefully planned schedule, and proper controls, and is meant eventually to be used as support for an application for registration. However, there are intermediate situations. When, for instance, a hospital physician asks for permission to conduct a clinical trial, it may be sometimes more or less obvious that his primary interest is in treating patients rather than in performing a scientific trial.

Postmarketing Control of Drug Utilization

Virtually the only control on drug utilization that exists in Sweden, once a drug has been registered for use, is the availability of means to check prescriptions at the pharmacy level and to act as a result of such checks. The pharmacists themselves occasionally report to the Department of Drugs what they consider to be unusual prescriptions. Also, regular inspections of pharmacies by the inspectors of the Department of Drugs include, among other things, a check of prescription forms stored at the pharmacies. All prescription forms on narcotics are, by law, kept at the pharmacies, making it possible to check on previous narcotics prescriptions. If the inspections reveal large or unusual prescriptions by a physician—for example, repeated prescriptions of hypnotics corresponding to a consumption higher than the recommended levels—the Department of Drugs investigates the matter, and the physician is asked to comment upon and explain his prescribing habits. If, for example, overprescription of narcotics persists, the physician's entire license or just his right to prescribe narcotics may be withdrawn. For overprescription of ordinary drugs, such actions are never taken, first, because it is difficult to define "overprescription" and, second, because letters from the Department of Drugs regarding the prescription habits are thought to be warning enough. Formally, however, the possibility does exist of withdrawing the physician's license to practice on the ground of overprescription.

The Department of Drugs also has access to the sales figures for all pharmaceutical specialties in Sweden and thus has the means to analyze the situation, to see whether sales are increasing or decreasing, and to follow shifts between various groups of drugs. Such analyses are regularly performed and may result in information being provided to the physicians. For example, two years ago the National Board of Health and Welfare advised physicians to be careful and restrictive in prescribing all sedatives and hypnotics. This was a generally worded recommendation that did not mention any specific drug.

Prescription checking is a time-consuming, laborious, and ineffective way of controlling drug utilization, and can be used only to get at the most flagrant cases of mishandling narcotic drugs. So far, however, nobody has come up with a better system applicable to the Swedish situation. The measurement of drug consumption on a per capita basis is a subject of growing interest for which methodology is being developed. Studies on drug consumption have been carried out in one small town in Sweden. All prescriptions filled for a certain proportion of the population (6 to 10 percent) are entered into a computer, along with information on the sex and age of the patient, the name of prescribing physician, and the name and quantity of drug or drugs prescribed. Diseases so far have not been included in the data base, and the project must be regarded as a pilot study only. Enlargement of the study is being discussed, but no decisions have been made.

As stated earlier, a patient pays only fifteen Swedish crowns for any number and any amount of drugs prescribed at the same time. Over-the-counter sale of drugs has always been rather limited in Sweden, and only simple drugs such as analgesics (acetylsalicylic acid), cough drops, and vitamins are available as over-the-counter drugs. The sale of these preparations dropped after the introduction of the last prescription reform, which has made it cheaper for the patient to buy such preparations with a doctor's prescription than without a prescription (over-the-counter).

Controls on Advertising

Government regulations control the advertising of drugs. In addition, there are also internal advertising rules written by the joint organization of the pharmaceutical industries. The main government limitation on drug advertising is that prescription drugs may only be advertised in the medical, not in the lay, press.

Advertising is permitted only for approved indications. The exact composition or generic name of the drug must always be given, and the information must not be "exaggerated or misleading." In general, advertising must conform to the FASS statements about the drug, although there is no legal wording to this effect. A breach of these rules may form the basis for withdrawing the registration of the drug.

Discussion

It is difficult to compare the Swedish system of drug control with those in other countries, because drug systems are intimately connected with the entire structure of medical care, which, in turn, is dependent upon the socioeconomic structure of the country. Also, historical developments play an important role in the creation of any system of this type. What functions well—and is readily accepted—in one country may not work at all in a different setting.

Various ways of facilitating control over drug utilization are now being discussed in Sweden. Thus, registration for a limited time only—for example, three or five years—could be one way to make it easier to provide modern and up-to-date drugs to the physicians and, in particular, to get rid of old and obsolete preparations. Under the present situation, the Department of Drugs must prove that a registered drug has no effect in order to get the registration withdrawn—and such negative proof is not always easily obtained. A time-limited registration would leave it entirely to the manufacturer to defend a drug whose efficacy had been questioned during the registration period. In the absence of a valid defense, the registration would be automatically withdrawn.

Another change that has been suggested is the use of an official so-called Phase IV, or monitored release, system under which the registration would be valid only if certain criteria, for example, those regarding the reporting of adverse reactions, were fulfilled.

The time involved in performing the preregistration evaluations is unfortunately long: the mean processing time in the Department of Drugs is at present approximately two years. This is a definite drawback and causes annoyance to the public as well as to the medical profession. International cooperation in this field may well help to shorten such time periods, and steps to start such cooperation between the U.S. Food and Drug Administration and the Swedish Department of Drugs have been taken.

As may be seen from the description of the Swedish system in this paper, most control of drugs and drug utilization occurs before registration. Once a drug is registered, any physician may prescribe it for any patient. There is no limited registration as, for example, there is in Denmark, where drugs may be registered for use only in hospitals, by certain specialists, et cetera. The Swedish government, mainly through the Department of Drugs and with final approval by the Board of Drugs, puts drugs at the disposal of physicians. How they use them is mainly a matter of medical school education and training, postgraduate courses, and the receipt of regular information. With the rapid development in drug therapy during recent years, however, this has been found insufficient and new ways to disseminate information have been sought. The *FASS* has proved valuable, as have the booklets published by the Central Drug Information Committee. Limited mechanisms exist for controlling prescribing, but this is a rather inefficient way of controlling drug utilization. I believe that frequent information from official sources and, more important, continuing education through the physician's entire postgraduate life is the best way to achieve better, more effective, and safer pharmacotherapy.

8

DENMARK

Steen Antonsen and Eigill F. Hvidberg

Drug control in Denmark is part of a longstanding tradition, dating back to 1772 when the first legislation on medicines was enforced. The Danish Pharmacy Act of 1954, followed by several amendments and a number of administrative orders, was the basis for control of production of drugs and registration of new ones until June 1975. At this time the Danish Parliament (Folketinget) passed the new Medicines Act of 1975, valid from January 1, 1976. This act is in many ways different from the Pharmacy Act of 1954, and it will take some time before its exact influence on the drug control system and the number of registered specialties is known.

The main content of the definition of a drug is the same as in the previous law: "Articles which are intended to be administered to human beings or animals to prevent, diagnose, alleviate, treat or cure disease, symptoms of disease and pain, or to affect bodily functions (medicinal products). The provisions of this Act shall also apply to contraceptives." The law does not cover food, cosmetics, dietary supplements, or feed supplements for animals.

As a rule, drugs are sold in Denmark through some 330 pharmacies, which serve a population of 5 million inhabitants. The new law states that iron and vitamin preparations and antiparasitic preparations for animals may also be sold through other approved outlets. Furthermore the law stipulates that preparations made from pure natural products, which have no harmful effects on consumers, may be sold outside pharmacies; these drugs are not controlled by the National Health Service.

A pharmaceutical specialty (that is, a drug) is defined as a medicinal product intended for sale and supplied to the consumer in the manufacturer's original package under a name selected by the

171

manufacturer. The other group of medicines defined under the new law consists of those made up for the individual patient by a pharmacy. A pharmaceutical specialty shall be sold under a name approved by the National Health Service. This can be either the generic name or a special brand name. In the case of a brand name, the generic name must appear on the label in an easily read form at least half as large as the brand name.

All pharmaceutical specialties on sale in Denmark must be registered with the National Health Service, which in these matters is advised by the Registration Board (Registreringsnaevnet).

At the time of marketing, the National Health Service will publish the name and indications for the registered product, and it will be included in the official Danish Register of Specialties (Specialitetsregistret). The registration can be cancelled at any time the drug is no longer considered effective or safe or if the composition of the product or its appearance is changed without permission from the National Health Service.

According to the previous law (Pharmacy Act of 1954) preparations from pharmacies as described in official monographs, such as the Nordic pharmacopeia, were exempted from registration, but this stipulation has been altered in the Medicines Act of 1975. The National Health Service now includes such products in the official Register of Specialties.

Certain low-dose vitamin preparations are classed as dietary supplements and need not be registered; they are not controlled by the National Health Service. Serum and vaccines produced or imported by the State Serum Institute (Statens Seruminstitut) are exempted from registration. If, however, a similar preparation is marketed by another manufacturer, the corresponding product from the State Serum Institute must also be registered within one year according to the normal procedure (that is, accepted by the National Health Service).

As Denmark has been a member of the European Economic Community (EEC) since 1973, Danish drug legislation must be in conformity with the three EEC directives on drug specialties, issued in 1965 and 1975 (official numbering: 65/65, 75/318, and 75/319). These directives stipulate the main contents of the legislation on specialties in the member states (for example, the grounds on which an application for a product may be refused). In other cases they have the character of a guideline (for example, on the requirements for pharmacological, toxicological, and clinical documentation). The purpose of the directives is to harmonize the legislation in the member states, and the decision on whether to accept a product is still left to the health authorities in each member state. One of the objectives of the EEC is to facilitate the free circulation of all goods within the community, and, in the field of drugs, the goal is to allow a manufacturer to market his products simultaneously and according to equal requirements in all member states.

In the drafting and adoption of the Danish Medicines Act of 1975, the EEC directives were taken into consideration, fulfilling Denmark's obligation to transform the requirements of the directives to national law before their entry into force in November 1976.

Sources of Information

Postgraduate Education in Clinical Pharmacology and Therapeutics. Clinical pharmacology is not an independent discipline in Denmark. The first separate chair was established in 1973 at the University of Copenhagen under a temporary grant from the Danish State Medical Council. This chair is now in the process of being changed to a permanent position. In 1975 two permanent chairs (within the departments of pharmacology) were established at the universities of Odense and Aarhus, which, with the University of Copenhagen, have the only medical schools in Denmark. Separate departments in clinical pharmacology may eventually develop from these chairs. In Copenhagen there is a formal connection with the university hospital.

The undergraduate course in basic pharmacology is given during the first one and one-half years of clinical training, while clinical pharmacology is deferred until later and is integrated into the clinical courses conducted by predominantly clinical teachers. Few trained clinical pharmacologists have taught therapeutics in the medical schools until recently.

Although there is no formal postgraduate education in clinical pharmacology, it is included in many programs arranged for specialist training and for general practice. The universities are not officially responsible for these clinically oriented programs (in contrast to training programs in basic medical sciences), but university teachers are usually in charge. These teaching activities are administered and financially supported by the National Health Service, in collaboration with the various scientific societies (such as the Danish Society of Internal Medicine, the Danish Society of Surgery, the Danish Cardiological Society, and the Danish Society of General Practice), and with the Danish Medical Association. These bodies initiate and conduct the teaching through their permanent educational committees.

At present there are only a few postgraduate courses in clinical pharmacology taught at the universities, but there are proposals for more extensive programs. In addition to courses taught at the universities, there are local courses, lectures, and symposia arranged by clinical and scientific societies in which clinical pharmacology plays an integral part. Frequently, university teachers are also in charge of these courses, and they are often carried out in collaboration with the local hospitals. Interdisciplinary courses covering various clinical pharmacological fields have been arranged on the initiative of the Danish Medical Association. These intensive courses usually last four to six days and are open to specialists of various clinical disciplines. The subjects covered have included clinical drug evaluation and rational drug therapy. Teachers may be invited from abroad. Postgraduate courses covering similar fields have been arranged by the Danish Association of Pharmacy Proprietors and the Danish Association of Dentists for their respective members.

Drug Information. There is not yet any officially organized system through which information about the merits of new or established drugs can be obtained in Denmark. A few years ago, however, a committee under the National Health Service and the Ministry of the Interior reviewed the question of drug information. This committee suggested, among other things, that a state drug information board be appointed. The Medicines Act of 1975 ordered such a board to be set up. The Drug Information Board is composed of nine members appointed by the Minister of the Interior. Three members are recommended by the Danish Medical Association, two members by the pharmaceutical industry and importers, respectively, and one by the Association of Pharmacy Proprietors. Detailed plans for the board's competence and working fields have not yet been established because it was originally planned to have other objectives than were finally incorporated in the new act.

The drug information presently available comes from various sources. Occasional reviews are published in the *Weekly Medical Journal* (*Ugeskrift for Laeger*) issued by the Danish Medical Association. A panel of experts assists the editorial board in publishing industry-independent drug information and in encouraging specialists to provide opinions and evidence on the relative value of newly marketed drugs. Considerable emphasis is placed on comparisons with drugs marketed for same diseases.

Two other medical journals, the *Scandinavian Medical Journal* (*Nordisk Medicin*) and the *Monthly Journal for General Practice*

(*Månedsskrift for praktisk laegegerning*), also provide industry-independent drug information. The Danish Medical Association issues a comprehensive catalog of medicines (*Laegeforeningens Medicinfortegnelse*) as a pocket-sized book every second year with interim supplements. It is provided free to the 9,000 members of the Danish Medical Association, and 14,000 to 16,000 copies are sold to hospitals, nurses, pharmacies, dentists, and pharmaceutical houses. This catalog contains brief descriptions of all medicines on the Danish market, arranged according to therapeutic groups, and includes pharmacological action, indications, contraindications, side effects, dosages, precautions, dispensing forms, and prices. A short, critical, and comparative description is given of the clinical value of each therapeutic group, stating its relative value in relation to other therapeutic groups, and including descriptions of adverse reactions. Subsequently, the various brand names of each drug are listed. This arrangement provides the physician with the means to choose rapidly the most suitable and cheapest drug. Older remedies regarded by clinical pharmacologists as useless are listed with a statement to that effect. Previous editions were based mainly on material supplied by the pharmaceutical industry, but the 1975 edition was edited by an independent editorial board, with sole responsibility for the content. The next edition has been scheduled for 1977.

Recently, a new source of drug information has appeared in Denmark. The producers, importers, and distributors of drugs (which had issued separate drug catalogs) collaborated to issue a large catalog (*Laegemiddelkataloget*) covering all registered medicines in Denmark. It is a very comprehensive work, giving quite detailed information on pharmacological actions, indications, and side effects. It is divided into several parts, including a general description of the various therapeutic groups and a detailed description of the single preparations listed alphabetically. A separate volume gives the prices. In many ways it resembles the *PDR* (United States) and *FASS* (Sweden), but the Danish editorial board is independent of the companies and is solely responsible for the content. The book is financed by three organizations: the Association of Pharmaceutical Manufacturers in Denmark (MEFA); the Association of Importers of Pharmaceutical Products in Denmark (MEDIF); and the Association of Danish Pharmacy Proprietors (DA), which includes distributors as well as producers of drugs. The main catalog will be issued yearly, while the price list will be issued twice a year. It is sent free of charge to all physicians, dentists, and pharmacies in Denmark. Besides these sources of information, the pharmaceutical producers/importers provide a large part of the drug information through advertising and—in particular—through visits to doctors by their representatives. Meetings and symposia on specific products are frequently sponsored by the industry.

Control of Introduction of Drugs to the Market

No pharmaceutical specialty may be sold in Denmark before it has been accepted by the Danish National Health Service. To obtain registration of a pharmaceutical specialty the following conditions must be satisfied:

(1) It must be manufactured by a firm that has at its disposal the necessary professional knowledge, and that can ensure the satisfactory manufacture of this specialty.

(2) It must be of satisfactory quality and, in comparison with specialties already approved, be suitable from a health point of view.

(3) It must not, under normal conditions of use, result in side effects that are disproportionate to the intended effect or that constitute a danger to health.

(4) Sufficient information on, and documentation of, the pharmaceutical, pharmacological, toxicological, and clinical work shall be provided to show that it is reasonable and warrantable to release the product in accordance with the indications contained in the application.

(5) If the product contains several active ingredients, any increased health risk that may exist must be shown to be negligible in relation to the therapeutic value offered by the combination preparation.

The decision of acceptance is based on a report given by the Registration Board, which now includes nine members. All are professors or chief physicians in full-time positions at universities or hospitals, using their spare time to work at the Registration Board for a nominal fee. The members must, of course, be independent of all commercial activities related to distribution and manufacturing of drugs. The Registration Board meets approximately once a month, and before each meeting all members have been through the total documentary material for the applications to be dealt with at that meeting.

Applications for marketing of new drugs in Denmark must be filed by a Danish manufacturer or, in the case of imported specialties, by the manufacturer's authorized representative domiciled in Denmark. This representative will receive all official correspondence concerning a marketed drug. The application fee is 600 Danish kroner (U.S.$100), which covers all dosage forms of the product.

Before an application is circulated to the Registration Board, it is evaluated by the secretarial staff in the National Health Service. The pharmaceutical evaluation is done by pharmacists employed by the National Health Service's Pharmaceutical Laboratories, taking care of the applications as a part of their normal work (chemical and biological analyses of existing pharmaceutical products). Evaluation of the clinical and toxicological part of the application is done by a junior staff of hospital doctors. At present, this staff consists of seven M.D.s, whose contract includes ten hours' work a week at the National Health Service.

The complete application, accompanied by the secretariat's evaluation, is circulated to all the members of the Registration Board and finally to the chairman of the board, who will present it at the next meeting. The results of the board's discussion of each application are sent to the National Health Service, where a reply on behalf of the general director of health is drafted and sent to the applicant.

The applicant does not receive information about the handling of his application until he receives the reply from the National Health Service, which has taken about ten months. More than half of first-time applications are refused. In the reply all reasons for refusal are carefully stated to let the applicant know what is needed for the application to be successful.

The application must include full documentation of both active and inactive substances used to make the product. It must include test methods for specific quantitative determination of the active ingredients and results of stability tests. On the whole the pharmacological requirements are commensurate with those stated in the various World Health Organization Technical Reports. All necessary information about absorption, distribution, and elimination of the active compounds in man must be available.

The amount of clinical data necessary for a new drug registration depends on the nature of the drug. In the case of cough syrup, comparisons with placebos might be the proper way to prove the value of the new pharmaceutical specialty. If it is a new antirheumatic compound, comparisons of both effect and adverse reactions with existing remedies are required, and documentation for safety during longtime treatment is extremely important. If an effect against a malignant disease is proven for a new drug, the requirements for safety testing are regarded as less important.

It should be noted that a "lack of need" (in the Registration Board's opinion) is not a valid reason for refusal of an application for registration of a new drug. This concept represents a fundamental difference between the Danish and the Norwegian systems.

If a drug is already on the market, the requirements for registering a generic equivalent made by another manufacturer are normally confined to complete chemical and pharmaceutical documentation and a comparison of absorption, blood levels, and excretion between the new applicant's product and the existing one, done in ten to fifteen healthy volunteers.

The results of all clinical trials must be submitted in a scientifically analyzed form, preferably in a form ready to be published in the medical journals. Detailed patient records and laboratory notebooks are not wanted.

Clinical investigations performed outside Denmark are accepted if they are of a sufficient scientific standard, but if these investigations have been done on a substantially different racial group, comparisons with trials done in the Danish population are required.

Even though the detailed patient records are not included in the documentary material, the amount of paper to be circulated among the members of the board is considerable—about 250,000 pages (1,300 pounds) yearly. The number and nature of the applications are shown in Table 1.

A new drug can be advertised only for the specific indications for which its efficacy has been established. Only accepted indications officially published by the National Health Service when the drug is marketed may be used in the promotion material and advertisements.

Under the previous law, the National Health Service was not informed about clinical trials underway in Danish hospitals, but this was altered in the Medicines Act of 1975. Clinical testing may not be initiated until notification to the National Health Service by both the doctor (or dentist or veterinary surgeon) who is to carry out the testing and by the manufacturer of the specialty or his representative. The National Health Service may specify conditions of such testing and may at any time demand that it be stopped or modified. The doctor who carries out the investigation shall immediately notify the National Health Service in the event of serious side effects in the course of the testing. On completion of the testing the doctor shall submit the results of the investigation to the National Health Service. How much manpower the National Health Service needs in order to exert an effective control of all such clinical trials has not yet been settled.

Table 1
NEW DRUG APPLICATIONS IN DENMARK, 1971–75

	Applications 1971		Applications 1972		Applications 1973		Applications 1974		Applications 1975	
	Total number	Approved	Total number	Approved	Total number	Approved	Total number	Approved	Total number	Approved
New preparations ("originals")	23	3	49	13	46	9	34	10	61	29
New preparations (analogues)	32	15	39	16	24	10	24	14	16	8
Reapplications (supplementary documents)	80	45	73	53	80	45	98	70	71	45
Changes in dispensing forms, new strengths, etc.	57	42	68	46	83	60	78	52	86	72
Total	199	109	249	144	240	127	242	150	239	158

Control of Drug Utilization after the Stage of Marketing

Prescription Regulations. As soon as a new drug is registered and put on the market, the conditions of its sale (rules for prescribing) are specified by the National Health Service. Generally, these rules divide the drugs into the following categories:

(1) those dispensed from the pharmacy without a prescription ("over-the-counter drugs");

(2) those dispensed on a doctor's prescription as often as wanted for five years on the same prescription;

(3) those dispensed on a prescription only once, unless the doctor has indicated on the prescription that it can be refilled a specified number of times at particular intervals;

(4) those dispensed only once on a prescription;

(5) those drugs leading to addiction, such as morphine and amphetamine, dispensed only once and prescribed on a special form (a copy attached to the form must be returned to the National Health Service, and doctors who abuse their authority in this area are deprived of their license to prescribe narcotic drugs for periods of five years or more).

Almost all drugs fall into one of these categories, but in special cases registration may be granted for a limited period. Such *limited* registration applies mainly to promising, but toxic, new remedies often with an action on cancer or similar serious diseases. Such drugs are usually registered for a period of two years, during which time they can be used in hospitals only. After this period expires, the drug must be reevaluated by the Registration Board. Depending on the supplementary clinical and toxicological documentation then available, the registration may be cancelled, renewed for another two years, or referred for normal registration.

According to the Danish Medicines Act, registration of a new drug is valid only for a period of five years. Because of shortages of staff, there has not yet been an efficient reevaluation of older drugs (that is, remedies accepted on the Danish market when the criteria for registration were considerably less strict than at present). Rules for re-registration of older drugs are in the process of being established, and the Registration Board may in the future follow the following guidelines: If newer therapeutic compounds for the same disorder have been registered which have definite advantages over the older preparations (as determined by an evaluation of therapeutic and toxic effects), the older ones will probably not be re-registered. How large the difference should be will, of course, be a matter of individual judgment in each case.

Payment for Drugs. As a part of the social legislation, the Ministry of Social Affairs has laid down rules according to which medicine may be subsidized, thereby making essential drugs less expensive for the consumer. As a result of this measure the government may also have some influence on drug consumption.

In Denmark, about 50 percent of the nation's expenses on medicine are defrayed by public funds, mostly through the National Health Insurance System, the annual cost being just below 500 million Danish kroner (about U.S.$80 million).

Registration of a new drug does not, however, automatically imply that its cost will be subsidized. The manufacturer or importer must submit an application to the Medicine Committee, an advisory agency under the National Health Service, which will recommend whether a drug should be subsidized.

The subsidies on medicine fall into the following groups: Group A, for which 75 percent of the price is reimbursed. This group includes the particularly important remedies normally used in the treatment of severe, acute, or chronic diseases; Group B, for which 50 percent of the price is reimbursed. This group includes drugs whose therapeutic value is documented, but which are less important than the value of the drugs in Group A; Group C consists of drugs that will not be reimbursed because, for example, their therapeutic value cannot be considered sufficiently substantiated.

The committee must also take into consideration the price of the drugs concerned. If the therapeutic value of chemically identical preparations is identical, but prices vary, the more expensive products may not be subsidized unless they can be shown to have distinct advantages over the less expensive products.

Patients who purchase drugs in the pharmacy pay only the reduced price, and the rest is paid directly to the pharmacy by the national insurance system. If required, the social security system will pay the patient's share. In all Danish public hospitals (about 90 percent of all hospitals in Denmark) all medicine is free of charge for the patients; this costs the taxpayers approximately 200 million Danish kroner.

Monitoring of Adverse Drug Reactions. Spontaneous reporting of adverse reactions (that is, reporting on the doctors' own initiative) was started in Denmark in 1968 and a report on the five-year period through 1973 was published in January 1974. A special board is appointed to supervise this spontaneous reporting, but the work is carried out in close collaboration with the Registration Board. So far, the board has published twenty-two communications on adverse drug reactions in the weekly *Danish Medical Journal*. The rate at which reports are received from physicians, hospitals, and other sources is about the same as in Norway and Sweden. During the first five years, 3,720 reports were received from all parts of the country (35 percent from general practitioners, 52 percent from hospitals, and 12 percent from other institutions). About 30 percent referred to anti-infective drugs and 7 percent to antirheumatics. The Danish Adverse Drug Reaction Board works in close cooperation with the Adverse Drug Reaction Center of the World Health Organization in Geneva, Switzerland.

Control of Advertising. The law states that advertisements of medicinal products shall be sober and factual and may not give an exaggerated, incomplete, misleading, or deceptive picture of the product. Advertising medicines directly to the public is only permitted for certain over-the-counter drugs, and must be approved in advance. Medicines requiring a prescription must not be advertised in the lay press (or to the public at large) at all.

Professional journal advertisements of medicines need not be approved in advance, but the National Health Service may order the manufacturer or advertiser to issue corrections. Since the National Health Service does not monitor advertisements as a matter of routine, enforcement of the ban on incorrect advertising is usually prompted by complaints from a third party. A committee was recently established by the pharmaceutical industry to administer voluntary standards of drug advertising.

"Basic information sheets," used in England in connection with drug promotion activities, are not available in Denmark, but they are under consideration by the National Health Service.

Free Drug Samples. In principle, samples of registered specialties cannot be supplied free of charge to physicians. The manufacturer (importer) is, however, allowed to give free samples of a new pharmaceutical specialty for a maximum period of twelve months from the date of marketing and only in the smallest package size. Naturally, control of such activities is difficult.

Drug Committees. Only twenty-four drug committees are functioning at present, mainly in hospitals. At the time they were introduced in other countries, there was no tradition for such activities in Denmark. Drug committees are now being planned in many hospitals, and the authority of existing ones is being expanded.

Drug Consumption Recording. Precise recording of the consumption of drugs has not been established in Denmark, though some research on consumption has been published recently. A system for collection of such data will probably be established in the near future, partly in cooperation with other nations and the World Health Organization.

Special Danish Demands for Registration. At present about 1,400 pharmaceutical specialties are available on the Danish market. Many of them appear in several dosage forms (tablets, ampules, ointments, and the like), so there are about 2,300 pharmaceutical items in all. These figures are lower than those in most other countries outside Scandinavia for the following reasons.

Nearly all of the 2,300 items were registered under the previous law (Danish Pharmacy Act of 1954), according to which a preparation could not be registered if its only active content was a substance already available on the open market. The only exceptions to this rule were allowed to manufacturers who had been the first to prove a compound had a hitherto unknown therapeutic effect, or who needed special equipment to manufacture it in a dispensable form. This restriction, which undoubtedly reduced the number of new specialties being registered, was written into the previous law to encourage the production of medicine by Danish pharmacies. The pharmacies at that time had production facilities and skilled manpower, but they had no experience in research, drug development, or promotion. The intention was to provide price competition for drugs produced by the pharmaceutical industry.

Another special Danish regulatory mechanism in the previous law was control over registration of fixed combination drugs. Two conditions had to be fulfilled in order to have such preparations registered: (1) at least one of the active components should not be available in the open market, and (2) the applicant had to establish that a particularly satisfactory therapeutic effect was obtained if the active ingredients were combined in one preparation instead of being administered separately to the patient. This rule was administered very strictly—with the result that only a few combination prepara-

183

tions were registered in Denmark during the twenty years the Pharmacy Act of 1954 was in force.

Another limiting factor on the number of pharmaceutical items was that the Pharmacy Act of 1954 granted permission to use a brand name only to manufacturers who had contributed essentially to the development of the medicine. In practice such a brand name was allowed only for one Danish medical company and one foreign company. All other producers had to market the generic product under the generic name. This rule applied also to products manufactured by the pharmacies.

All the above-mentioned special regulations disappeared with the introduction of the Medicines Act of 1975, but its influence on the number of pharmaceutical specialties cannot yet be judged. Any manufacturer can use his own brand name if the product fulfills the conditions for registration, but with a population in Denmark of only 5 million, there is a limit to how many different brand names of the same product can be profitably marketed. Besides the economic aspects, the number of pharmaceutical items that come to be marketed will depend on how the new law is administered. It is the intention of the Registration Board to require that the ratio between intended effect and risk of side effects be high.

Drug legislation in Norway, Sweden, and Denmark differs on some essential points, but on the whole the requirements for registration and for the control of existing drugs have been similar in the three countries for many years. The health authorities in the three countries have worked closely together, exchanging information on such matters as unexpected side effects and preparations which did not fulfill the required control standards. Normally, a pharmaceutical company tries to introduce a new product in all three markets and often uses the same designations and packing material throughout the Scandinavian area.

Advantages and Disadvantages of the Danish System

The advantages of the system as it functioned under the Pharmacy Act of 1954 was that it allowed a limited, but sufficient, number of brand-name drugs on the market, and few combinations. Production of medicinal products other than brand-name preparations could be achieved by the pharmacies. The administration of the Danish system required only a small number of people for several reasons: only a limited number of applications for synonymous drugs were received; there was no control of clinical trials; control of the labeling material was easy because only technical information was allowed, and there was no package insert to control. The National Health Service needed only a small amount of manpower to publish medical information and to control the informational material given to medical doctors by the producers. Because the members of the Registration Board did investigate the full application material themselves, they were able to make prompt decisions on evaluations made by the administrative staff. Control of the medicine produced by the pharmacies, which has been a substantial, but declining, part of the whole market (approximately 25 percent in 1975), was carried out by a small staff from the National Health Service.

Several disadvantages of the system can be mentioned. Physicians have lacked information from the authorities about new drugs introduced on the market, and they have lacked comparative information about the value of existing drugs. The reevaluation of existing drugs was not done in a fully satisfactory way. Many of the clinical trials performed on new drugs could have been better if planning of the trial had been scrutinized.

The producers felt at a great disadvantage because lack of manpower made it impossible for the administrative staff to take up personal discussions or correspondence concerning the quality of an application before it was fully evaluated by the Registration Board some nine to eleven months later. The public has undoubtedly missed information about drug effects, side effects, and dosage, particularly for the over-the-counter medicines.

It is not yet possible to know exactly how much the Medicines Act of 1975 will alter the system. The intention of this law is that the National Health Service must have more substantial control over the various aspects of drugs, and that it shall initiate and control more extensive information both to physicians and to the public. All manufacturers of medicines in Denmark must be supervised by the National Health Service, and they have the right to market generic preparations if these are of sufficiently high standard. One thing is clear, however: the National Health Service will need increased staffing, even though the staff has already been enlarged since the new law took effect in January 1976.

The new law, taking into consideration that Denmark has entered the European Economic Community, provides for harmonizing the conditions for drug control with the other members of EEC. Representatives of the national drug control bodies in the different EEC countries have held meetings in Brussels to enable producers to use the same application for filing in all nine EEC countries.

9

NORWAY

Magne Halse and Per Knut M. Lunde

Drug Control Systems

Brief History. Traditionally, Norwegian society has tried to control the quality and use of medication in order to safeguard the public and to ensure proper medical treatment. The first official legislative measure within this field dates from a 1679 royal decree on pharmacy inspection. Before the industrial era of ethical drug production, the major efforts toward control were in the education of medical personnel, the establishment of drug standards in official formularies, the control of the production and distribution chain (mainly the pharmacies), and the introduction of general and special prescription rules.

With the industrialization and commercialization of drug production and marketing, new control measures became necessary. The first regulations to control the industrial production of drugs were set as early as 1914. In 1928, those regulations were extended by an act of the Parliament (Stortinget), according to which the marketing of each drug product must be approved by a government authority. Ever since the act was passed, the basic parameters for drug evaluation and registration have been safety, efficacy, need, and cost. Drug advertising was regulated and restricted by the same act. In 1930, a government agency to administer the regulations was established, with a quality control laboratory, and a laboratory for drug standardization was added in 1948. In 1974, these services were reorganized and fused into the National Center for Medicinal Products' Control (Statens Legemiddelkontrol).[1]

[1] B. Jøldal, "Norwegian Drug Control, Organization and Tasks," in *Report from the Norwegian Drug Monopoly*, ed. Magne Moe (Oslo: The Norwegian Drug Monopoly, 1974), pp. 32-43 (in Norwegian), and Committee on the Future Organization of Drug Control in Norway, *Norwegian Public Reports*, no. 28 (1972) (in Norwegian).

In the field of distribution a major reorganization took place in 1958 with the nationalization of the drug wholesaling system, including pharmaceutical specialties (that is, prepackaged pharmaceuticals, as opposed to those prepared at the pharmacy) as well as bulk therapeutic materials. The state company thus established—the Norwegian Drug Monopoly (Norsk Medisinaldepot)—is an important part of Norway's drug control and information system. The drug legislative and regulatory rules were revised and consolidated in the Poison and Drug Act of 1964.

Present and Future Drug Control Systems. All public health matters in Norway are under the responsibility of the Ministry of Social Affairs and are handled by the Health Directorate of that ministry. The National Center for Medicinal Products' Control deals with drugs, acting on behalf of the director general of public health. Figure 1 illustrates the overall structure of the drug control system with special emphasis on the relationship between this center, the Health Directorate and the various advisory and decision-making boards. Figure 2 further outlines the organization and major activities within the National Center for Medicinal Products' Control projected in the reorganization started in 1974.[2] The main idea behind this reorganization is to strengthen government drug control through improved coordination and better use of the available resources *within the present institutions and professions.* The deciding body in questions concerning drug registration is the Specialties Committee (Spesialitets nemnda). Its members, appointed by the minister of social affairs (Sosialministeren), are experts in different fields of medicine and pharmacy. The director general of public health (Helsedirektøren) is ex officio the chairman of the committee.

As was mentioned above, the main legal criteria for the registration of drugs in Norway are therapeutic efficacy, safety, and medical need—together with standards on product composition and quality. The price is formally considered after the drug is registered, but before it is marketed. A drug registration application must include documentation of the chemical, pharmaceutical, toxicological, and pharmacological properties of the actual product, as well as results of clinical tests. General application forms and written guidelines for the further contents of such applications have been worked out. In addition to the general product documentation, the application must be accompanied by a brief drug/preparation specification proposing indications, contraindications and special precautions, known adverse

---

[2] Ibid.

Figure 1

STRUCTURE OF THE DRUG CONTROL
SYSTEMS IN NORWAY
(as reorganized from January 1974)

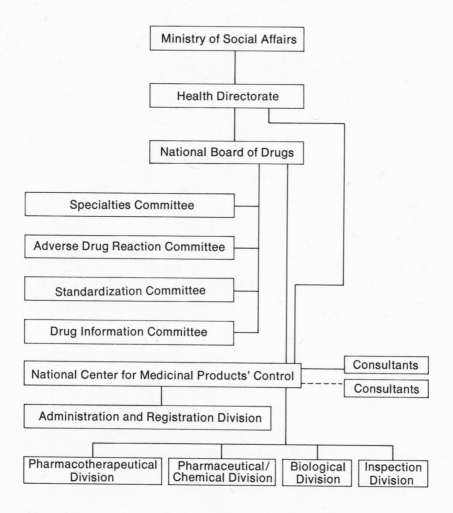

Source: B. Joldal, "Norwegian Drug Control, Organization and Tasks," in *Report from the Norwegian Drug Monopoly,* ed. Magne Moe (Oslo: The Norwegian Drug Monopoly, 1974), pp. 32-43 (in Norwegian); and Committee on the Future Organization of Drug Control in Norway, *Norwegian Public Reports,* no. 28 (1972) (in Norwegian).

Figure 2

STRUCTURE OF THE NATIONAL CENTER FOR MEDICINAL PRODUCTS' CONTROL

(as reorganized from January 1974)

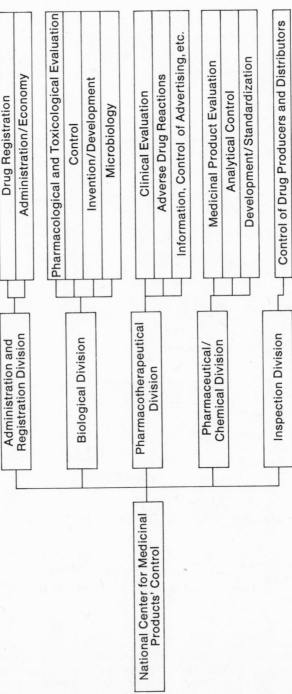

Source: B. Joldal, "Norwegian Drug Control, Organization and Tasks," in *Report from the Norwegian Drug Monopoly*, ed. Magne Moe (Oslo: The Norwegian Drug Monopoly, 1974), pp. 32-43 (in Norwegian); and Committee on the Future Organization of Drug Control in Norway, *Norwegian Public Reports*, no. 28 (1972) (in Norwegian).

reactions and side effects, interactions, and dosage. When the drug is registered, this specification, which is often revised by the control authorities before being approved, is published in the annual catalog of drugs on the Norwegian market. This catalog is under continuous review and revision by the drug manufacturers and is distributed to all physicians and pharmacies in the country.

Package inserts are occasionally allowed in Norway, generally when technical instructions on the handling of the drug and special equipment for its administration are needed. Proposals for other indications and changes in the dosage schedules of the drug must be approved by the Specialties Committee before they can be promoted. Thus, if a physician is extending the use of a drug to nonapproved indications, or prescribes doses widely different from those officially recommended, this has the character of a clinical trial, with its possible legal implications.

Upon receipt, applications for registration are considered by the staff of the National Center for Medicinal Products' Control. For further evaluation, independent experts outside the organization are often selected. If necessary, additional laboratory tests or clinical trials in Norwegian hospitals are also performed before the national center gives its recommendation to the deciding body, the Specialties Committee.

The relatively low number of registered drugs in all the Scandinavian countries may reflect similarities in Scandinavian legislation as well as in its implementation. The number is, however, lower in Norway than in Sweden: in 1973, there were 1,933 specialties with 770 different active ingredients in Norway, compared with 2,836 specialties with 900 active ingredients in Sweden. The lower number in Norway may be due in part to a special clause in the Norwegian legislation which states that approval of registration "shall only be given for preparations which are medically justified and which are considered to be needed." By this clause it has been possible to limit the number of drug products that are chemically identical and biologically similar. The policy has been to permit five to seven different brands of each substance. Thus, there are five oxytetracycline preparations and five phenoxymethylpenicillin potassium preparations on the market. It should be stressed, however, that the number of such "synonyms" is more strictly limited for drugs still under patent. Because the patent has expired for chlorpromazine, but not for thioridazine, we have five brand-name preparations of the former but only one of the latter.

The same clause has made it possible, for forty-five years, to implement a requirement for comparative efficacy and thus to limit the number of "me too" preparations.

The resulting administrative practices varies with the therapeutic area and depends on the assumed need—that is, the relative sizes of the patient groups for treatment. Thus, only three cephalosporin derivatives have been accepted, while the number of phenothiazine derivatives in the neuroleptic group is thirteen. The differences and the policy adopted will, however, to a large extent reflect the opinions of the leading specialists consulted in the various fields of medicine. It cannot be claimed that all drug groups are handled identically.

There is no formal restriction on the exact number of different chemical entities that can be marketed within a given therapeutic class. However, this is covered by the "clause of need," as described above. Perhaps more important is the fact that the policy of the Specialties Committee has been to consider with skepticism registration applications for combination preparations. Arguments by the applicants that the ingredients are well-defined and well-known substances from a chemical and pharmacological, as well as from a clinical, point of view, or arguments for convenience of use, have generally not been accepted. It is worth noting that the differences mentioned between the number of drugs in Norway and Sweden is particularly marked in the case of combination preparations, especially analgesics, psychopharmaceuticals, antihistamines, and similar classes. Of course, the limited market possibilities for drugs in Norway—the total annual drug sale being approximately U.S.$120 million in 1973 to a population of 4 million—may also contribute to the low number of drugs on the Norwegian market.

The philosophy behind the relatively rigorous restrictions put on drug registration and marketing in Norway has been—and is—that this will promote rational drug therapy with a reasonable number of drugs, in order to avoid confusion among the prescribers, the patients, and the parts in the chain of control and distribution. There is, of course, a potential danger that the drug selection will not always be sufficient. So far, however, we have no real indication that our regulatory system has resulted in an inadequate range of therapy available to the patients. An example of the drugs available in one therapeutic group of cardiovascular drugs, the diuretics, is given in Table 1.

For drugs not registered in Norway the physician can obtain a special license for prescription to named patients for given indications. Quantitatively, however, this represents only a minor portion of all drugs registered and used in Norway. The normal procedure in cases

Table 1
REGISTERED DIURETICS IN NORWAY, BY GENERIC AND BRAND NAMES

Thiazides

Bendroflumethiazide	Centyl "Leo" injection, tablet
	Centyl with KCl "Leo" tablet
Hydroflumethiazide	Rontyl "Leo" tablet
	Rontyl with KCl "Leo" tablet
Hydrochlorthiazide	Dichlotride "MSD" tablet
	Esidrex "Ciba" tablet
	Esidrex-K "Ciba" coated tablet
	Esidrex-K mite "Ciba" coated tablet
Chlorthiazide	Chlotride "MSD" tablet
Polythiazide	Renese "Pfizer" tablet
	Renese mite "Pfizer" tablet
Trichlormethiazide	Fluitran "Schering Corp." tablet

Sulfonamides (thiazides excluded)

Furosemide	Diural "A.L." injection, tablet
	Impugan "Dumex" injection, tablet
	Lasix "Hoechst" injection, tablet
Quinethazone	Aqvamox "Lederle" tablet
Clopamide	Brinaldix "Sandoz" tablet
Chlorthalidone	Hygroton "Geigy" tablet
Mefruside	Baycaron "Bayer" tablet
Bumetanide	Burinex "Leo" injection, tablet

Aldosterone antagonists

Spironolactone	Aldactone "Searle" tablet
Canrenoate potassium	Soldactone "Searle" injection

Others

Ethacrynic acid	Edecrin "MSD" injection, tablet

where a special license is desired is for the physician to write a prescription and, in addition to the usual requirements, give the indication for the actual drug prescribed, as well as the active ingredients of the preparation and the name of the producer. When this prescription is presented to a pharmacy, it will be forwarded to the drug wholesale company, which applies for the license and also places the order with the foreign company. The time of delivery will vary from one to four weeks. An examination of the licenses reveals that only a minor portion of specially licensed drugs represents important drugs urgently

193

needed in rare cases in hospital practice. (These drugs are ordinarily kept in stock by the drug wholesale company or at the hospitals, and the sales volume in these cases is estimated as being too low to allow profitable marketing.) The greater part of these special-license prescriptions are for drugs which the patients have persuaded their doctors to prescribe. An example is pills of procaine in combination with twenty-three different minerals and vitamins in very small quantities. This preparation is advertised as being effective for various geriatric purposes.

Such a license system tends to improve the communication between the prescriber and the central authorities, and advice and comments can, if necessary, be given to the physicians.

Registration Period. All drugs in Norway are registered for a period of five years unless problems of a special nature develop. On the expiration of the registration period for the drug, a new application for registration is demanded by the control center. This renewed application goes through the same procedure as the application for new drugs.

In the case of drugs which are of questionable efficacy, but which have been used extensively for a long period, and are still considered safe, withdrawal from the market may be postponed for another period of five years. In this five-year period there will be a ban on all promotion of the drug, and experts will be asked to express their views on its use (the views being expressed through medical forums). During this period, physicians will have time to change their prescription habits and to prepare their patients for alternative therapy. A recent example is long-acting alkyl nitrates, based on slightly soluble compounds (as, for example, pentaeryturitol tetranitrate) as well as sustained release glyceryl trinitrate preparations. If new evidence appears on the efficacy or safety of a drug, the drug's registration may be withdrawn at any time during the five-year registration period. Recent examples of this kind are the withdrawal of sedatives containing a combination of methaqualone and other ingredients, and prohibition against promoting barbiturates and their combinations as well as on meprobamate and glutethimide. Here it can be mentioned that the Adverse Drug Reaction Committee (Bivirkningsnemnda) is organized within the same framework as the registration board (Figure 1). The Adverse Drug Reaction Committee, which is an advisory board, registers, classifies, and to a certain extent evaluates the adverse reactions reported by the hospitals, general practitioners, private specialists, and dentists. For assumed lethal complications of drug therapy the reporting is an *obligatory* task for all physicians and dentists, while the reporting of non-lethal complications is voluntary.

Special priority is given to reports on new drugs, less-recognized reactions to older drugs, and to the more serious adverse reactions—that is, those leading to hospitalization or major therapeutic problems. The reports, which may require further investigations at various levels before they are accepted and classified, are subsequently handed over to the WHO Research Center for International Drug Monitoring, and a copy (that does not identify patient and physician) is also sent to the respective pharmaceutical firms for their orientation and eventual comments. The reporting system, as linked to the international monitoring system of WHO, forms the base for the Adverse Drug Reaction Committee's advice to the drug registration authorities on the possible withdrawal of a preparation or the setting of special restrictions on its use, labeling, and promotion. Furthermore, the Adverse Drug Reaction Committee publishes yearly overall reports on its activity, as well as information on adverse reactions of special interest. In this connection it is of great value for the control organization that the Adverse Drug Reaction Committee cooperates with the Institute of Pharmacotherapy.

Pharmacy Production of Drugs. The pharmacies have traditionally done a considerable amount of their own drug compounding, and their compounds still account for about 8 to 10 percent of total drug sales in Norway. Their production has gradually become more centralized. Drugs compounded in pharmacies have so far not been covered by the registration and control rules given here. This situation will be changed in the near future and a reevaluation of these products will take place. A number of the present pharmacy products are considered obsolete and their efficacy doubted or at least not entirely documented. Such products are mostly manufactured according to the pharmacopeia and the authorized national formularies, and many of those obviously need revision.

Restrictions on Drug Advertising. The Norwegian Drug and Poison Act of 1964 and the Royal Decree of 1966 sets rules and control procedures for drug advertising. All drug promotional literature, including pamphlets, advertisements in medical journals, and drug catalogs published by the drug producers or their societies must be approved by the drug control authorities before they are distributed. This portion of the legislation may, depending upon the degree of vigor with which it is implemented, also have an impact on drug utilization.

The pharmaceutical industry spends a substantial amount of its budget on marketing efforts. It is, however, a permanent problem for the control authorities to handle the huge amount of drug promotion literature. As a whole the pharmaceutical industry uses detail men to approximately the same extent per capita as in the United States.

Drug prices. Under Norwegian law, the director general of public health has the authority to approve and to control drug prices. The drug prices to the public are the same throughout the country. Officially approved price lists are printed and distributed quarterly. Prices from the drug industry to the Drug Monopoly are approved by the National Center for Medicinal Products' Control. The markup by the Drug Monopoly amounts to 15 percent. The pharmacies' markup is also regulated: at present it is 30 percent on purchasing prices. Furthermore, the pharmacies receive Norwegian kroner 1.05 per drug package sold, and Norwegian kroner 1.50 as an additional fee on prescribed drugs (N.Kr. 5.25 are equal to U.S. $1). Thus, if the price from the manufacturer is Norwegian kroner 20.—, the consumer has to pay Norwegian kroner 33.—plus value added tax (20 percent).

The pharmacies must pay a fee, based upon their turnover, to a central fund, which is used to subsidize small unprofitable pharmacies in rural areas. The itemized income and expenditures of each pharmacy are scrutinized annually by a group of experts in the Directorate of Public Health, and the need for profit regulation or financial support is considered. Before a drug approved by the Specialties Committee can be marketed, its price to the Drug Monopoly must be sanctioned by the National Center for Medicinal Products' Control, as described above.

General guidelines for price setting are production costs and comparison with similar products from other producers, domestic as well as foreign. Price alterations during the five-year registration period must also be approved by the same body. Furthermore, the National Center for Medicinal Products' Control has the authority to call for a price reduction during the registration period. In price discussions, the control center has the legal right to demand all relevant information from the producer.

For new drugs, protected by patent, the industry has a strong bargaining position and will in most cases receive approval of its price proposals. A comparison of drug prices in different countries shows that prices in Norway are at approximately the same level as in neighboring countries. However, for some important drugs, Norwegian prices are almost twice as high as the prices in the United Kingdom, and also substantially higher than in the United States. Examples are α-methyldopa and ampicillin. For drugs not protected by patent, such marked price differences do not exist.

The situation in Norway illustrates the difficulties of the smaller nations in price negotiations with international pharmaceutical companies.

The social security system in Norway, which covers approximately 40 percent of the nation's drug bill, does not exclude the more expensive drugs. Free drugs are given to all hospitalized patients as well as to patients suffering from serious or chronic diseases like tuberculosis, cancer, diabetes, hypertension, rheumatoid arthritis, Parkinson's disease, and so on—irrespective of the price of the drug. This policy must be seen in connection with the official approval required for drug prices. The other 60 percent of the total drug cost for the most part represents drugs prescribed for disease treated outside hospitals, and is paid by the patients. If necessary, these drugs may be subsidized by the local communities. It is difficult to determine how drug price levels as such influence physicians' prescribing and patients' drug consumption. The physicians' choice between alternative drugs may be influenced by the source of payment—whether the preparation is paid for by the patient or by the social security system, the local community, or a corporate insurance plan. In general, it is a rule of economics that low prices ought to increase the sales of a product, but in the drug market there is also a tendency for highly priced products to have greater sales. This may be due partly to the fact that the marketing efforts by the pharmaceutical industry seem to be focused on the relatively expensive—and often new—products.

Clinical Trials. Official control of clinical drug tests performed in Norway is limited to a compulsory notification of the test to the drug control authorities. This requirement was introduced in 1971. The notification must be made in advance, on a standardized form which facilitates examination and comparisons of the tests. This system gives the control authorities the opportunity to intervene, if necessary, but to date the system has mainly functioned to provide notification, the whole responsibility for the test resting with the physicians in charge.

A recent survey of the first three years of the notification system will determine whether the system should be extended to require a formal approval plus direct guidance and coordination at the planning stage of trials. The survey showed that preclinical and early clinical tests (phase I) are relatively rare in Norway. Indeed, the number of drugs and preparations primarily developed in Norway is quite limited. However, with the increasing interest of the Norwegian pharmaceutical industry in research, more tests of this kind are expected. The survey also indicates that a relatively large number of tests—mostly phase II-III—are initiated and planned by international pharmaceutical companies, possibly as a part of their efforts to have preparations registered and introduced in Norway. Thus, the registration record shows examples where some pharmaceutical companies have initiated from fifty to eighty clinical "tests" on one single preparation at the stage of its registration. Reports on such tests are rarely sent to the registration authorities, and they are only occasionally published in medical journals. Extensive efforts of this type are hardly defensible, either from a scientific or from an ethical point of view. Furthermore, it might tend to reduce the physicians' awareness of the important distinction between clinical investigation and routine therapy.

Drug Quality Control. Drug standards are set in the Nordic pharmacopeia, which is produced and continuously revised jointly by the four countries involved (Denmark, Finland, Norway, and Sweden). Cooperation in this field is especially advantageous and necessary for the smaller countries. In addition, Norway has subscribed to the Pharmaceutical Inspection Convention of the former European Free Trade Association (EFTA) countries and has thus participated in its Good Manufacturing Practice (GMP) rules. These are guidelines for the pharmaceutical industry as well as for governmental inspection. The countries that have joined the convention may ask for inspection reports on pharmaceutical companies in other member countries. The mutual exchange of inspection reports based upon established criteria and principles is of great value for the control organizations in these countries. Since about 75 percent of the medicinal specialty products used in Norway are imported, Norwegian control authorities have welcomed the opportunity to obtain official statements on the quality standards of a number of foreign pharmaceutical companies. Registered drugs are checked at intervals by Norwegian biological and chemical control laboratories for content, content uniformity, dissolution, bioavailability, purity, pyrogens, sterility, microbiological contamination, and so on. By European standards these laboratories are well equipped. Samples for examination are drawn from various levels in the distribution chain.

In addition, a drug recall system is established in cooperation with the Norwegian Drug Monopoly. This system is based for the most part upon reports from pharmacists in hospitals or in retail services on drug batches judged—from their appearance—not to fulfill acceptable quality. Examples are particulate matter in infusion fluids, discolored tablets or solutions, and unusual size or color of tablets. Sometimes atypical reactions in patients may throw suspicion on a certain drug batch. A recall of a batch of local anesthetics, where analysis showed that the epinephrine was degraded, had its origin in such a report. Mislabeling of some packages of a batch, which may give rise to serious disasters, is one of the most frequent faults reported. Drug recalls can also be initiated by the quality control departments of the pharmaceutical firms.

Surveillance of Drug Utilization

With the nationalization of the drug wholesaling system in Norway in 1957, the exclusive rights to import and distribute drugs of domestic as well as of foreign origin were given to the state company established for that purpose, the Norwegian Drug Monopoly (NMD). A unique opportunity then arose for obtaining data on the overall sales of pharmaceutical specialties and bulk materials, both for the country as a whole and for its twenty administrative counties.

The NMD has its headquarters in Oslo with subdivisions in various major regions of the country. Since the start of its activities, an integrated on-line computerized system for drug purchasing, sales, invoicing and stock inventorying, as well as for drug "consumption" statistics, has been gradually developed. Knowledge of actual drug consumption is, of course, vital to the NMD's own purchasing and stockkeeping, as well as to the pharmaceutical companies in the Norwegian market, both for their production planning and for the evaluation of their sales efforts.

The NMD has also paid attention to the medical advantages of having convenient drug sales and utilization statistics. A drug classification system has been developed, based upon the international EPhMRA (European Pharmaceutical Market Research Association) anatomical classification system, as extended to include chemical groups and substances. A comprehensive list of the drugs on the

Norwegian market, classified according to that system, is revised annually.[3]

As part of an international collaboration under the aegis of the World Health Organization, the NMD has also contributed to developing a convenient methodology for establishing comparable drug statistics within and among countries. For this purpose a "defined daily dose" is used as a unit of comparison. A complete list of daily doses for all drugs given for systemic use in Norway has been available since 1975.[4]

With the data for drug sales in terms of defined daily doses per unit time and population, it is possible to estimate roughly the number of patients being treated with a drug or group of drugs in the country or within a region. Another advantage of using this unit of measurement (rather than a monetary unit) is that the unit is independent of price and currency variations with time and among countries. A simple illustration on the utilization pattern of digitalis glycosides, and its development with time, is given in Figure 3.

Data from this system are now used by the public health authorities, by the drug control, registration, and information bodies, by hospital drug committees, and by individual research workers as *one* base—among others—for their decisions and planning. The use of psychotropic drugs, especially sedatives and hypnotics, has been followed with special interest. Steps have been taken to reduce the rapid rise in the overall consumption of such drugs, and to alter prescription patterns inexpedient from a medical point of view. This is done mainly through general warnings and information to the prescribers, or through special restrictions put on the prescribing and marketing of certain drugs, or both. Recent examples are some intensified warnings on the slow elimination and potential hangover risks of a number of hypnotics, and the withdrawal from the market of the methaqualone combinations. The number of adverse drug reactions are also considered in relation to consumption figures.

Another example of the use of drug statistics is illustrated by "the reserpine case." When in autumn 1974 the reports arrived of a possible connection between reserpine use and the development of breast cancer, it was immediately possible to estimate the number of patients on reserpine therapy in the country. On the basis of this estimate, and of advice from the medical consultants, the problems

---

[3] *Terapeutisk Kjemisk Legemiddelregister* (Oslo: Norsk Medisinaldepot).

[4] I. Baksaas Aasen, P. K. M. Lunde, M. Halse, I. K. Halvorsen, T. J. Skobba, and B. Strømnes, *Drug Dose Statistics: List of Defined Doses for Drugs Registered in Norway* (Oslo: Norsk Medisinaldepot, 1975) (in English).

Figure 3

OVERALL SALES OF THE MOST IMPORTANT DIGITALIS GLYCOSIDES IN NORWAY, 1964–73

(as given in dose statistics)

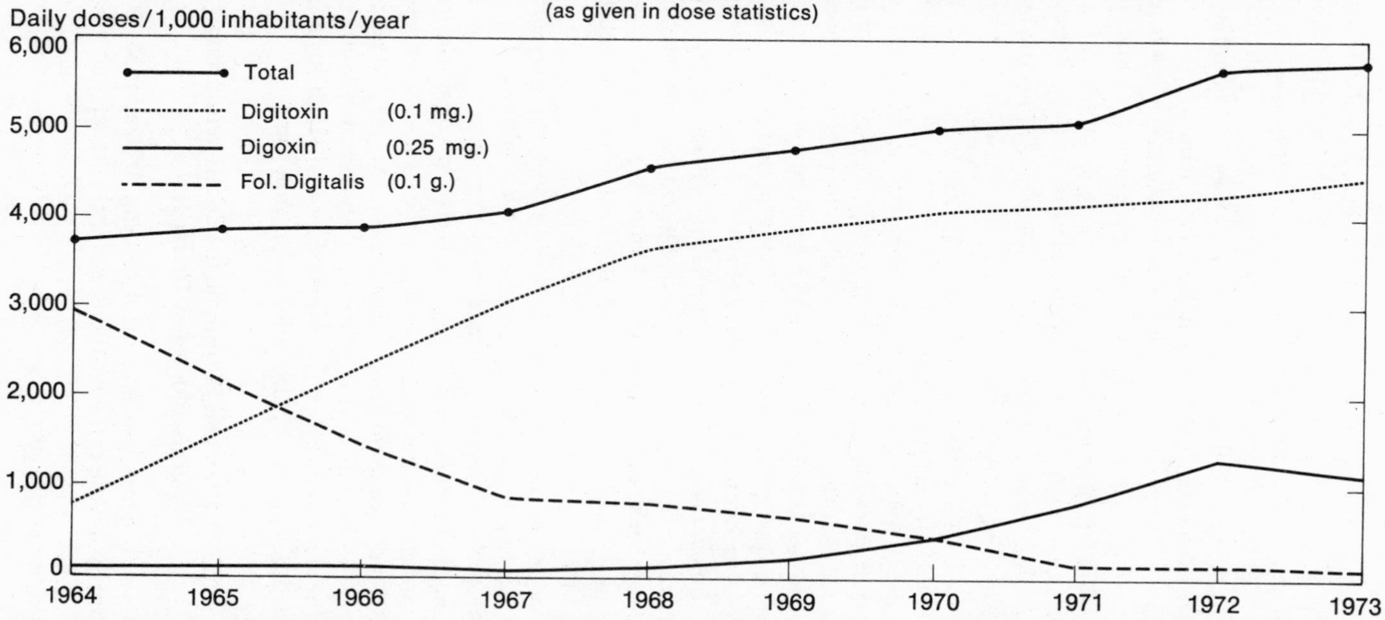

Note: The daily dose defined for each glycoside is indicated in parentheses. The digoxin dose used represents the average one given to a series of 100 digoxin-treated inpatients subject to routine plasma analysis, and found to be within therapeutic range. This dose, as compared to that of digitoxin, may be somewhat underestimated, given the general dosage recommendations for digoxin in patients with unimpaired renal function.

Source: *Report from the Norwegian Drug Monopoly, 1974*

201

associated with changing therapy were considered small. In spite of the inconclusive nature of the association, it was considered correct to send a warning letter to all physicians and pharmacies, advising the prescriber to change, if possible, the regimen in female patients from reserpine to alternative drugs. The sales figures for reserpine then decreased by 60 percent over a period of three months.

As was mentioned above, hospital drug committees are using the drug statistics to review and revise their prescribing. Thus, in one hospital, knowledge of their extensive use of ampicillin (much greater than that in other hospitals) precipitated thorough discussions. As a result, ampicillin prescriptions were halved and phenoxymethyl-penicillin was used instead, resulting in more considered therapy as well as reduced drug costs.

A detailed data processing system especially developed for "narcotic" drugs (strongly addictive analgesics and central stimulants) makes it possible to follow the prescribing pattern down to each single drug, doctor, and patient, and thus enables the necessary precautions to be taken.[5] Through this system, the prescribing of narcotic drugs was greatly reduced. Over a period of one year the sales figures for hydrocone tablets were reduced by approximately 50 percent, ketobemidone by 15 percent, and methadone by 20 percent. Simultaneously, a rise in the sales figures for pentazocine and dextropropoxyphene was registered. A number of excessive prescribers, some of them addicts themselves, have been detected by the system.

The narcotics system could, if it were deemed necessary, be extended to other groups of drugs, for the whole country or for certain regions. At present, without an adequate mechanism by which to define the need for detailed surveillance—and to supervise its consequences through continuous evaluation of the data—the gains would hardly justify the cost of such surveillance. At the present stage further formal and practical strengthening of the postmarketing control of drug utilization in Norway is hampered not so much by a lack of technical facilities as it is by limitations of manpower.

Drug Information and Postgraduate Education in Clinical Pharmacology and Therapeutics

Most efforts at postmarketing control of drug utilization in Norway are traditionally devoted to education, under the belief that education

---

[5] B. Jøldal and I. K. Halvorsen, "Electronic Data Processing in the Control of Legal Consumption of Narcotics in Norway," *Bulletin of Narcotics*, vol. 24 (1972), pp. 55-57.

of and information to the medical professions—and the public—form the basis for rational drug therapy.

In addition to the heavy load of drug product information a physician receives from the pharmaceutical industry, there are several sources of independent drug information in Norway, as well as opportunities for postgraduate education. These are listed in Table 2. It will be apparent from Tables 2 and 3 that these systems are organized in a more or less pragmatic manner.

From the State Health Authorities. Traditionally the information provided by the state health authorities has been at a regulatory, technical, and pharmaceutical level. In addition there has been general public information through the mass media. Upon the reorganization and strengthening of the National Center for Medicinal Products' Control, more efforts have been made to provide information on the use of drugs, especially for patients and the community at large. Instead of individual "patient package inserts," which may provide nonuniform information, the authorities are now working out simple but systematic guideline pamphlets for patients on drug therapy. These pamphlets are generally meant to be given to the patients when they receive the drug for the first time at the pharmacies, or upon request. They are also meant as a help for the pharmacies in responding to patient requests for information. For drugs sold without prescription, this will represent the only systematic information the patients receive. Such pamphlets must therefore consider criteria for the appropriate choice and use of these drugs alone, as well as in

---

Table 2

MAJOR SOURCES OF INDEPENDENT DRUG INFORMATION AND POSTGRADUATE EDUCATION IN CLINICAL PHARMACOLOGY AND THERAPEUTICS IN NORWAY

1. The state health authorities (the Health Directorate, the National Center for Medicinal Products' Control)
2. The Norwegian Drug Monopoly
3. Postgraduate courses (sponsored by the universities, the Norwegian medical and pharmaceutical associations and their subdivisions)
4. Institute of Pharmacotherapy (see Table 3)
5. Swedish/Norwegian collaboration (booklets with systematic and extensive drug therapy reviews, primarily worked out by the Swedish National Board of Health and Welfare)
6. Hospital drug committees,[a] pharmacies, and clinical pharmacology units

---

[a] Now established at about forty Norwegian hospitals.

Table 3
INSTITUTE OF PHARMACOTHERAPY,
ORGANIZATION AND FUNCTION

Organization

Formally an independent university institute, mainly supported by the Norwegian Drug Monopoly, to some extent also by the Norwegian Medical Association and the pharmaceutical industry

Staff (full time)

Head: university professor in pharmacology
Administrative leader: pharmacist
Other employees: two pharmacists, two or three secretaries

Staff (part time)

Drug information groups [a]
    Drugs in infectious diseases
    Drugs in rheumatic diseases
    Drugs in psychiatry (includes hypnotics and analgesics)
    Drugs in neurology
    Drugs in endocrinology/metabolic disorders, hematology and
      oncology
    Drugs in cardiovascular diseases
    Drugs in allergic and autoimmune diseases
    Ad hoc groups

Functions

Written drug information (therapy notes) in most issues of the local medical journal
Pre- and postgraduate courses in drug therapy
Central for requests about drugs and therapy problems
Collaboration with state health authorities and drug industry and coordination of Swedish/Norwegian collaboration (see Table 2)

---

[a] Each group is guided by a senior pharmacologist and involves from eight to twenty physicians, pharmacists, and younger pharmacologists.

relation to alternative drugs within the same group and to other possible drugs. For drugs primarily subject to prescription, more general pamphlets, intended to supplement the information given by the physician, are also considered important. In addition, pamphlets referring to specific situations such as drugs and driving, and accidental poisoning in children, are being worked out, as well as a pamphlet with general rules on drug handling and intake. It is hoped that these efforts will also result in an improved contact between the various links of the therapeutic chain. At the same time, the labeling of the actual preparations will be revised accordingly. Furthermore, to assure more effective and comprehensive information about new drugs, there will be regular distribution of data sheets to the physicians and the pharmacies, giving them sufficient information to allow prescribing. Finally, distribution of regular drug letters to physicians, pharmacists, and the public, as well as systematic drug information through mass media, is being considered.

Through the Drug Monopoly. Because of its unique position, the Norwegian Drug Monopoly can serve as an important source of information for the overall drug sales figures (cost and amount), and for more detailed data suitable for further analysis and research. These data have been available through yearly reports or upon specific request by the authorities and independent research workers, and there is also an annual report on drug retailers. Such data are of value in the planning of educational and informational activities at various levels.

The NMD also provided funds for the establishment and continued support of the Institute of Pharmacotherapy at the University of Oslo. In addition, the NMD also funds distribution of the booklets from the Swedish National Board of Health and Welfare to all Norwegian physicians and pharmacies.

The total yearly cost of keeping these two information channels open was about $180,000 in 1974. By comparison, the estimated cost to the pharmaceutical firms in Norway of keeping their detail men alone was $7 million to $8 million. (As was noted earlier, the total annual drug bill as calculated from the pharmacies' sales figures is about $120 million.)

Postgraduate Teaching and Training. About 100 different general postgraduate courses are sponsored by the medical faculties at the universities in Oslo, Bergen, and Tromsø each year. In 1973, ten of those were concerned mainly with drug therapy, and drug therapy was an important ingredient in another fifteen courses. In addition, a great number of regional and local courses were arranged, taught by university teachers and others; most of these included drug therapy. Many of the courses were aimed at specialists as well as at general practioners.

All general practitioners, practicing specialists, and clinicians are expected to attend at least one course for three to six days every year, but there is no systematic planning of the postgraduate courses in clinical pharmacology and therapeutics, and the physicians (as well as pharmacists and others) participate on a voluntary base. In some of the courses the participants are subject to a small examination to obtain the course certification, but, unfortunately, most courses are rather passive. Norway is still lacking a complete and optimal apparatus for postgraduate teaching in general, and for drug therapy in particular. The work by the course organizers, including the central course committees at the universities and in the medical association is, however, of tremendous value. Drug firms are increasing their efforts, often in collaboration with university teachers, to improve the quality and pertinence of their offerings.

In the education of clinical pharmacologists, Norway's three universities have approved a common educational program.[6] The M.D. candidates are subject to a postgraduate program of six years, consisting of two years of pharmacology, two years of clinical pharmacology, and two years of clinical medicine (such as internal medicine, pediatrics, or psychiatry). In the developmental phase, and because clinical pharmacology is not formally accepted as an established specialty, candidates pursue pharmacology or clinical medicine. One unit of clinical pharmacology has been at work since 1972 at Ullevaal Hospital (at the University of Oslo), and another unit is under development at the University of Tromsø. A unit has been established at the University of Bergen, and another at the Rikshospitalet (at the University of Oslo). The major limitation has been a lack of qualified personnel. According to agreements entered into by three of the four universities, the clinical pharmacologist in Norway is not assumed to have direct patient care responsibility, and much weight is put on his pharmacological training. On the other hand, the need for educating chemical or analytical pharmacologists, that is, nonmedical academics, is much stressed. The interest among chemists, biochemists, and pharmacists is considerable. The wide tasks in clinical pharmacology obviously call for collaboration among qualified personnel in different categories.[7]

Through the Institute of Pharmacotherapy. This institute, established in 1964, is formally an entity within the University of Oslo, and functions as a general information center in drug therapy (see Table 3). It is now located within the Institute of Pharmacology. The head of the institute, Professor Knut Naess, M.D., is a permanent professor in pharmacology, but the rest of the staff is provided through economic support from the NMD, as was mentioned above. Until 1971 the institute's information output, regularly published as "therapy notes" in Tidsskrift for Den norske laegeforening (Journal of the Norwegian Medical Association), was mainly the work of the

---

[6] *Joint Committee on Clinical Pharmacology: Its Scope and Organization in Norway* (Oslo/Bergen/Tromsø: Universities of Oslo, Bergen, and Tromsø, 1971) (in Norwegian).

[7] World Health Organization, *Clinical Pharmacology: Scope, Organization, Training,* Technical Report Series, no. 446 (1970).

head of the institute and a number of selected senior and younger clinicians acting as consultants. In 1972 the institute was reorganized with the primary responsibility for drug information given over to seven or more drug therapy groups (see Table 3). An open invitation to participate in the informational work was extended to clinicians with special interests in pharmacotherapy through the medical journal. The final selection of the members of the various therapy groups was carried out by a committee of pharmacologists and pharmacists established at the Institute of Pharmacotherapy and the Institute of Pharmacology, in collaboration with the clinical departments. Each group has been supplemented by general practitioners. The therapy groups meet regularly to decide which subjects within their fields deserve attention; they also choose those inside or outside the group who will cover the topics. Literature documenting drug use is obtained through the institute. Depending upon the subject, discussion meetings are sometimes held in the presence of twenty to thirty pharmacologists, pharmacists, and physicians from various clinics throughout the country. After thorough review by the therapy groups, the result appears as "therapy notes"—that is, four to eight pages in most issues of the journal. These notes are written primarily for general practitioners and busy clinicians. The subjects are therefore presented in digest form, and—if possible—guidelines and recommendations are given. The journal strives for a combination of systematic short reviews and brief notes about actual therapy problems. A group of three senior pharmacologists forms the editorial board, which decides—together with the editor of the journal—what is to be published and when. In collaboration with the institute and the therapy groups this board also plans future work.

This group organization brings fundamental knowledge about pharmacology and drug therapy directly to a considerable number of physicians and others, and, above all, improves the contact among pharmacists, pharmacologists, and clinicians. It also represents a valuable educational opportunity for younger pharmacologists, and increases the potential for pre- and postgraduate teaching in clinical pharmacology and therapeutics. The burden of this teaching now tends to exhaust the limited number of clinical pharmacologists. The know-how created around the Institute of Pharmacotherapy is also of importance for the state health authorities and others who need comments on drug therapy problems from a broad forum.

Scandinavian Collaboration on Drug Information. Since 1970 the Swedish National Board of Health and Welfare (Socialstyrelsen) has taken the initiative in producing a series of information booklets on drug therapy, covering the main drug groups and fields of therapy. The booklets are published in pairs, with a main volume, containing an extensive review of clinical pharmacological background material, and a summary volume, with supplementary pharmaceutical data. They are distributed free of cost to all Norwegian physicians and pharmacies as well as to students of medicine and pharmacy. The manuscripts for the books, as prepared by two or three selected authors (clinicians, pharmacologists, pharmacists), are sent to a dozen referees in Sweden and Norway before publication. In Norway their work is coordinated through an independent committee with members from a variety of institutions (the state health authorities, the universities, the Drug Monopoly, the Medical Association, some hospitals) and representatives from the national and foreign pharmaceutical industry. The main volume is the same in the two countries, but the summary volume, including some recommendations, is somewhat different, as a result of variations in the drug preparations available and differences in therapeutic traditions between Sweden and Norway. Before the Norwegian summary is worked out in its final form (usually by one or two of the Norwegian referees), a broad discussion meeting is arranged. To this meeting additional clinicians, pharmacologists, and pharmacists are invited, as well as representatives from the drug manufacturers involved. Controversial points are elucidated and, if of sufficient significance, eventually discussed in the final version of the summary. The impact of the drug industry in this forum has been no greater than the validity of their arguments. We have also found it of value that so many groups concerned with improving the quality of drug therapy are brought together. The discussions show where we have common interests, but also indicate where the interests of drug firms may differ from those of the "therapeutic professions" and society.

Hospital Drug Committees. During the past decade an increasing number of clinicians have called for assistance and advice on choosing among registered alternative drugs and preparations in their routine prescribing. Along the same lines as in Sweden, drug committees are now established at about forty Norwegian hospitals. Some of these committees, especially those organized at university hospitals, have been working on a rather fundamental level reconsidering the basic pharmacological, pharmaceutical, and clinical documentation behind the actual drug products. Drug manufacturers and a number of other sources are used to obtain this documentation. Where possible, the choices made and the recommendations given are based primarily upon accepted clinical pharmacological criteria. If such criteria alone are insufficient, the local therapy tradition and (to some extent) price differences become important guidelines. In some committees, products developed by the national drug industry may be preferred, if found equivalent to products developed abroad. The preference may sometimes be on grounds of price, but generally it is due to the fact that the Norwegian manufacturers' part of the national drug market has been steadily decreasing during recent years.

The work done by the hospital drug committees has primarily a local impact, one important aspect of which is the generally increased drug therapy "conscience" among the staff at each hospital. The future may bring up a need for additional regional collaboration, not least to avoid duplication of much of the time-consuming review and evaluation work. Close contact between the committee and the hospital staff is imperative, and centralized decisions may reduce much of the value of the review and evaluation, which is primarily of an informative, rather than restrictive, character. On the other hand, the drug committees as a whole may offer positive feedback to the central drug control authorities as an apparatus for increased contact.

The drug committees illustrate the potential for collaboration among the different professors in the field of drug therapy. Most committees include physicians, nurses, pharmacists, and (if available) pharmacologists. The work of the hospital pharmacist, who is primarily responsible for the technical and administrative handling of drugs in Norwegian hospitals, has a much firmer base if it is linked to the drug committee. It should be stressed, however, that the recommendations from the committee are suggestions to the physician, not orders.

Comments and Conclusions

The basic aims of drug control, information, and therapy are: (1) to allow drugs to occupy an appropriate place in medical treatment and patient care, taking into consideration the existing alternatives—including the alternative of no treatment at all, and (2) to ensure—when drug treatment is preferred—a proper choice between, as well as an optimal handling and utilization of, the available products at all levels of the therapeutic chain.

The basic problems arising from these simple statements are, however, extremely complex and heterogeneous. From a global perspective, the level of sophistication in the developed countries, as represented by the contributions to this publication, may appear irrelevant to the needs of the less developed countries. In the developed countries, one major problem is how to study physicians' prescribing and patients' drug consumption habits, as influenced by the efforts of drug manufacturers, independent information sources, and control bodies. In the less developed countries, the major problem may still be a desperate lack of proper facilities, including professional manpower at most levels, money, and even the most important drugs. From this point of view, the question is, How we can assist and give advice to others (if desired), on the basis of our new experiences.

Before being tempted to impose or transplant one set of views or systems to others, however, we should perhaps clarify where we ourselves stand. To what extent are our criteria for the evaluation of drugs generally valid? How much is fact and how much is still claim? Is it possible to discriminate between scientific criteria and general attitude based upon moralistic and political background? To put it simply, What is right and what is wrong? To find the truth in medicine is difficult—so also with regard to drug therapy.

It is regularly asserted, by the public as well as by members of the medical professions, that an increasing "overconsumption" of drugs and therapeutic substances occurs in our societies, especially of sedatives, analgesics, hypnotics, vitamins, and antimicrobial agents. If this is correct, it would be an important task for state health authorities to counteract the overconsumption by limiting the number and use of these drugs. The lack of precise criteria to undertake general precautions against overconsumption makes these matters difficult to handle, however. First, adequate cost-benefit analyses have not been carried out. Second, our attitude on drug treatment of less defined symptoms and diseases may also depend on nonmedical factors such as those mentioned above.

In our enthusiasm to solve such problems we should never forget that the remedies themselves are not necessarily so bad as our mode of using them. Moreover, frontal attacks on certain drugs or groups of drugs may leave the public with the false impression that all drugs are dangerous and should therefore be avoided. Positive elements in drug information, especially information provided to the general public, may be as important as warnings.

We believe it is correct to strengthen the drug control and information bodies to make them able to function in the wide variety of tasks demanded by society. In a small society, only limited resources are available. These limitations may, however, be an advantage in flexibility and reduced distance between the decision bodies and "the consumer." On the other hand, extensive programs for the continuous evaluation of all kinds of drug therapy problems are—and will presumably continue to be—beyond reach.

10

NEW ZEALAND

William M. Wardell and A. W. S. Thompson

The social security medical program in New Zealand was forced through by a Labour government in the face of determined, persistent, and often bitter opposition by the medical profession. Its legislative basis is the Social Security Act of 1938. In that year a government White Paper proposed, among other things, the establishment of a universal general practitioner service to provide free medical care and free medicines to all members of the community. Opposition by the medical profession led to compromise and delay. The General Medical Services Scheme, which eventually came into being in 1941, is a subsidized fee-for-service system that permits the doctor to make a reasonable extra charge to any patient, over and above the government subsidy, should the doctor consider the charge justifiable. In line with a time-honored phrase, it preserves the doctor's right to charge a fee "commensurate with the service."

History of the Pharmaceutical Benefits Program

The Pharmaceutical Benefits Scheme, inaugurated in May 1941, is another part of New Zealand's medical care program. It has never been entirely free in the sense that a doctor could prescribe any or every medicament as a full charge on public funds. In over thirty years, however, it has proved itself to be a flexible system which, on the whole, has been accepted as satisfactory by the public and the medical profession. The only serious criticisms ever leveled at it have been that it "wastes" drugs and public money and is increasingly costly to the taxpayer.

The basic principles of the drug program have been altered little over the years, although its method and scope have developed considerably. Its objectives, which have never been spelled out officially, have also undergone certain changes with the passage of time.

The first *Drug Tariff*, a publication listing all drugs payable through public funds and effective May 5, 1941, consisted of two printed pages, and authorized the use of official (generic) drugs only. The first unofficial (brand-name) drugs—a total of ten—were included the following year. The schedule of approved items, listed by official name, in the current *Drug Tariff* runs to forty-four pages.

The primary intention of government at the outset was simply to keep expenditure within bounds by limiting the scope of the drug program. This was exemplified by the decision not to include items such as bandages and dressings, a policy that has been adhered to ever since. Since 1955, however, various controls originally aimed at limiting costs have been increasingly used in a manner intended to promote safety in prescription and medical treatment. Early in 1956 the *Lancet* published a lead article, entitled "Restriction of Antibiotics?," which discussed the New Zealand government decision that "from February 1, New Zealand doctors shall be able to get erythromycin only through hospitals and only for the treatment of diseases which do not respond to other remedies." [1] The writer of the article indicated that the purpose of this restriction was to keep erythromycin in reserve, since it would often work where other antibiotics had failed. While conceding that this was "a course of action which most doctors will acknowledge to be sound scientifically, and necessary for the good of patients," he pointed out that it might be regarded "as an interference, by a government, with the doctor's freedom to treat his patients in whatever way he chooses."

At the time, some New Zealand doctors took a similar view, but fears of a "therapeutic dictatorship" did not last long. Today, even when doctors resent certain restrictions, most are prepared to admit that they are of value in carrying out the objectives of the program. These objectives are to provide doctors with a comprehensive range of effective therapeutic drugs, free-of-charge to the patient, under controls aimed at (1) keeping expenditure to an acceptable level and (2) ensuring so far as possible that drugs are used with due regard for safety.

The program has been examined critically on several occasions, one being an "efficiency and economy review" by the State Services Efficiency Review Committee, which reported to the government in December 1974. The committee found that, in general, "the Pharmaceutical Services are well conducted and administered . . . . within the

---

[1] "Restriction of Antibiotics?" *Lancet*, vol. 1 (1956), p. 193.

limits of the resources at present available." The report commented that the Department of Health "provides a low cost administrative and technical service which is materially assisted by the voluntary contributions of several members of the medical profession. The New Zealand system is characterized by this voluntary assistance together with reliance on overseas countries for drug evaluation."

Postgraduate Education in Clinical Pharmacology and Therapeutics

Within the Universities. The first formal postgraduate course of training in clinical pharmacology was established in 1970 when the Department of Pharmacology at the University of Otago Medical School at Dunedin started to offer a one-year diploma course in clinical pharmacology. The first candidate graduated in 1972.

The Department of Health. In 1957 the Department of Health instituted, with considerable trepidation, a system of issuing information leaflets called *Prescribers' Notes* to doctors. These were at first regarded with suspicion and even hostility by some senior members of the Medical Association, who saw them as a further intrusion of bureaucracy into private practice; others took the view that the Department of Health was indulging in an academic activity which should properly be a function of the Medical School. Gradually, however, the system won acceptance. In 1973 a survey carried out by the visiting practitioners, who explain national drug policy to doctors, showed that 74 percent of general practitioners claimed to read every issue and that 88 percent rated them as good to excellent.

Most doctors have come to reply upon the notes as an important aid in the struggle to keep their knowledge of drugs up to date. The notes are distributed at the rate of about twenty a year, and are now supplied to dentists as well as to doctors—and, where relevant, to pharmacists. They are of three kinds:

Notes on prescription costs. These include cost comparisons of different drugs within given categories, as well as price lists for selected groups of drugs. This information is surprisingly well received by doctors, who constantly urge the department to supply more.

Therapeutic notes. Short, practical articles provide information on drug treatment, aimed particularly at the general practitioner. The majority of the articles are specially written by local experts, while others are based on articles published in the U.S. *Medical Letter*, the British *Prescribers Journal*, or other periodicals.

Clinical services letters. These contain information on changes in the regulations by which drugs are controlled and on various aspects of drug usage. Warnings of sudden increases in the cost of pharmaceutical benefits have been included from time to time, usually towards the end of a financial year when the Department of Health is faced with the necessity of applying to the government for extra funds on a supplementary estimate. These warnings appear to have had some effect in the short-term in stimulating cost consciousness among doctors; the department believes they produce a temporary slow-up in expenditure, but this impression has not been assessed.

In addition to these publications, the Department of Health facilitates the distribution of relevant information from other sources. Warnings and advice about adverse drug reactions from the Health Department's Committee on Adverse Drug Reactions are printed and circulated in the same format as *Prescribers' Notes,* as is the *Annual Report* of the National Poisons Information Centre. This report also includes warnings, for example, about untoward reactions to Lomotil (diphenoxylate) in children and about the gravity of the prognosis for patients poisoned by the herbicide paraquat.

The visiting practitioners also play a limited educational role in regard to drugs. These officers are in a position to explain to doctors why certain drugs have not been made available under the program or have been subjected to various restrictions. The Department of Health also supplies copies of the British *National Formulary* to doctors and dentists. This publication is a useful compact handbook of practical therapeutics.

Independent Sources of Drug Information. A remarkable development that has taken place in New Zealand (and Australia) over the past decade is the establishment of an independent system of information on therapeutic drugs by a privately owned company not affiliated with any pharmaceutical manufacturer or association. Known as the Australasian Drug Information Services Pty. Ltd., the company began this activity in 1964 with the publication of a catalog of prescription drugs and dose regimens. Since then its scope has expanded vastly until it has evolved into a system of drug information services that is an instrument of considerable importance in the postgraduate education of physicians in clinical pharmacology and therapeutics. The heart of this system consists of two monthly journals, *New Ethicals and Medical Progress* and *Patient Management,* along with a *Catalogue of Drugs* issued twice yearly. These are controlled-circulation periodicals which carry advertising. They are distributed free-of-charge to almost 4,000 medical practitioners throughout New Zealand (and more than 17,000 in Australia). In New Zealand, they are also sent to all sixth-year (final-year) medical students and hospital head pharmacists. Editorial content is prepared by a small qualified editorial staff under the editorship of Mr. G. S. Avery. There is a large panel of honorary specialist consultants from all fields of medicine, predominantly in Australia and New Zealand, but also, increasingly, from abroad.

New Ethicals and Medical Progress contains several sections. First, there is prescription information on new products, with separate independent review articles (often exhaustive in content) discussing the clinical pharmacology and therapeutics of selected items. Second is a section of wide-ranging review articles on general areas of clinical pharmacology and therapeutics. These are usually written by outside consultants, and often take the form of a series of articles on a particular field, beginning with physiology and pharmacology and subsequently dealing with clinical pharmacology and therapeutics. Third are interpretive abstracts of the literature, grouped under nearly twenty topic headings ranging from clinical pharmacology and all the medical subspecialties to pathology, radiology, and surgery. The high quality and usefulness of this periodical have led to further success: the articles and abstracts in it are updated and expanded to form the substance of a new journal, *Drugs*, published in Europe.

Patient Management consists largely of review articles dealing with various aspects of patient care and medical treatment, abstracts from the literature, a section on diagnostic trends, and another on new items of medical equipment.

Further use is now being made of the resources of this private company for other purposes, including the provision of teaching and bibliographic services to the medical community.

Controls over Access of Drugs to the Market

Until 1962, when the thalidomide disaster stimulated action, New Zealand had no official controls over the admission of any drug to the market. The largely ineffective controls hastily introduced by the Department of Health at that time were replaced in 1970 by more stringent measures, and administration of these was transferred to the department's Division of Clinical Services, which is responsible for running the Pharmaceutical Benefits Scheme, in addition to the General Practitioner Services.

Since 1970, the sale, distribution, and advertising of new drugs has been prohibited without the specific consent of the minister of health. The minister is advised by the Drug Assessment Advisory Committee, which is the New Zealand equivalent of regulatory bodies in other countries. Established under the Food and Drug Act of 1969, this committee concerns itself with the quality, safety, and efficacy of new drugs. Its eight members are selected from the following disciplines: administration, academic medicine, general medicine, clinical pharmacology, pharmacology, pathology, pharmacy, and chemistry. If a member resigns, a successor from the same discipline is sought; in practice, the retiring member suggests a replacement, who is usually accepted by the department and other concerned organizations. (The Medical Association and the Pharmaceutical Society are invited to nominate members, but all appointments to the committee are made by the minister of health.) Committee members serve as individuals, not as representatives of particular interests or organizations, and their recommendations are purely advisory and have no status in law. The Department of Health accepts the ultimate responsibility for any action recommended.

New Zealand is a small country with limited resources of medical expertise, and its policy is to take due note of expert opinion in other countries where regulatory agencies of standing and reliability have been established. Drugs that have been approved in Great Britain, the United States, or Australia do not have great difficulty in being accepted for distribution and marketing in New Zealand. Indeed, such drugs may be approved by the staff of the Department of Health without reference to the committee. When doubts arise, or a drug has not been approved by the regulatory authority in one of the above countries, the new drug application is referred to the committee.

The pattern of drug admissions to the New Zealand market is generally similar to that in Great Britain. As will be seen, however, drug use is determined more by the *Drug Tariff* than by the simple fact of marketing.

The Investigational Use of New Drugs. The Food and Drug Act of 1969 placed the clinical investigation of new drugs under the jurisdiction of the director-general of health, assisted by the Medical Research Council. Investigations on new drugs may be conducted only by persons with the appropriate qualifications and facilities, as assessed and recommended to the director-general of health by the Standing Committee on Therapeutic Trials of the Medical Research Council. At present, therefore, controls are concerned with the credentials of the person investigating a drug, rather than with the drug itself and the nature of the investigation. Further controls over the drug and the investigation are to be introduced shortly.

Controls over Drug Use

The main controls over drug use stem from third-party (government) payment for drugs through a formulary system known as the *Drug Tariff*. The *Drug Tariff* lists under official (generic) titles all drugs that may be prescribed at the cost of public funds and sets out the conditions under which they may be ordered. The *Drug Tariff* is issued as a ministerial direction under the authority of the Social Security Act, and not as a regulation, a fact that gives it considerable flexibility. Amendments to the *Drug Tariff* are issued three times a year. The principal feature of the tariff is a schedule that lists all the available drugs in alphabetical order and indicates the restrictions (if any) that govern their being supplied free of charge. For the convenience of prescribers, the Department of Health also issues a pocket-sized, comprehensive *Alphabetical List of Drugs*, which includes brand names as well as official titles, but in practice most doctors rely upon the *Catalogue of Drugs* issued twice yearly by the Australasian Drug Information Services.

The *Drug Tariff* has an important influence on drug use in New Zealand. As is explained below, while most drugs may be prescribed by any doctor and dispensed by a retail pharmacist, some are subject to various restrictions in their use. These restrictions are aimed at encouraging general practitioners to make their first choices from the longer-established drugs, and to use certain new drugs or drugs with unusual hazards only under specialist supervision or advice. The system also reduces promotional pressures on the general practitioner to use these restricted items, because the drug firms do not find it profitable to promote them while they are subject to restrictions.

There is no legal bar to the prescription of therapeutic drugs that have not been included in the *Drug Tariff*, but if they are prescribed the full retail cost must be borne by the patient. Since the tariff is revised three times a year, and since the drug companies almost invariably seek to have new drugs included as soon as they become available on the market, it is kept reasonably up-to-date. Little use is made of drugs not listed in it. Only 2,820 applications from doctors for free supplies of nontariff items were made in 1974, which comes to 1.4 per private practitioner in active practice. No figures are available to show the extent of prescription outside the tariff, where the patient must meet the full cost, but it is believed to be minimal. A few doctors make a practice of ordering nontariff items from time to time in the belief that certain patients do better on treatment for which they have to pay.

The process whereby drugs are admitted to the tariff is separate and distinct from the controls on marketing. The committee responsible for admitting drugs is the Pharmacology and Therapeutics Advisory Committee. It was set up in 1941. The chairman, who does not exercise a vote, is the director of clinical services. Members are independent persons in active practice, serving in an honorary capacity. At present they consist of two consultant physicians, a surgeon, a professor of pediatrics, a clinical pharmacologist, and a general practitioner, along with two other physicians who are prepared to act as stand-in members as necessary. At first, members were nominated by the Medical Association and appointed by the minister of health under the Social Security Act of 1938. The practice now is for the committee itself to recommend replacements for members as they retire. Before being referred to the minister of health for approval, the recommendations must be endorsed by the Medical Services Advisory Committee, which is the central advisory committee on health benefits whose members are appointed for a limited term on the advice of the Medical Association.

The Pharmacology and Therapeutics Advisory Committee functions in the manner of a discussion group, and unanimity of opinion is reached before positive action is taken on any issue of importance. If only one member is displeased with any proposal, the matter is dropped or deferred. The committee meets three times a year to consider additions and amendments to the *Drug Tariff*.

In considering new candidates for the *Drug Tariff*, the factors taken into account (in order of importance) are "therapeutic value," safety and side effects, and cost. The question of therapeutic value deals with the way the apparent virtues of the new drug compare with those of other similar items already in the tariff or previously rejected by the committee. This is a matter of opinion and judgment which must take into account all recent relevant decisions of the committee. Occasionally a ruling on a new submission necessitates reconsideration of an action taken previously.

Information on the drugs to be considered is distributed to committee members about two weeks before each meeting. A complete set of all information available on each drug is sent to three members selected according to their interests, while summaries are supplied to the other three. At the meeting the members who have made a special study of a drug speak first, and a general discussion follows. In a doubtful case, further advice may be sought from specialists, particularly when the relevant specialties are not represented on the committee.

In addition to deciding whether a drug is admissible to the tariff, the committee also makes decisions on whether any further controls or conditions should be imposed on the way in which a drug must be used if it is to qualify.

Drugs not included in the tariff may still be obtained at the cost of public funds if the doctor applies for a special supply for a particular patient, giving brief clinical details and stating that in his opinion it would be unreasonable for the patient himself to be asked to pay for the drug. These applications are sent directly to the Division of Clinical Services, accompanied by a prescription for endorsement. Such free issues of drugs are regarded as supplementary benefits under the Social Security Act, and no reasonable application is refused.

Nearly all applications for the inclusion of new drugs on the tariff come from the pharmaceutical industry. The policy of the Department of Health is that New Zealand cannot afford to allow the *Drug Tariff* to lag behind medical progress. For the past three years the numbers of applications received and accepted are set out in Table 1.

Table 1
NEW DRUG APPLICATIONS, 1972–75

Year	Received	Accepted
1972–73	50	25
1973–74	56	24
1974–75	43	12
Total	149	61

Of about 3,000 brand-name ethical drugs currently on the market in New Zealand, some 2,700 are in the *Drug Tariff*. (This figure does not include galenicals.)

Influence on Price. Since the Department of Health is the monopoly purchaser of most drugs used in the country and plays a part in determining whether and how a drug will be used, it is in a powerful negotiating position when it comes to determining the price to be paid. Continuous checks are made on the prices at which drugs are sold abroad, and on the prices of other drugs in the same therapeutic class.

Nearly all items in the *Drug Tariff* are accepted as a full charge on public funds. The price paid by the department is based on the cost of the cheapest reliable brand, and generally the other brands fall into line. Any more costly brand is subject to a partial charge to the patient. When a manufacturer's price for a new drug is higher than the prices for other items in a therapeutic category and when in the opinion of the Pharmacology and Therapeutics Advisory Committee a therapeutically equivalent drug is already available in the list, the item may be accepted only as a partial charge drug. In that case, the patient has to pay the difference directly to the pharmacist.

The Department of Health maintains that whenever a drug is subject to a partial charge, an equivalent preparation is available in the free list or else some alternative form of treatment is available that is not subject to a charge (an example would be the use of diet as an alternative to an antiobesity agent). The department concedes that some drugs carrying a partial charge may have unique advantages, but takes the view that these are not such as to justify the extra cost to public funds.

These attitudes have not gone unchallenged, with the challenges coming mainly from drug firms and in some instances from doctors. An example is the controversy sparked off when the department put a partial charge on capsules of tetracycline with nystatin, on the ground that the use of antifungal agents with tetracyclines was not routinely necessary, and that when they were considered desirable, the drugs could be prescribed separately. On the whole, however, the committee's recommendations have seldom been seriously disputed. In 1971 the department supplied doctors with a schedule of free alternatives to each of 112 brand-name drugs subject to partial charges. Only one item—an antiobesity agent—was seriously challenged. It was later transferred to the free list.

It will be seen that absolute and relative efficacy, safety, and price are all explicit considerations in the cost-benefit argument. The subtleties of these issues have not become matters of great concern to the academic or practicing medical community in New Zealand. They have always, however, been of paramount importance in the negotiations between the pharmaceutical industry and the Department of Health.

International comparisons have shown that the prices paid for drugs by the New Zealand Department of Health are among the lowest in the world.[2] Considering the country's relative isolation and the small size of its market, the system of price negotiation that has been developed over the years appears to have attained a considerable level of efficiency. New Zealand's bill for pharmaceutical benefits in 1973–74 amounted to $NZ15.08 per head of population, and 0.53 percent of the gross national product. It represented 11.32 percent of total government expenditure on health, a little higher than in the National Health Service in Britain, where it was 10.1 percent in 1969.[3]

Other Measures of Control. When pharmaceutical benefits were first introduced, various measures were adopted in an effort to control the cost of the program. It was soon realized, however, that some of these measures are capable of influencing drug use according to the safety of the drugs, and this is now regarded as the most weighty consideration involved in drug control. Examples of drugs controlled primarily because of questions of safety rather than questions of cost are the amphetamines, tuberculostatics, cytotoxics, clindamycin, the cephalosporins, oral and parenteral neomycin, and gentamycin.

The control measures fall into six categories.

(1) *Restrictions on the period of supply.* Much thought and trial have gone into seeking the optimal way to regulate the period of supply (and, to a lesser extent, the quantity) of drugs ordered in a single prescription. Over the last three decades a dozen different variations have been tried. Under the present method, an ordinary prescription is designed to allow short-course treatment of an acute illness, this being seven days with one refill. For prescription of drug amounts for one month or more, the number of months must be handwritten on the prescription form, using the exact words, "extended supply one (or two or three) month(s)." This creates a distinct and intentional gap between short and extended courses of treatment. Recently this restriction has been relaxed to permit prescription of quantities for more than seven days and less than one month, provided the form is endorsed with the words "extended supply," and the total quantity to be issued is stated.

---

[2] E. M. Jacoby, Jr., and D. L. Hefner, "Domestic and Foreign Prescription Drug Prices," *Social Security Bulletin,* May 1971.

[3] Kings Fund Hospital Centre, *Do We Spend Enough on Health Care?* (London, 1971). Percentages of GNP spent on health services in 1969 were as follows: Canada 7.3 percent, United States 6.8 percent, Sweden 6.7 percent, France 5.7 percent, New Zealand 5.7 percent, U.K. 4.8 percent (Office of Health Economics, *Information Sheet,* no. 22 [May 1973]).

These restrictions are a source of some irritation to prescribers, but there is good evidence that they have kept prescribing costs down. In 1962–63, the Department of Health conducted the now-celebrated and probably unique South Island experiment. For nine months, all period-of-supply and quantity restrictions were abolished in the South Island of New Zealand, and the prescribing costs per capita were compared with those in the North Island (which contains three-quarters of the country's population). A circular letter announcing the experiment to all doctors said, "If all went well for twelve months, consideration would be given to rescinding the period-of-supply restrictions altogether." Doctors were enjoined to order no more than the patient needed, "with due regard to economy and the avoidance of waste." In the North Island, the restrictions continued to apply as before.

> The result was remarkable. In the 36 months up to the commencement of the experiment, the cost of drugs per head of population in the South Island averaged only 90% of the cost in the North Island and this relationship had shown no tendency to alter. In the nine months of the experiment it went up to 95.6%. When the experiment was stopped the situation returned to normal. The experiment cost about a quarter of a million dollars. This was despite the fact that all the doctors concerned knew how important it was that the experiment should succeed and every doctor we spoke to maintained that his prescribing pattern had not changed.[4]

The reason the experiment failed is probably simple enough: the period-of-supply restrictions create an artificial pattern of quantities ordered, which tend to be rounded to higher figures if the restrictions are lifted. Seven days' supply of a tablet taken three times a day is 21 tablets; a month's supply is 90 tablets; three months' supply is 270. Most doctors when freed from restrictions would order 30, 100, or 300, respectively, or even more.[5] This experiment is one of the few empirical demonstrations of the size of the effect of supply restrictions on drug utilization.

(2) *Restriction of outlets to other than retail pharmacies.* The supply of certain drugs is restricted to public hospital pharmacies.

---

[4] A. W. S. Thompson, "Controlling the Costs of Community Medical Care," *The Organization and Evaluation of Medical Care* (Dunedin, New Zealand: University of Otago, 1970).

[5] During the course of the experiment, a patient reported for admission to a public hospital in the South Island with two bottles, each containing 1,000 Librium capsules.

The restriction was originally adopted to save money, inasmuch as hospital boards purchase drugs at contract prices and dispense them at cost. It was soon found that drugs restricted in this way were always modestly prescribed, for two reasons. First, it is less convenient for the patient to take the prescription to a public hospital than to the nearest pharmacist, and doctors are reluctant to put their patients to inconvenience unless there is good reason for doing so. Second, pharmaceutical firms seldom make great efforts to promote these drugs. The result is that this method of supply has become a powerful way of ensuring that a drug is used only in moderation. Examples of drugs whose use increased considerably when transferred from the hospital board category to retail pharmacy are doxycycline, ampicillin, lincomycin, and co-trimoxazole.

This has obvious implications for safety in the case of new drugs. During the period of limited use, the drug can be reassessed and its position evaluated, leaving the Pharmacology and Therapeutics Advisory Committee free to justify making certain drugs available earlier than might otherwise be desirable. Drugs placed in the restricted category long before they would otherwise have been added to the tariff include tamoxifen, pimozide, clindamycin, some of the newer anticonvulsants, the cephalosporins, ketoprofen, and pentazocine. (These examples are in fact still restricted to hospital dispensaries, and some also require specialist recommendation.) With few exceptions, the question of safety is the primary, and usually the sole, reason why drugs are now placed in this restricted category.

(3) *Recommendation by specialist.* This is a tighter category than restriction to hospital board dispensaries. Drugs in this category can be prescribed only by—or on the recommendation of—a specialist. A general practitioner may order such a drug if he endorses the prescription with the words "Recommended by (name of a recognized specialist)." This requirement is, however, administered with a light hand. A general practitioner is not obliged to refer his patient formally to a specialist: it is sufficient if he consults him by telephone, and most New Zealand specialists are willing to provide their services gratis in this way. The approval of the specialist is, however, accepted for this purpose only for drugs related to his own specialties.

There are now two forms of this restriction depending on where the prescription may be dispensed: "Retail Pharmacy (Specialist)" and "Hospital Board (Specialist)"—that is, a dispensary administered by a public hospital board.

This form of control depends on the existence of a system of specialist registration. It specifically affects general practitioners and is resented by many of them on this account alone. In fact, it is the single most common cause for complaint disclosed during interviews with visiting practitioners inasmuch as the general practitioners believe it treats them as second-class doctors. The department replies that the important difference between specialists and general practitioners is that the specialists *must* find the time to keep themselves up-to-date in their specialties, while most general practitioners will readily admit that they have little or no time for regular study. The department also points out that this system permits the new drugs in question to be made available at a much earlier stage in the monitoring process than would otherwise be possible.

These two forms of control—restriction to hospital dispensaries and the required recommendation of specialists—have several effects believed to be desirable. New and expensive drugs tend to be used sparingly and presumably for indications more specific than if their use were unrestricted. Also, drugs that are dangerous (for example, antimitotic agents) or for which widespread use would impair efficacy (for example, rifampin and clindamycin) may be used with greater safety or benefit. The safety function is emphasized by the fact that it is not only new drugs that are restricted in this fashion. Recently, chloramphenicol was placed in the specialist-only category, a move that represents an obvious solution to the perennial problems experienced with drugs of this type. As yet, however, the effects of this restriction on the quantity and quality of chloramphenicol prescription are unknown. In addition, the specialist is placed in the role of educator to the general practitioner in the use of new drugs at the crucial time when patterns of use are being established. There is also some evidence that the beneficial effects of this process continue for long after new drugs have been de-restricted. For example, when first introduced, the corticosteroids were closely controlled. Prescriptions were scrutinized and had to be endorsed by local ad hoc specialist committees, and one large hospital board appointed a senior consultant physician specifically for this purpose. It was feared that when these restrictions were lifted, the drugs would be used unwisely and to excess, and there were sharp differences of opinion among the experts consulted by the department as to whether or how the controls should be relaxed. In fact, however, no evidence of widespread misuse has ever come to notice, and the advisory committee, which watched the situation with some anxiety for a considerable time after the restrictions were lifted, attributes this to the caution engendered among doctors by the initial restrictions.

The Department of Health recognizes the vulnerability of this system to criticism.

It is hard to defend a system of keeping the prescribing of drugs within bounds which depends for its success on the fact that it is more trouble for the patient to go to a public hospital for his supplies than to go to the local chemist. On the whole, this measure works well, but it is wrong in principle. Similarly, it is an undeniable interference with professional freedom to make it mandatory for a doctor to consult a specialist before he prescribes any particular drug. . . . The fact that, up to a point, it achieves the desired result is almost its only justification.[6]

(4) *Restriction to approved indications.* From time to time drugs have been approved for inclusion in the *Drug Tariff* only when used for certain purposes. One example is the oral contraceptive. Several years ago, when the matter was regarded as a potentially awkward political issue, a ministerial ruling was given that oral contraceptives must not, in any circumstances, be supplied to healthy women at public cost. This policy directive has not yet been rescinded. If, however, there are medical reasons for recommending contraception, and a doctor is prepared to state that in his opinion the patient could not reasonably be expected to pay the cost, application may be made for a special approval of a free supply. If, on the other hand, a doctor prescribes a contraceptive drug for reasons other than contraception (for example, menstrual problems), the drug may be obtained free-of-charge if he endorses the prescription with the words "approved condition." This amounts to a certificate that the drug is not for contraceptive purposes. In theory, the accuracy of this certification is liable to be challenged, but unless a doctor uses it frequently, this is unlikely to happen. This kind of restriction is disliked both by doctors and by the department, and is seldom used. At present it applies only to contraceptives.

(5) *Disciplinary action.* The Department of Health regards disciplinary action as a last resort. In 1957, following the advice of a Special Committee on Pharmaceutical Benefits, drug regulations were extended in an effort to control excessively expensive prescribing. Grounds for complaint against a physician to the Disciplinary Committee were held to exist when "the average cost of prescriptions issued by him during any period of three months has been unduly high in comparison with the average cost of prescriptions issued

---

[6] A. W. S. Thompson, "Aspects of Pharmaceutical Benefits," *Pharmaceutical Journal N. Z.*, March 1968, pp. 9-12.

during the same period by other medical practitioners engaged in similar practice." Disciplinary action has been enforced on rare occasions, but it has never become a widely applied method of control, in part because the Department of Health enjoys a good relationship with the medical community and has chosen to use education and exhortation, rather than disciplinary measures, to achieve compliance.[7] In any case, the marshaling of the data necessary to mount convincing disciplinary proceedings is so time-consuming that only occasionally could it be achieved without the help of a computer system of pricing. Plans for a computer system have been deferred indefinitely for economic reasons.

(6) *Visiting practitioner program.* In 1957 a special committee recommended the appointment of a senior practitioner to visit doctors and advise them on prescribing, with special reference to cost. The proposal was implemented in 1959 with the appointment of one doctor. This officer was a highly respected senior general practitioner turned consultant physician, well known to the profession and well received in this appointment. His personal influence put the program on a sound basis, and it was later expanded to three visiting practitioners, who now visit all general practitioners in the country at least once a year, and also pay visits to specialists.

It was emphasized from the beginning that the visiting practitioner was not associated with any concept of discipline or surveillance. His assistance and advice would be available, however, when a doctor's prescription was under scrutiny because of cost, if asked for by the doctor concerned. As with the issuance of *Prescribers' Notes,* one objective of the visiting practitioner was to balance, in some small degree, the one-sided advertising directed at the doctor, and thus to foster better habits of prescribing.[8] Over the years, the emphasis on the role of the visiting practitioners has changed from giving advice on prescription to the more general function of improving liaison between general practitioners and the Department of Health. The visiting practitioner tells the doctor that he wishes to hear any complaints, criticisms, or suggestions he may wish to make about the administration of the program, and to know of any difficulties he is meeting in practice. There is evidence, however, that these visiting practitioners have had a substantial effect in reducing prescription costs.[9]

---

[7] Special Committee on Pharmaceutical Benefits, *Report 1961-1962* (Wellington, New Zealand: Government Printing Office, 1963).

[8] Thompson, "Controlling the Costs of Community Medical Care."

[9] Ibid.

When the first visiting practitioner died after three and one-half years in office, an analysis was made of the prescribing costs in Auckland, where he had been stationed, and Wellington (400 miles away), where his influence was necessarily much smaller. The monthly average cost per prescription had always been higher in Auckland than in the rest of New Zealand. The Wellington figure had always been relatively low. Eighteen months after the officer was appointed the relationship changed. In the sixty-eight months up to that time the Auckland figure had been lower than that in Wellington in only four months. From then on it was lower than Wellington's in twenty-two months out of twenty-five. At the same time the number of prescriptions issued per unit of population in Auckland was falling, while in Wellington this figure was on the increase. After this officer's death, difficulty was encountered in replacing him, and the Auckland/Wellington relationship gradually returned to its former pattern. It was calculated that in his short period of service this officer saved the country at least $NZ1,200,000. The medical impact of these savings in prescription costs is believed to be favorable, but no formal cost-benefit study involving hospitalization rates and duration, morbidity rates, and work time lost has been made.

Studies of Drug Use and Experience

Patterns of Drug Usage. Through the prescription pricing program of the Department of Health, a considerable amount of information has become available on patterns of prescription throughout the country. Regular surveys have been made in which the cost of drugs per patient attended per month is worked out for every general practitioner in a given area. Each doctor receives a schedule which shows how his costs compare with those of his neighboring colleagues, individual doctors being designated by reference numbers only and not by name.

Studies have also been designed to detect the abuse of narcotic prescription. In a recent example, the use of Palfium (dextromoramide) was suddenly found to have increased dramatically in one South Island city, with prescriptions exceeding the total for the rest of the country. This situation was brought to the notice of the Medical Officer of Health, who, with the cooperation of the local medical association, succeeded in correcting it. Moreover, descriptive studies based on these data have been made. For example, Thompson has shown how the pattern of hypnotic, sedative, and tranquilizer use in the whole country has changed over a thirteen-year period.[10] (Of course, a large-scale experimental study on the effect of removing restrictions on the period and quantity of drug prescribing is seen in the South Island experiment.)

If electronic data processing is introduced for prescription pricing, much more detailed information on prescription will be available. If this information can be used to support experimental approaches to the study of controls now in effect, New Zealand would offer a unique situation for research into these aspects of drug use.

Surveillance of Adverse Drug Reactions

Spontaneous Reporting Systems. The Committee on Adverse Drug Reactions has had a register of spontaneous reports operating for nine years.[11] New Zealand has the highest reporting rate of all twelve countries reporting to the World Health Organization Drug Monitoring Project, with a reporting rate per capita double that of Great Britain and about twenty times that of the United States.[12] This is due largely to the organization of Professor E. G. McQueen, University of Otago, the medical assessor of the committee.

Liaison between the committee and general practitioners throughout New Zealand is good. Annual summaries of reports received by the committee are published in the *New Zealand Medical Journal* and other professional journals in the country, and further details are available on application to the committee office. Since few other countries publish their reports in comparable detail, these reports are useful for research purposes, and they also serve an important educational role in keeping members of the profession aware of the current prevalence and nature of adverse drug reactions. Moreover, in addition to the publicity given to adverse drug reactions in these reports, specific problems are referred to in the Department of Health's *Prescribers' Notes.*

The public also seems to be fairly well informed about the possibility of harm from drugs, and accepts the fact that potent drugs generally have side effects. There has not, so far, been a strong tendency for patients in New Zealand to resort to litigation if drug side effects occur.

---

10 A. W. S. Thompson, "The Prescribing of Hypnotics, Tranquilizers and Stimulant Drugs in New Zealand," *N. Z. Board of Health Report Series, 1973,* no. 18 (Wellington, New Zealand, 1972).

11 New Zealand Committee on Adverse Drug Reactions, "Ninth Annual Report," *New Zealand Medical Journal,* vol. 80 (1974), pp. 305-11.

12 World Health Organization, "Research Project for International Drug Monitoring," Report No. 5 (January 1972).

Intensive Prospective Drug Surveillance. Dr. Gavin Kellaway at Auckland Hospital has instituted an intensive surveillance program in a medical ward of the Auckland Hospital, one of the participating hospitals in the Boston Collaborative Drug Surveillance Program. This participation has now been extended to the Hutt Hospital (near Wellington) and will be expanded, if possible, to more hospitals throughout the country. This link provides a useful contact with prospective surveillance schemes in use abroad.[13]

Discussion and Conclusions

The New Zealand Pharmaceutical Benefits Scheme has a number of distinctive features. First, it covers an entire country, embracing virtually all prescription outside public hospitals. Second, it has been operating and evolving for more than thirty years, so that it can now be seen as well tested and workable. Third, controls over the use of drugs in general practice are more extensive and detailed than in most other countries. Some of these controls may be unique to New Zealand, and while they are certainly restrictive, the restrictions are closely geared to medical reality and provide enough flexibility so that physicians can respond appropriately to unusual medical situations. That these controls appear to achieve their purpose without causing excessive reaction from the medical community is remarkable, given the debate prompted by these issues in other countries.

Some points of interest deserve special mention. When a third-party payment system (as distinct from a regulatory agency) makes decisions on the availability and use of drugs, the kind of information demanded from clinical pharmacology is vastly more complex than for "simple" decisions on safety and efficacy. For example, relative efficacy—not normally regarded as the purview of a regulatory agency—becomes a topic of immediate concern, particularly as it relates to cost. Since few data are available on relative efficacy, committee judgments on these issues include a large subjective component.

Many of the current difficulties surrounding the regulation of new drugs in any country arise because the methods of clinical pharmacology are not yet capable of providing unequivocal answers to questions of safety and efficacy. It would appear, therefore, that the same methodology is far less able to cope with the more subtle demands that are being placed upon it. There is a clear need to

---

[13] New Zealand Committee on Adverse Drug Reactions, "Ninth Annual Report."

improve the methods of clinical pharmacology if it is to provide a scientific way of solving these problems as more third-party control over drug use and finance is exerted. In New Zealand, the government pays between two and three times as much for the drugs prescribed as for its contribution to the services of the physicians prescribing them.[14] If similar patterns develop in other countries, drug-related issues will probably bear the brunt of the control measures arising from third-party sources.

The second main point of interest is the whole question of the control of drug marketing as against the control of drug use in therapeutics. So long as control over the admission of a drug to the market remains the main weapon of a regulatory agency, and so long as the function of this agency is viewed as one of reducing harm to the community as a whole, then the policy of a regulatory agency will tend to be conservative. If a drug that could greatly benefit the few is also likely to harm the many, then consideration of the overall good of the community would dictate that the drug should not be released. The corollary to this is that, if one could ensure that a useful drug will be wisely used, then it should be released, even if it is hazardous. The significance of the controls over use in New Zealand is that they demonstrate that the way a drug is used can be directed through monitoring during the early stages, restricting use to that under the supervision of specialists, and confining employment to certain indications. In principle, then, controls over use could be a beneficial alternative to blanket controls over the admission of a drug to the market. The latter can be relaxed at the expense of stricter control over use. The New Zealand situation demonstrates some feasible methods of control over drug use and how a medical community reacts to the imposition of these controls.

The New Zealand model is probably most feasible in a small country with a system of medical practice that already recognizes distinctions between the general practitioner and the specialist and between the physicians practicing within and outside the hospital system. It also depends on a flexible administration with responsive links to the medical community. In principle, the freedom of physicians is not infringed, because any physician can still prescribe any therapy. In practice, however, since patients become used to receiving drugs at no cost, a physician's freedom to prescribe whatever he wishes is to some extent curtailed.

Finally we need to examine the objectives and performance of the system. Its main objectives are twofold: (1) to reduce the costs

---

[14] Thompson, "Controlling the Costs of Community Medical Care."

of the drugs prescribed in general practice while maintaining the availability of modern and medically appropriate therapy and (2) to reduce the inappropriate use of toxic, new, or expensive drugs.

To a certain extent, these goals have been achieved. Savings have been made in prescription costs in general practice, and some inappropriate drug use in general practice has been reduced. But there are wider questions that have not generally been examined. Are the controls causing drugs to be used in a manner that is most cost-effective for the health system as a whole? Do controls that involve specialist endorsement of prescriptions lead to inefficient use of the time of the limited number of medical specialists in the country? The real issue is whether the controls ensure that drugs are being used in the most cost-effective way for reducing morbidity and mortality in the community. Moreover, what is the effect of the controls on the number of patient visits to general practitioners and specialists? On the frequency and duration of hospital stays? On the work time lost through sickness? In none of these areas have the effects of controls been examined. More information is needed on these wider effects of controls.

PART THREE

AN EASTERN EUROPEAN SYSTEM

11

CZECHOSLOVAKIA

Zdeněk Modr and Ludvík Štika

The swift expansion of modern drug therapy, pharmacy, and the pharmaceutical industry, together with social changes that give the population access to drug therapy, have evoked many economic and social—as well as medical—problems in Czechoslovakia. These problems concern the health care not only of individuals but also of the population as a whole. To solve some of these problems, Czechoslovakia has gradually developed a special system for the control of drug use.

Historical Introduction

The present system for the control of therapeutic drug use in Czechoslovakia has been developing since 1951. In that year, the foundations were laid for a socialist health care system which, according to law, must ensure that health care is generally available. Health care must be preventive and curative, consistent with modern standards of medical science and society's economic capability, and free of any charge to the patient at the time of service. To attain these goals, a uniform system of health care institutions was gradually established, and the pharmaceutical industry, the wholesale drug trade, and (later) the pharmacies, were nationalized. In this way, Czechoslovakia became the first European socialist country to supply medicines free of cost in both hospital and ambulatory health care.

Organization. In the Czechoslovak health care system, the basic unit of preventive and curative care is the Community Health Center, which supplies services for approximately 3,500 persons. At each center a full-time physician and nurse, and a part-time pediatrician, pediatric nurse, gynecologist, and dentist are employed. Similar health centers exist at major plants and institutions. In the cities, the health centers are mostly concentrated in policlinics which employ additional specialists in all major medical disciplines.

A policlinic, together with the appropriate hospital, forms a functional and administrative unit. In most districts in Czechoslovakia, several such hospitals with policlinics, along with additional health care institutions, constitute the District Institute of National Health. Similarly, in each region, there is a Regional Institute of National Health; its hospitals and policlinics supply highly specialized care in all medical disciplines. These institutions are subject to both medical and administrative guidance and control by the Ministry of Health, operating through the departments of health of the regional or district national committees. National committees are organs of socialist state power and administration, and their responsibilities include supplying the necessary funds for the health care they provide.

Planning for the funds for all health care costs, as well as supervising the expenditures, requires the above-mentioned departments of health to obtain data on all medical and health care activities. Therefore, at every district institute of national health, a statistician collects the following data monthly: the number of patients seen in consulting rooms and the number of home visits made by each community health center physician or specialist, the number of inpatients treated, the numbers of diagnostic tests and procedures performed in laboratories and X-ray departments, the average duration of hospitalization classified by diagnoses (International Classification of Diseases, 1966), the utilization and costs of hospital beds, and the consumption of such things as blood and blood derivatives, chemicals, prosthetic and orthopedic devices, X-ray materials, dental materials, and drugs. These data serve for both the planning and the supervision of the health care furnished at all structural levels of the Czechoslovak National Health Service.

With these changes in the character and structure of the Czechoslovak health care system, the state health authorities became responsible for a systematic solution of all domestic social, professional, and economic problems connected with the production, distribution, prescription, and utilization of drugs. Many legislative and organizational measures had to be instituted. Some had their roots in the previous system, but most had to be newly created and then adapted in the light of experience.

Once the pharmaceutical industry was nationalized, the first step in controlling drug use was an appraisal of the entire production program by a committee of experts. On the committee's recommendation, production of all duplicate and obsolete preparations was discontinued. Out of an original total of about 3,000 items, the expurgated production program contained only 370 preparations. Simultaneously, a new act ruled that the only pharmaceutical preparations that could be produced and marketed in Czechoslovakia were those which had passed an expert appraisal by a special committee of professionals and had been approved by the Ministry of Health. The authority of the State Institute for the Control of Drugs was also strengthened. This institute systematically supervises the quality of pharmaceutical products used in Czechoslovakia, as well as compliance with the rules and specifications of the Czechoslovak pharmacopeia, which is prepared and systematically revised by a special expert body, the Pharmacopeia Commission.

In the field of drug distribution, the commercialism of the pharmacies was suppressed. Beginning in 1960 these enterprises were incorporated into institutes of national health and financed by the state budget.[1] In this connection, the principle established in the new state is that, in socialist economics, medicines are not commercial merchandise. A drug's price is now determined primarily by the therapeutic significance of the drug. The general rule is that drugs acting against the cause of a disease (for example, antibiotics, chemotherapeutics) and drugs counteracting pathogenesis (for example, cardiotonics) are priced lower than symptomatic drugs and, especially, preparations of questionable therapeutic value—for example, tonics, rubefacients, multivitamin preparations. Another example of this policy is the lower retail prices of analgesics with relatively few adverse side effects—for example, aspirin and its simple combinations—compared with those that cause more frequent or major adverse side effects—for example, compounds containing aminopyrine or phenacetin. This policy is especially important because many analgesic combinations, tonics, rubefacients, multivitamins, and similar preparations may be sold over the counter in pharmacies.

The weightiest control measures had to be taken to ensure rational and economical prescription and utilization of drugs in medical practice [2] because of society's interest in how, and for what drugs, the socialist state's financial resources were being spent. Moreover, an answer had to be sought to questions about the effects of the drugs

---

[1] J. Jirout et al., *The Pharmaceutical Service in the Czechoslovak Socialist Republic* (Prague: Ministry of Health, State Publishing House of Medical Literature, 1964), pp. 1-59 (in English).

[2] Z. Modr et al., "Problems of Reasonable Prescription of Pharmaceutical Preparations," *Československé zdravotnictví*, vol. 7, no. 9 (1959), pp. 518-32.

on the state of health of the whole society, as well as that of individuals.

To accomplish these tasks, the first Regulations for Control of the Utilization of Drugs, medical devices, and health supplies were issued as early as 1955, and advisory boards for drug utilization were constituted to deal with economic and administrative factors rather than with the medical aspects of drug use. Thus, the boards issued regulations concerning only the formalities of drug prescription and the methods used for financial supervision, gathering evidence, and regulating drug consumption. No attention was paid to the medical concerns of prescription or to a rational approach to drug therapy.

In 1958, when the activities of these boards had been critically appraised, a government decree was issued directed at the medical aspects of the drug use. On the basis of the decree, the Central Committee for Rational Drug Therapy was established in 1959. This committee, which consisted of prominent clinicians, pharmacologists, pharmacists, and economists,[3] drew up rules for the active guidance, regulation, and control of drug prescription. Analogous committees were constituted in individual regions and districts and even at hospitals.

Objectives. The basic guidelines covering the activities of these committees emphasize that the crucial criteria to be considered in seeking a solution to all problems connected with the control and regulation of drug prescription are professional medical criteria. In the committees' guidelines, rational drug therapy is defined as drug therapy which, on the basis of contemporary medical science and of all expert knowledge available for use, achieves the desired therapeutic effect in the best, quickest, and simplest way possible. Rational therapy is economical, even if high-priced drugs have to be used. Conversely, any superfluous therapy is irrational, even if its financial cost is low. Finally, it is stressed that concern for rational drug therapy must be an integral part of the tasks of all socialist health workers.

A major role is given to the specialists responsible for guiding physicians working in health centers, policlinics, and hospitals. Such specialists are obligated, when consulting and when paying supervisory visits to physicians, to judge not only the physicians' diagnostic skills, but also their pharmacotherapeutic activities, from both the administrative and medical points of view. The objective of this supervision is to correct any faults and to improve the medical knowl-

---

[3] Z. Modr, J. Boukal, and J. Partiš, "Some Questions of Rational Pharmacotherapy and Drug Utilization," *Praktický lékař*, vol. 40, no. 20 (1960), pp. 913-16.

edge, particularly of health center physicians. Moreover, in 1959 a request was made by the Ministry of Health that the problems of rational drug therapy be systematically included in all special courses organized by the Institute for Postgraduate Medical and Pharmaceutical Training in Prague.

Committees for rational drug therapy have been active in Czechoslovakia for many years; they have contributed considerably to raising the professional level of drug therapy in our country. These committees, however, are not competent to solve all problems connected with the therapeutic use of drugs in medical practice. To serve special needs, special working groups had to be constituted: the Drug Importation Committee, the Committee for Adverse Drug Reactions, and others. Thus a system was created which enables the national health administration to maintain effective control over the prescription and utilization of drugs in medical practice.

With the creation of a federal organization for the Czechoslovak Socialist Republic in 1968, separate ministries of health were constituted in the two states—namely, the Czech and the Slovak Socialist republics. The administration of health policy, including control of drug utilization, is identical in each republic. The boards and committees of the two ministries of health correspond to each other in structure and competence. Each committee collaborates closely with its counterpart in the other state, and common recommendations are formulated in joint sessions so that uniform regulations will be in force and valid in both republics. In view of this fact, subsequent descriptions here will not distinguish between the two republics.

Controls Prior to Drug Marketing

Each drug or pharmaceutical substance intended for use in medical practice in Czechoslovakia must first be approved by the Ministry of Health. This rule applies to drugs manufactured in Czechoslovakia as well as to those imported from abroad. An approved drug is included in the pharmacopeia, and an approved mass-produced pharmaceutical preparation is included in the *Register of Approved Pharmaceutical Preparations*.

An application for inclusion in the register (that is, for registration), is submitted to the Ministry of Health, and must be accompanied by a complete set of documents on the composition of the preparation, its physical and chemical properties, the methods used in its analysis, and detailed reports on the results of its preclinical and clinical trials. The technical documentation is reviewed by the State Institute for the Control of Drugs.

239

The results of preclinical and clinical trials are critically evaluated by the Drug Committee, an advisory body of the Scientific Advisory Board of the Ministry of Health. The Drug Committee consists of selected specialists—pharmacologists, clinical pharmacologists, clinicians, and pharmacists. It deals with requests for registration of mass-produced pharmaceutical preparations and with applications to undertake the several stages of clinical trials required for any new drug, domestic or foreign. No drug can be clinically tested in Czechoslovakia without previous clearance by the Ministry of Health. The Drug Committee also evaluates applications for approval of drug manufacture in Czechoslovakia. The recommendation, submitted by the Drug Committee to the appropriate Ministry of Health, must also include the committee's decision on whether the preparation to be approved is a drug and may therefore be dispensed at the cost of the state health administration. (All medicines are issued free of cost, while certain classes of preparations having the character of adjunctive remedies, such as some dietetic, cosmetic, and similar products, are paid for by the consumer; therefore, this decision determines who pays for the preparation.)

When evaluating a pharmaceutical preparation, the Drug Committee appraises its safety (relative to that of other specifics) and its efficacy. The criteria now used are in line with the requirements for preclinical and clinical appraisal of drugs used by the World Health Organization.[4]

Registration of each mass-produced pharmaceutical preparation must be renewed at five-year intervals. When applying for renewal, the manufacturer must submit to the Drug Committee any new information which might be relevant for the committee's decision on the drug's safety and efficacy. In making a decision on such an application, the Drug Committee also consults the National Committee for Adverse Drug Reactions.

For drugs of foreign manufacture, registration is only a prerequisite for their possible use in Czechoslovakia. The decision whether the drug will be imported into Czechoslovakia rests with the Drug Importation Committee, another body constituted by the Ministry of Health. Its task is to select from foreign pharmaceutical preparations those that are indispensable for preventive or therapeutic use and for which no domestic equivalents exist. When several chemically

---

[4] World Health Organization Scientific Group, *Principles for Pre-Clinical Testing of Drug Safety*, World Health Organization Technical Report Series, no. 341 (Geneva, 1966), and World Health Organization Scientific Group, *Principles for the Clinical Evaluation of Drugs*, World Health Organization Technical Report Series, no. 403 (Geneva, 1968).

or pharmacologically related preparations exist for a given indication, the committee requires the results of comparative controlled studies. If the necessary data are not available, the committee recommends that the studies be made in Czechoslovakia. The approved foreign pharmaceutical preparations intended for wide medical usage are then included by the committee in the *List of Regularly Imported Pharmaceutical Preparations*. Individual health institutions plan their requirements for the preparations from the list and order them from special institutions of the State Pharmaceutical Service.

Most imported drugs are reserved for selected indications only. Therefore, the Drug Importation Committee, in collaboration with additional specialists, also submits to the Ministry of Health its recommendations on the distribution, prescription, and use of such drugs. For example, certain drugs are reserved for use in hospitals or in specified hospital wards or specified outpatient departments where patients with the appropriate indications are concentrated. These drugs include most cytostatics, and also selected antibiotics, tuberculostatics, psychotropic drugs, antidiabetics, certain hormones, antiasthmatics (for example, cromolyn sodium, which is reserved exclusively for asthmatic children), and dietetic preparations for the treatment of phenylketonuria, in addition to some others. For other imported products, restricted indications and conditions may be specified for which, on the recommendation of a specialist (or sometimes without a recommendation), the drug may also be prescribed by a physician in a community health center. Other foreign pharmaceutical preparations, registered but not included in the *List of Regularly Imported Pharmaceutical Preparations*, can be obtained in individual cases of proven necessity by a procedure known as extraordinary importation. This procedure requires special approval issued, after expert appraisal, by the director of the District Institute of National Health. The attending physician must then submit to the Ministry of Health a written report describing the results achieved with the needed preparation. If adequately documented, such reports occasionally help the Drug Importation Committee and the Committee for Rational Drug Therapy on each level to make decisions when additions to the *List of Regularly Imported Pharmaceutical Preparations* are being considered. The reports vary considerably in quality, and most are simple case reports.

The *List of Regularly Imported Pharmaceutical Preparations* is revised annually. In addition, every three to five years, the Ministry of Health critically reviews the schedule of drugs manufactured in Czechoslovakia. Representatives of all expert committees of the Ministry of Health and of special medical societies participate in this review. The review is aimed at eliminating production of drugs that can be replaced by drugs that are more efficient and safer and at critically appraising the development plans for new drugs in Czechoslovakia. Examples of drugs eliminated include preparations combining theobromine with digitalis, caffeine, papaverine, or valerian extract; a preparation containing a complex of crystalline digitalis lanata glycosides; several analeptics (synephrine, coretonin, hydroxamphetamine, pentetrazol, lobeline); combined sulfonamides, sulfamethoxypyridazine, penethamate hydriodide, the haemostyptic naphthylamine, the ganglion blocker dimecamine, expectorant syrups, benzocaine, tetracaine, antihistamines antazoline and mepyramine; and diiodinated contrast media. Most of these were replaceable by more potent and safer drugs manufactured in Czechoslovakia. These include generic versions of modern drugs of foreign origin (for example, digoxine, acetyldigitoxin, sulfamethoxydiazine), as well as Czechoslovak inventions (for example, the antihistamines moxastine, embramine, embramine theoclate, methiaden, and dithiaden, and the pyrazolidine derivatives, kebuzone and tribuzone).

Almost 2,000 pharmaceutical preparations are currently registered in Czechoslovakia. Of this number, 665 are manufactured in Czechoslovakia and are on the *List of Czechoslovak Pharmaceutical Preparations*, while 309 are included in the *List of Regularly Imported Pharmaceutical Preparations*. The remaining 1,000 or so registered drugs are not included in the *List of Regularly Imported Pharmaceutical Preparations*. They may be obtained by the extraordinary importation procedure. The number of different kinds of drugs used in Czechoslovakia is low in comparison with other countries, because no duplication of identical or too-similar drugs is permitted within therapeutic areas. For example, of the antistaphylococcal semisynthetic penicillins, only oxacillin has been released. Of the broad-spectrum drugs, only ampicillin and carbenicillin have been released. Nevertheless, the Czechoslovak assortment of pharmaceutical preparations fully covers the requirements of preventive and curative care.

Most pharmaceutical preparations may be dispensed only on medical prescription. Over-the-counter (OTC) drugs are enumerated in a special list, subject to regular revision. During the last revision in 1974, the following groups of drugs were deleted from the list: all antiasthmatics, some vitamin preparations containing the vitamins A and D, and, for considerations of toxicity, some compound analgesics containing aminopyrine and phenacetin. The current list contains no more than 175 preparations, mainly certain simple and compound vitamin preparations (C, B [complex]), mild analgesics, medicinal cosmetic preparations, medicinal mixtures of herbs, dietetic preparations, and similar items. Even such OTC preparations, however, are dispensed or sold exclusively by pharmacies.

Special regulations are in effect for oral contraceptives. These preparations must be indicated, and their use supervised, by a physician. Unless used in a therapeutic indication, contraceptives are not dispensed at the cost of the state health administration and have to be paid for by the consumer in the pharmacy.

Controls of the Use of Drugs after Their Introduction into Medical Practice

Administrative Regulations. To promote the rational use of drugs in therapeutic practice, the Ministry of Health regularly issues special guidelines, which physicians, pharmacists, and health care institutions must follow. The guidelines concern the prescription, dispensing, handling, and use of drugs and the professional, economic, and administrative control of these activities. Analogous rules apply to blood and blood derivatives and to such medical devices and health supplies as orthopedic and prosthetic devices, spectacles, artificial (glass) eyes, dental needs, dressings, X-ray materials, and chemicals. Only those regulations directly concerning the conditions and proper control of drug prescription are described here.

The state health administration pays for all drugs prescribed by physicians working at state health institutions. In private medical practice—rare in Czechoslovakia today—drugs may not be prescribed at the cost of the state health administration.

No more than two different drugs or preparations may be prescribed on the prescription form. The amount that may be prescribed on one form depends on the character of the patient's illness. As a rule, a quantity is allowed that will last until the next medical visit—about seven to fourteen days in acute diseases. In chronic diseases, an amount covering a longer period may be prescribed. There is an exception in the case of psychostimulants (for example, phenmetrazine), of which only one package may be prescribed on one form. Narcotics are prescribed on special forms and are handled in accordance with special regulations, consistent with the appropriate international convention. All prescriptions issued at the cost of the state health administration are retained at the pharmacy after the medicine has been issued to the patient.

For dispensing and processing the prescription, a handling charge of one Czechoslovak crown (U.S.$.10) per form is collected at the pharmacy. The introduction of this charge in 1964 temporarily decreased the number of prescriptions issued, but did not influence the total amount of drugs prescribed.

If a patient expressely demands an amount that will last longer than one to two weeks in order to cut down on frequent visits for refills of a prescription needed for long-term treatment, the physician may write out a prescription on a special form, but the patient then has to pay full price at the pharmacy. In this case, the prescription remains the patient's property. The physician, however, must indicate on the prescription how many times it may be refilled.

Professional Regulations. Professional regulations concern only the medical aspects and the rationale of prescription. The principle is that a physician is authorized to prescribe (1) only those drugs that he himself deems to be indicated for a disease that he is capable of diagnosing with the facilities available to him, and (2) only those drugs whose effects he himself is capable of checking and controlling.

In principle, all physicians may prescribe any drugs listed in the Czechoslovak pharmacopeia and all preparations registered in Czechoslovakia. As stated above, the physician may prescribe without administrative restrictions only those registered preparations listed in the *List of Czechoslovak Pharmaceutical Preparations* and in the *List of Regularly Imported Pharmaceutical Preparations*. The physician must respect certain professional limitations dictated by the character and indications of the drug in question. An example of a medically dictated limitation on prescribing may be found in the procedure for antibiotics, which is ruled by the principles of all-state policy applied to the use of antibiotics.[5] According to the present regulations, antibiotics are divided into three classes:

Class 1—which includes antibiotics that may be prescribed without limitation by all physicians: penicillin G (benzylpenicillin), penicillin V (phenoxymethylpenicillin), oral tetracyclines and chloramphenicol, nystatin, and topical antibiotics (for example, neomycin combined with bacitracin), and similar items; Class 2—which includes antibiotics that may be prescribed by hospital physicians only on special order forms: erythromycin, streptomycin, kanamycin, oxacillin, griseofulvin, and injectable tetracyclines and chloramphenicol;

[5] Z. Modr, "Principles of Antibiotic Policy in Czechoslovakia" (Paper delivered at a conference of the University of Pavia, Library of IKEM, Prague, May 8, 1974).

Class 3—which includes all remaining antibiotics. These may be prescribed by physicians in hospital practice (and in exceptional circumstances, by physicians in ambulatory practice), on a recommendation issued by an antibiotic center.

(These centers are advisory and technical institutions responsible for performing specialized laboratory examinations, maintaining surveillance over resistant microorganisms, planning and distribution of Class 3 antibiotics, giving advice on all problems connected with the practical use of antibiotics, and enforcing the principles of antibiotic policy in accordance with actual epidemiological conditions in their catchment area. There are, in each region of the Czech Socialist Republic, at least one such center and usually two to four.)

These professional regulations of antibiotic usage are strictly followed and have proved to be valuable. This is evident, for example, from a relatively favorable trend in the development of resistance patterns, from a relatively lower occurrence of side effects of these drugs, and from a decreased frequency of antibiotic misuse in general practice. In view of our recent experience of a nonuniform development of resistance patterns of pathogenic microorganisms in different regions, the authority of the centers will soon be extended so that they will directly specify the antibiotics to be used in hospital practice in accordance with local conditions. Consequently, the antibiotics included in Class 2 will be given more flexible usage than they are now.

Specific limitations are also imposed on the prescribing of certain other groups of drugs: antidiabetics (prescription of these drugs is concentrated in the diabetic dispensaries which provide long-term therapeutic care for all registered diabetic patients in every district; a community health center physician may prescribe these drugs only in emergencies); cytostatics (most are reserved for oncological departments and dispensaries); tuberculostatics (only for tuberculosis departments and dispensaries); psychostimulants (to be prescribed only by psychiatrists and neurologists who provide care for narcolepsy); anorectics (only for medical departments); corticosteroids in topical application forms (only for dermatologists, ophthalmologists, and pediatricians); low-phenylalanine preparations (only for special pediatric dispensaries); and so on. Such preparations may be indicated and prescribed by competent specialists only. On the recommendation of these specialists, however, health center physicians may also prescribe such preparations for specific mutual patients. With certain drugs, the limitation of prescription is dictated by their character—

for example, with general anesthetics—or by exactly demarcated indications.

The Control of Information about Drugs. The control of information to physicians about pharmaceutical preparations—especially new preparations—begins during the drug-registration procedure. The Drug Committee reviews the draft text of the package insert and, in the case of domestic drugs, the draft text of the informative monograph for the *List of Czechoslovak Pharmaceutical Preparations*. This list is issued by the state trust of pharmaceutical manufacturers— United Pharmaceutical Works (Spojené Farmaceutické Závody, or SPOFA)—and disseminated free of cost to all physicians, pharmacists, and senior medical and pharmacy students.

SPOFA also possesses a special medical information department. Its activity, however, is professionally supervised by the Ministry of Health, and it collaborates closely with that ministry. It issues several publications: for example, the periodical *News in Drug Therapy* (*Farmakoterapeutické zprávy*); a series of monographs entitled *Information on Therapy* (*Terapeutické informace*) dealing with individual drugs, groups of drugs, or certain therapeutic problems; and minor informative bulletins. Before publication, these materials are reviewed by experts commissioned by the Ministry of Health.

A plan approved in advance is also obligatory for the expert informers of SPOFA (equivalent to detail men and possessing a pharmacy degree), who directly inform physicians about new drugs produced in Czechoslovakia.

Drug advertising in medical journals is also subject to supervision by the Ministry of Health. This rule applies both to pharmaceuticals manufactured in Czechoslovakia and to those imported from abroad: they may not be advertised without the express approval of the ministry. Detail men of foreign firms must also adhere to ministry regulations.

Determination of Drug Prices. An important instrument for the regulation and desirable regimentation of drug consumption in Czechoslovakia is the determination of retail prices of drugs. These prices apply to payments made by the institutes of national health to the pharmacies for drugs issued on prescriptions and to cash purchases of OTCs.

The prices paid by the wholesale distributor to the manufacturer cover the production costs and planned profit, which in turn cover the manufacturer's production and development costs. Only part of the costs of new-drug research are paid by the pharmaceutical industry from its profit: a major part is financed by the Ministry of Health from its budget for medical and pharmaceutical research. This ensures that pharmaceutical research is oriented to tasks necessary for the development and improvement of health care, while commercial interests are restrained.

Pharmacies buy drugs from a wholesale distributor for retail prices less a margin. The difference between the wholesale and retail prices is governed by the imposition of a variable purchase tax. In consequence, the retail price can be modified by intentional variation of planned profits and the purchase-tax rate. In determining the prices for imported drugs, world market prices of these imports must be taken in account. The socialist economic system recognizes primarily medical criteria and real therapeutic efficacy when drug prices are being determined. In keeping with this principle, preparations possessing significant therapeutic activities (for example, cardiotonics) are relatively less expensive than drugs with less effective or symptomatic therapeutic activities (for example, expectorants, tonics). Another important criterion for determining drug prices is the principle of therapeutic equivalence. According to this principle, related drugs belonging to the same indication group have equal prices; this is true, for example, for all oral cardiotonics, antiasthmatics, and tetracyclines. This principle is also applied when prices are being determined for new preparations. The principle, however, is not absolute; in specific instances other criteria, for example, economic considerations, must be taken into account. For instance, the original uniform prices of oral corticosteroids were altered because of great differences in their production costs. In relation to the price of prednisone, the price of triamcinolone was raised and that of dexamethasone was lowered. The establishment of prices according to the principle of therapeutic equivalence is aimed at permitting the physician, when choosing a drug, not to have to take price into account but, rather, to choose from a given group the preparation believed to be most advantageous for the patient.

Committees for Rational Drug Therapy. These committees, which are the most important institutions of the state health administration, are responsible for the control of correct and economic utilization of drugs in therapeutic practice.[6] They are expert advisory boards with the following specific tasks:

---

[6] Z. Modr, "On the Working Method of Commissions for Expedient Pharmacotherapy," *Československé zdravotnictví*, vol. 9, no. 6 (1961), pp. 352-57.

(1) guidance of physicians and other health workers in adherence to principles of rational drug therapy;

(2) performance of expert analyses of prescriptions issued by individual physicians;

(3) performance of expert analyses of the prescribing of drugs, blood, medical devices, and health supplies at individual hospital departments or, if necessary, in entire health institutions;

(4) surveillance and expert appraisal, of both the quantity and the cost of development of the consumption of drugs, blood, devices, and necessities in the individual institutions of the institutes of national health;

(5) proposing suitable measures for correcting faults revealed by prescription analyses;

(6) supervision of the system for reporting adverse drug effects;

(7) estimation of the actual supply of drugs and devices;

(8) expert appraisal of the draft budget for drugs submitted by the appropriate regional or district institute of national health; and

(9) participation in the planning of drug consumption and, in particular, of imported preparations. (The committees assess future trends in the consumption of domestic drugs, classed into individual pharmacological groups, and advise what amounts of foreign drugs, included in the *List of Regularly Imported Drugs* issued by the Ministry of Health, should be imported in order to optimize the expenditure of allocated funds.)

Committees for rational drug therapy operate at all regional and district institutes of national health, as well as at major individual health institutions within a district. At the Ministry of Health, the Central Committee for Rational Drug Therapy gives expert professional guidance to lower-level committees. Each committee consists of specialists, physicians, pharmacists, and economists. The chairman is usually a specialist in internal medicine, and the secretary is the chief pharmacist. In each committee are represented all chief specialists who are entrusted with methodological guidance of their colleagues in the appropriate medical branch within the committee's domain.

The prime task of the committees is to help physicians adhere to the principles of rational, scientifically based, and economical drug therapy. To fulfill this task, the committees disseminate information and news on drug therapy as a means of raising the physicians' professional knowledge and of improving their practice of drug therapy. In addition the committees impart to the physicians a feeling of responsibility for the economics of their prescription practices. In addition, the Central Committee for Rational Drug Therapy publishes a bulletin *Rational Drug Therapy—List of Recommendations (Účelná farmakoterapie—Metodické listy)*, which is sent to all physicians and pharmacists. The bulletin carries information about new drugs, gives critical appraisals of current and new therapeutic procedures, discusses the drug therapy for specific conditions, describes newly discovered adverse drug effects, and promulgates regulations for procedures involved in the prescription of specified drugs. Its recommendations are not compulsory regulations; the idea of the bulletin, readily accepted by physicians, is to offer representative reviews of current medical knowledge in order to help physicians find their way through the complicated problems of modern drug therapy. In the past, the bulletin appeared irregularly; since 1973, it has been published six times a year in the form of printed booklets. Similar bulletins are also published by several regional committees.

The essential work of the district and institutional committees consists of making expert evaluation of prescription analyses of individual physicians or individual ambulatory or hospital departments. By means of such evaluations, the committees can demonstrate administrative faults (for example, violations of obligatory guidelines) and medical faults (for example, prescriptions involving drugs therapeutically or pharmaceutically incompatible or therapeutically not indicated) and point out solutions. In specific instances, the committees also suggest that appropriate seminars be organized or that a physician with a proven major deficiency in his professional competence take special individual training. The committees are also authorized to propose to the director of the Institute of National Health specified disciplinary measures (usually reduction of a discretionary salary bonus) against physicians who repeatedly, willfully, and without adequate reasons disobey valid regulations concerning the prescription and rational use of drugs. In practice, however, such events are rare.

Surveillance Procedures. To be competent in guiding physicians toward rational drug therapy, the committees must have information about physicians' standards of drug therapy, along with quantitative data on drug consumption by individual physicians, policlinics, hospital departments, all the way to entire districts and regions.

249

For its part, the central committee needs data about patterns of drug consumption within the whole republic. This is why special attention is paid to prescription analyses and surveillance of drug consumption within each territory.

Drug consumption has been systematically investigated in Czechoslovakia since 1952,[7] and precise quantity and cost data have been obtained on the consumption of individual drugs and whole groups of drugs. (The term *consumption* does not refer to the consumption of drugs by patients, but to the amount of drugs delivered from the wholesale distribution system to community and hospital pharmacies.)

Chronological Sequences of Drug Consumption. From these data, chronological trends in drug consumption emerge, making possible longitudinal follow-up studies and analyses of the consumption of individual drugs and whole classes of drugs. When endeavoring to quantify total drug consumption, one cannot easily compare and summarize different-sized packages of drugs, or compare the numbers of tablets with those of ampules or milligrams with international units. One simple way of getting around this problem is to compare drug expenditures according to retail prices. If prices are sufficiently stable, these data can be compared in relative terms—between drugs—as well as longitudinally in time. If, however, retail drug prices do change, then comparable, fictitious prices have to be obtained by multiplication by an appropriate coefficient. Thus, after two price changes had taken place in Czechoslovakia, the prices were converted to their original values in order to make possible comparisons of the general trend over time. Figure 1 shows the development of expenditure for drugs in the last eighteen years: drug expenditures rose by about 146 percent on the actual price basis (solid line), but by about 259 percent on the converted price basis (broken line).

Analyses of drug consumption based on expenditure figures always accentuate the economic aspect of this problem. Therefore, in basic analyses of the longitudinal development of drug prescribing from the medical point of view, it is more logical to express drug consumption in terms of dose units, or quantity. To a large degree such chronological sequences reflect the activities of physicians in the front line who stand closest to the patients and who, according to

---

[7] Z. Modr and B. Pechek, *Vývoj spotřeby některých lékooych skupin v ČSSR ou roku 1952 do roku 1969* [The development of consumption of certain drug groups in Czechoslovakia in 1952-1969], *Časopis lékařů českých*, vol. 110, no. 43 (1971), pp. 993-1000.

Figure 1

CHANGE IN NATIONAL EXPENDITURE ON DRUGS IN CZECHOSLOVAKIA, 1955–72

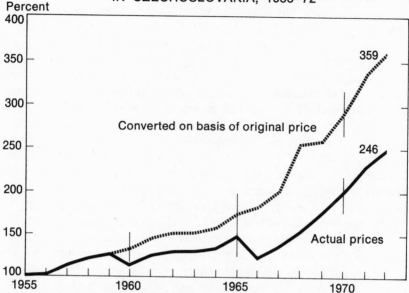

Percent

Converted on basis of original price

359

246

Actual prices

1955   1960   1965   1970

Source: Z. Modr and B. Pechek, "The Development of Consumption of Certain Drug Groups in Czechoslovakia in 1952-1969," *Časopis lékařů českých*, vol. 110, no. 43 (1971), updated until 1972 by the authors.

our findings, prescribe at least 60 percent of all drugs.[8] Furthermore, these figures also reflect the effects of the methodological and administrative measures intended to regulate the development of drug consumption, the effects of distribution and supply conditions, and also the effects of the structure, extent, and availability of the basic and the specialist networks of preventive and curative care.

The sequences enable us to find, for example, a continuously rising consumption of cardiotonics, mainly because life expectancy is increasing and, as a result, chronic patients take medicines over longer periods of time. Analogous trends are found with antidiabetics and numerous other drugs.[9] Another example is the change in the prescription of expectorants which occurred after a recommendation to

[8] K. Kubát, L. Štika, and Nekvinda, *Využití počítače pro hodnocení účelnosti farmakoterapie* [Use of computers for evaluation of adequacy of pharmacotherapy], *Časopis lékařů českých*, vol. 110, no. 31 (1971), pp. 721-26.

[9] Modr and Pechek, "The Development of Consumption," pp. 995-96.

prescribe syrups only for children: the prescription of syrups sank to one-quarter of its former level (Figure 2).[10]

Similar trends are seen in the consumption of analeptics such as synephrine, hydroxyamphetamine, pentetrazol, nikethamide, coretonin, and so on—which have been replaced by other, more efficient drugs—or of sulfonamides (Figure 3), the decline in whose consumption corresponds with the rise of the consumption of antibiotics. A transitory drop in the consumption of sedatives followed the introduction of psychotropic drugs on a major scale. Professional and administrative measures that restricted the prescription of psychostimulants resulted in a marked decline in their consumption.[11]

Longitudinal checking of the consumption of individual drugs has shown that some newly introduced efficient drugs rapidly displace older preparations. This was the case with a new antidepressant, the Czechoslovak drug Prothiaden (dosulepine), which within four years became the most frequently used antidepressant in Czechoslovakia. Its share of total antidepressant consumption rose from 3 percent to 34 percent between 1968 and 1972.[12] This antidepressant, however, also possesses anxiolytic properties, and the rate of increase in its consumption approaches the steep increase in the consumption of anxiolytics of the benzodiazepine type. Nevertheless, the consumption of the latter group did not rise so much in Czechoslovakia as it did in some other countries.

Longitudinal surveys of drug consumption have proved useful from the national point of view; therefore, they are used by the Central Committee for Rational Drug Therapy in its activities.

A different methodological approach to comparative studies of drug consumption is to calculate the daily doses per thousand of population per given period of time; this method makes it possible to compare and sum up approximately equipotent amounts of different drugs within a therapeutic group. On this basis a study was undertaken which compares the consumption of benzodiazepines and meprobamate. This study demonstrates that, despite a steep increase in the consumption of the former, their per capita amount reaches only about one-third of that found in Scandinavian countries.[13]

---

[10] Ibid., p. 999.

[11] Ibid., pp. 994, 998, 999.

[12] M. Haaszová, O. Vinař, and L. Štika, "Prescriptions on a Newly Introduced Drug," *Activitas Nervosa Superior* (Prague), vol. 16, no. 3 (1974), pp. 232-33 (in English).

[13] L. Štika et al., "Longitudinal Trends in Prescribing Psychotropic Drugs," *Activitas Nervosa Superior* (Prague), vol. 16, no. 3 (1974), pp. 230-32 (in English).

Figure 2

CHANGES IN PRESCRIBING OF EXPECTORANTS

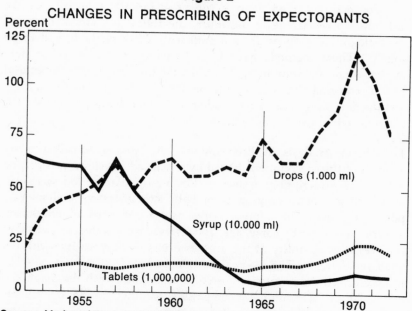

Source: Modr and Pechek, "The Development of Consumption."

Figure 3

CHANGES IN THE CONSUMPTION OF SULFONAMIDES AND ANTIBIOTICS

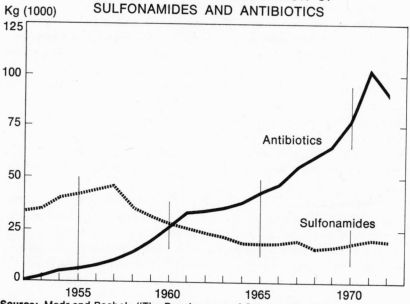

Source: Modr and Pechek, "The Development of Consumption."

For more detailed analyses of prescriptions, especially at the individual physician level, however, the follow-up and analyses of chronological sequences are not sufficient. New methods had to be sought. These methods have been based on the analysis of data marked on prescription forms. In this way, the checking and appraisal of drug consumption was close to both the physician and the patient, and the data thus express more adequately than higher-level data the patients' actual drug consumption.

The Direct Analysis of Prescriptions. At first, a so-called direct analysis of the prescriptions issued by a selected physician was carried out.[14] The prescriptions issued within a particular period were collected, sorted, and analyzed from both administrative and medical points of view. The administrative aspect consisted of checks on whether the patient's name, age, and address were stated and whether the prescribed quantity of the drug or drugs was compatible with the valid regulations. The medical criteria included checks on whether the prescribed drugs were indicated in accordance with the diagnosis, whether they were mutually compatible, whether the dosage scheme was correct, whether the directions for use were adequate and comprehensible to the patient, and so on.

After they were sorted, the prescriptions were classed by indication groups; in this way, a pharmacotherapeutic profile of the physician was obtained.

Along with this quantitative analysis, a qualitative analysis was also possible. Attention was focused on the drugs prescribed for a particular patient by the given physician and possibly by other physicians as well. The prescription analyses were carried out either by members of the committees or by physicians delegated by them. The information thus gained could then be compared with the patient's other health documents on the occasion of what is called a supervisory visit paid by appropriate specialists to the physician analyzed. Excellent results were also obtained when the physicians analyzed their own prescriptions; these results were then checked by experienced specialists.

Although the methods described proved to be good in practice and contributed considerably to an improvement in the level of drug therapy in our republic (obsolete drugs have been abandoned, the use of symptomatic remedies has markedly decreased, therapeutic incompatibilities have become rare, polypharmacy has declined, the prescriptions issued have been better documented in medical records

---

14 Modr, "Working Method of Commissions," p. 354.

than they were before), many drawbacks still persisted. The major drawback was the enormous tediousness of manual prescription processing, with the result that relatively few physicians could be analyzed. Furthermore, the manual system did not allow comparison of more than three criteria per analysis out of many (for example, the sort of drug prescribed, its price, the patient's age or sex, the prescribing physician's identity, and so on). Any additional criterion required a new sorting: evidently, the number of analyzable factors was small. To expand the number of items that could be checked and to involve more (or all) physicians in the checking, we sought new means of processing and appraising prescriptions. Such means were found when modern electronic data processing techniques were introduced.

Electronic Data Processing of Medical Prescriptions. The first project to apply electronic data processing to prescription forms for follow-up and analysis of drug consumption was carried out as early as 1967.[15] Work with this project emphasized that the electronic data processing project should also serve the needs and interests of drug manufacture and distribution in inventory control, automated ordering and billing, marketing purposes, and so on. The basic data source is still the prescription form, on which new data could now be added, including the patient's identification number (giving his birth date and sex) and the code number of the diagnosis. The WHO ICD code number is written on the prescription form by the physician; additional data, such as the code number and the amount of the drug issued, are coded by skilled pharmacists either in pharmacies or at the computer center. The computer permits storage of data in a convenient form and the determining of interrelationships among a great number of criteria. The storage of the patient's identification number makes possible linkage with other sources of information—work incapacity records, patient histories filed in hospitals, data in registers of births and deaths. Correlation of data stored in the computer memory offers a rich information base for medical inquiries and investigations. The primary aim of electronic data processing in this area is to obtain the information contained in the prescription form and find appropriate correlations among the data.

The goal to be achieved by such investigations must be clear in advance, in order to obviate "information inflation" and a flood of

---

[15] Z. Modr et al., "The Proposal for Use of Computerized Data on Prescription and Consumption of Drugs for Purpose of Rational Pharmacotherapy," *News of ÚZST* (1968), pp. 12-35.

figures which would hamper rather than facilitate evaluation. The extent of the data to be checked must be proportional to the goals intended, as well as to the level of authority for which the data are destined.

For the central authorities—the Ministry of Health and the Central Committee for Rational Drug Therapy—regular checks are needed of the structure, trends, and changes in the total drug consumption in the republic. These data, moreover, must be followed not only for the whole republic but also for individual regions. At the regional level, the requirements are analogous, and the data can also be supplied for individual districts. At the health institution level, even the activities of individual physicians or departments can be analyzed. At all levels, the effects of individual measures and regulations may be analyzed for feedback effects. All physicians can receive regular monthly information about their prescribing as early as the middle of the following month and can compare their patterns with those of their colleagues. This information flow represents the shortest feedback circuit.[16]

Apart from these regular investigations of the structure and development of prescription habits, the system also permits specialized selective investigations in which several criteria are processed in various combinations. For example, it can be determined what drugs are prescribed for certain diseases, for what diseases a certain drug is prescribed, how the therapeutic stereotypes of the individual physicians change, what drugs are prescribed for certain groups of the population (classified, for example, by age, sex, and occupation), and so on. (It is known that stereotyped physician behavior, even the repetitive prescribing of proven drugs, may hamper the introduction of new and more effective preparations.)

Such selective investigations produce a wealth of additional information when special programs are applied. For example, to determine how much of the new antiparkinsonian agent, levodopa, would probably be needed, use was made of computer-stored data covering the diagnoses and types of patients for whom current antiparkinsonian agents have been prescribed. It was found that only one-third of antiparkinsonian agents were prescribed for patients whose illness was diagnosed as parkinsonism. Another third was prescribed for patients with arteriosclerotic diseases. The remainder was prescribed

---

16 M. Kubásek et al., *Nový způsob rozboru preskripce v okrese* [New method of analysis of prescriptions in districts], *Československé zdravotnictví*, vol. 18, no. 1 (1970), pp. 3-13; and L. Štika, M. Hovorová, and J. Kratochvíl, "Automated Processing of Medical Prescriptions," *Activitas Nervosa Superior* (Prague), vol. 13, no. 3 (1971), pp. 229-30 (in English).

for mental diseases to correct the adverse side effects of the neuroleptics. When prescriptions for antiparkinsonian agents were analyzed by the patient identification number, it was found that one woman had prescriptions for trihexyphenidyl issued by several physicians; the physicians knew that the patient was being treated with neuroleptics, but were not aware that she had prescriptions for trihexyphenidyl issued by other physicians and was abusing the drug. Her drug dependence on trihexyphenidyl led to dosage gradation up to ten tablets daily and to an exacerbation of toxic psychosis requiring her hospitalization.[17]

So far electronic processing of prescription forms has been carried out in the Czech Socialist Republic in only a few health institutions in Prague, in the regions of central Bohemia, eastern Bohemia, and southern Moravia, and in the health care system of the state railways. All these systems collect and store data on diagnoses according to which drugs have been prescribed. In the future, computer recording of diagnoses will be extended to the whole country. In most cases, this system is used for automated invoicing and billing of drugs. In the central Bohemian region, periodic studies are performed of the prescribing habits of specialists in different branches of medicine; these studies are carried out with different aims and to different extents. Altogether, they cover a territory with about 1.2 million inhabitants. In Prague, regular electronic data processing of medical prescriptions for invoice control has been gradually extended from one district to four, covering a territory of about half a million inhabitants. At the present time, using the experiences gained so far, work is underway on a project for a uniform system of computerized processing and evaluation of prescriptions (including diagnosis), to be incorporated in a uniform pharmaceutical and health care information system for the entire state.

Past experience has shown that electronic prescription processing offers a wealth of valuable data which are also useful for the activities of committees for rational drug therapy.[18] It is already evident that demands for the practical use of data obtained in this way will be steadily growing. Members of committees for rational drug therapy and the appropriate workers of national institutes of health must prepare themselves for this demand. Furthermore, operational chan-

---

[17] L. Štika et al., zjištění lékové závislosti s použitím děrnoštítkových receptů [A case of drug dependence traced by the means of punchcard prescriptions], Praktický lékař, vol. 53, no. 20 (1973), pp. 772-73.

[18] K. Kubát, L. Štika, and V. Nekvinda, Automatisované zpracování receptů a metodické vedení [Automated processing of recipes and methodological guidance], Československé zdravotnictví, vol. 20, no. 7 (1972), pp. 261-68.

nels must be set up for the rapid feedback of such information to the state for regulation of prescription, and thus for the control of drug consumption. For example, better control of prescribed psychotropic drugs, especially psychostimulants, has markedly reduced the consumption of both psychostimulants and appetite supressants; vitamins are no longer prescribed automatically with every antibiotic or as expensive placebos in various diseases. It has also become possible to find possible drug addicts. In this way, an objective base has been provided for methodological consultations on how to appraise the level of prescription for selected—mainly cardiovascular—diagnoses.

Monitoring of Adverse Drug Reactions. In Czechoslovakia, monitoring of adverse drug reactions is organized according to the principles of the World Health Organization's project on drug monitoring, a project in which Czechoslovakia participates.[19] From experience gained during the study phase of the project, steps were taken in 1973 for Czechoslovakia to enter the operational phase. A new Committee for Adverse Drug Reactions was constituted, and the reporting system for such adverse reactions was simplified.[20] The aim is to increase the number of reports submitted on adverse reactions. The Committee for Adverse Drug Reactions issues regular annual reviews of reported adverse effects, and these are published in medical professional journals. Data of major significance, whether established in Czechoslovakia or abroad, are discussed with the Central Committee for Rational Drug Therapy and the Drug Committee. Such discussions result in recommendations for adequate professional or, if necessary, administrative measures. Thus, information about drug dependence on certain combinations of analgesic or antiasthmatic drugs was made use of in the revision of the *List of Over-the-Counter Drugs*, from which phenisatine-type laxatives were also deleted. Physicians receive information of this kind with understanding and appraise its practical value. In the light of experience gained during recent years, such a regular supply of information is the best stimulus to increasing the physicians' reporting of adverse drug reactions.

Performance of the System

When evaluating the system for the control of drug use in Czechoslovakia, we wish to emphasize that the system has been developing

---

19 O. Uhlíř, "Monitoring and Evaluation of Adverse Drug Reactions," *Časopis lékařů českých*, vol. 106, no. 15 (1967), pp. 392-93.

20 J. Vaněček, "Monitoring of Untoward Drug Effects," *Časopis lékřů českých*, vol. 112, no. 26 (1973), pp. 819-20.

and operating under conditions of socialist health care. This fact determines both the principles and the practice of the system. From the administrative point of view, the prime feature of the system is the unity of regulation and control of the research, manufacture, and distribution of drugs as well as of the activities of all health institutions under the Ministry of Health. From the point of view of its content, a characteristic feature of the system is its consistent fulfillment of the principles of socialist humanism, imposing on the state health administration the duty to provide optimal preventive and curative care free of cost for all inhabitants. The administrative form does not prevail over the content in this system because the state health administration is responsible to the appropriate agencies of the people's power. In addition, the committees for rational drug therapy play a major role; it is important in this respect that these committees consist mainly of specialists not employed in agencies of the state health administration. Although they are advisory, the committees strongly influence the activities of the appropriate agencies of the state health administration as well as the activities of practicing physicians. Results of prescription controls and suggestions for regulating prescription and for doing away with any faults that may be revealed are presented by the committee to the director of the appropriate Institute of National Health, who may then base his decisions on the professional authority of the committees. This authority has now been recognized by general and hospital physicians, a majority of whom no longer consider the committees as merely supervisory institutions. Today, physicians accept the committees as institutions helping them raise their professionalism in drug therapy.

The levels of activity of the individual committees for rational drug therapy are not the same throughout our country. Nevertheless, a majority of the committees fulfill their tasks well, and they are the most important component of the system for control of drug use in Czechoslovakia.

Experience has also proved that the activities of the committees, especially in control and analysis of prescription, may serve research functions in one of the youngest branches of clinical pharmacology— the branch called social pharmacology. This discipline studies not only the structure of prescription and its changes, but—more important—the positive and negative consequences of the introduction of certain drugs or therapeutic procedures for major groups of the population. For example, a program is being devised to evaluate the effects of intensified prevention and therapy in patients with cardiovascular diseases. The creation of this branch of clinical pharmacology is not incidental; rather it was enforced by practical needs, as had been the case with the creation of clinical pharmacology itself.

Clinical Pharmacology

Clinical pharmacology has developed in Czechoslovakia as in other countries. At first, clinical pharmacologists were represented mainly by clinicians who began to occupy themselves systematically with clinical research on new drugs and by pharmacologists whose study of human pharmacology brought a closer collaboration with clinicians.

Organizationally, the greatest attention was paid to the creation of a special institute and facilities for clinico-pharmacological research; this topic has also been systematically incorporated into the state plan of research. These institutions collaborate closely with Czechoslovak institutes for the research, development, and preparation of new drugs. Within the system of research institutes of the Ministry of Health, the Institute for Clinical and Experimental Medicine has established the Research Center of Clinical Pharmacology. This center is entrusted with studies of selected drug groups, primarily phase I and II clinical studies, as well as with the design and organization of controlled clinical trials to be performed either at individual clinical departments of the Institute for Clinical and Experimental Medicine or at cooperating hospitals.

In Czechoslovakia, clinical pharmacology is primarily cooperative.[21] The clinical pharmacologist plays a role as a specialist solving specific tasks, especially during the initial stages of clinical evaluations of new drugs, and also as a coordinator of all the following stages. Of course, he must also fulfill his advisory and educational duties. (This view of clinical pharmacology was discussed at a special Symposium on Clinical Pharmacology in Socialist Countries, convened in Prague in 1972 on Czechoslovak initiative.) [22]

So far, education in clinical pharmacology has been included in the undergraduate curriculum at only three colleges of medicine. However, lectures dealing with clinical pharmacology have been included in a majority of educational courses organized by the institutes for postgraduate medical and pharmaceutical training in both the Czech and the Slovak Socialist republics.

---

[21] Z. Modr, "Clinical Pharmacology: Present Problems and Perspectives," Časopis lékařů českých, vol. 112, no. 26 (1973), pp. 803-6.

[22] Papers presented at the Symposium on Clinical Pharmacology in Socialist Countries, Prague, October 3-5, 1972, Časopis lékařů českých, vol. 113, no. 26 (1973), pp. 801-24.

Evaluation of the System

From the foregoing information it is evident that a complex system for the control of therapeutic drug use has been gradually created in Czechoslovakia: its principal task is to improve national health care. Under the guidance of the Ministry of Health, not only physicians and paramedical personnel, but also pharmacists, the pharmaceutical industry, and economists active in health care participate in accomplishing the task imposed. The complex program consists of the following items:

(1) systematic gathering of information about, and expert surveillance of, both qualitative and quantitative aspects of prescription for all physicians;

(2) expert guidance of all physicians in adhering to principles of rational and scientifically based drug prescription;

(3) control of expenditure of the funds supplied from the state budget for medicines;

(4) control of pharmaceutical research, manufacture, importation, and distribution by the state health administration;

(5) supervision by the state health administration of the maintenance of professional precautions for safe usage of drugs.

To serve all the above purposes, the following measures have been taken:

(1) creation of a system of committees for rational drug therapy. In the committees, the physicians actively participate in expert supervision of prescription and also in a search for solutions for problems arising in connection with drug prescription and usage;

(2) creation of a system of controlling prescription, including computer processing of prescription forms;

(3) inclusion of responsibility for an adequate medical level of drug therapy among the obligations imposed upon the head specialists. These physicians are entrusted with methodological guidance of other physicians in a given specialty, including the community health center physicians in their domain;

(4) the creation of a system for monitoring adverse drug effects;

(5) the setting up of a system for informing physicians of advances in drug therapy and adverse drug effects;

261

(6) the establishment of collaboration between medical experts and economists in the planning and control of expenditure for drugs and in the planning of drug manufacture, importation, and distribution;

(7) the institution of health education centers for public education in correct drug usage.

The effects of the whole system are best seen so far in the trends of prescription patterns and of the costs of drugs prescribed by individual physicians and at individual policlinic and hospital departments: in these a gradual rationalizing of drug therapy and economizing of the expenditure of funds are evident. At the district, regional, and state levels, only broad effects can be discerned so far. These include:

(1) a favorable trend in the consumption of individual drugs or groups of drugs, especially when checked in terms of conventional daily dosages;

(2) an improvement in certain morbidity and mortality indicators, as well as a decrease in the incidence and duration of work incapacity (sick leave);

(3) a shift of expended funds from symptomatic therapy to drugs counteracting the pathogenesis of diseases.

More exact and detailed correlations between prescription patterns and their effect on the state of public health will have to wait until computerized processing of prescriptions is extended over the entire state.

Estimating the operational costs of the system is not easy. Except for the computer processing of prescription, the system is not directly financed. Service on committees for rational drug therapy and the methodological guidance of physicians constitute an integral part of work of the specialists concerned, and they receive no special remuneration for these activities, which take about 10 to 20 percent of their working time. On each committee there are five to ten specialists. There are 2 central and 11 regional committees for rational drug therapy, and 118 district and 330 institute committees. Under the two ministries of health in Czechoslovakia, 30,800 physicians are employed (*Statistical Yearbook, 1973*); about 2,000 specialists are entrusted with methodological guidance.

Conclusion

The system for the control of therapeutic drug use in Czechoslovakia is consistent in both structure and function with the structure and aims of the socialist health care system. The drug control system derives from the professional and economic responsibility of the state health administration for ensuring conditions for safe, effective, and economical drug use in therapeutic practice. It is characterized by active participation of physicians in the solution of problems connected with the control of drug use in Czechoslovakia. Although this system is already fairly adequate in its organization and function, further development is necessary. For this purpose, use must be made of experiences gained not only in Czechoslovakia and in other socialist countries, but also in other countries of the world.

Cover and book design: Pat Taylor